THE FORBIDDEN CITY

OTHER BOOKS BY FRANK DORN

The Dorn Cookbook

Cooking with Herbs and Spices

Forest Twilight (a novel)

THE
FORBIDDEN
CITY

The Biography of a Palace

by *Frank Dorn*

Charles Scribner's Sons / *New York*

". . . THE WIND CUSTODIAN SINGS,
'I GUARD THE FRAGRANCE OF A THOUSAND SPRINGS.
DRAW NEAR! DRAW NEAR!
TEN THOUSAND YESTERDAYS ARE GATHERED HERE.' "
—*Yuan Mei*

CONTENTS

MAPS

(All maps drawn by the author)

ILLUSTRATIONS

The following illustrations lie between pages 54 and 55

PREFACE

This is the biography of a palace: the Forbidden City of Peking. Once a place of great riches and pomp, it remains today the most splendid imperial residence to survive the ravages of time and history. But can an account of the palace-city of the emperors of China—consisting of inanimate stone, brick, and tile—be rightfully called a biography? Perhaps not. Still, the Forbidden City of Peking, for centuries the symbol of a great empire, consists of far more than the base materials of its construction.

In simple terms the word "biography" is defined as "the written account of a person's life." One might add, "to include not only the facts and figures, but all of the psychological and external influences brought on by events and people that have contributed toward molding a life to its completion." In that sense the great palaces of Peking are a gigantic, living entity. Having endured for over five centuries and having absorbed the lives of myriad people, they have created a spirit closely akin to life itself—a life that still pulses with the warm blood of history.

While an army officer and Chinese-language student in Peking from 1934 to 1938, I developed an interest in the Forbidden City and other imperial residences, first from casual sightseeing and then from conducting important visitors and tourists through the palaces. A growing familiarity with the buildings and courts soon became an absorbing urge to learn more about the history and legends connected with those who had created and lived within the walls of the palace-city. The first result of my researches was a pictorial map of Peking, after which I was completely hooked on the whole fascinating subject.

Much of the extensive research required to put flesh on the brittle bones of the past was accomplished while I was in Peking. It was a task of many years that included day-by-day association with bearded scholars and historians in a search of records belonging to the Chinese Nationalist government, the National Library, the imperial archives, the dynastic archives, and private libraries. Because of the disruptions caused by the Japanese invasion of 1937, World War II, the subsequent take-over of mainland China by Communist forces, and deaths and changes in the lives of the small group of researchers with whom I worked, the rough draft, as originally planned, lay gathering dust for over thirty years.

Though neglected, the material was not forgotten. After more years of intensive research, this book has now been rewritten as a biography —an account of the life of a palace. It is not presented in the chronological order of its more than five-hundred-year-old history but in accordance with the pattern and plan of the huge and complex mass of buildings enclosed by its walls. The narrative and background revolve around each gate and hall, each garden and courtyard, as if one were able to proceed from one historical setting to another by moving about the vast enclosure of the Forbidden City.

FRANK DORN

Washington, D.C.
January, 1969

PRINCIPAL DYNASTIES
OF CHINA

SHANG	1766 to 1122 B.C.
CHOU	1122 to 255 B.C.
CH'IN	255 to 207 B.C.
HAN	206 B.C. to A.D. 264
FOURTEEN MINOR DYNASTIES	A.D. 264 to 618
T'ANG	A.D. 618 to 906
FIVE MINOR DYNASTIES	A.D. 907 to 960
SUNG	A.D. 960 to 1279
YUAN (MONGOL)	A.D. 1260 to 1368
MING	A.D. 1368 to 1644
CH'ING (MANCHU)	A.D. 1644 to 1912

MING AND MANCHU EMPERORS OF CHINA

From 1421 to 1924 the Forbidden City—or the Great Within, as it is also known—was the official residence of twenty-four successive sovereigns: fourteen emperors of the Ming dynasty; and ten of the conquering Manchu, or Ch'ing, dynasty—a number of whom ruled through regents during their minorities.

MING DYNASTY (1368–1644)
Hung Wu (1368–1398)

The founder of the Ming dynasty and a Buddhist monk, he became the symbol of leadership in the rebellion that overthrew the alien Mongol dynasty; in 1368 he enthroned himself at Nanking as the Supreme Lord of the empire of China.

Chien Wen (1398–1402)

Chien Wen's father, the Heir Apparent to Hung Wu, died before he had a chance to inherit the throne, and therefore Chien Wen, a grandson of the founder of the dynasty, took the throne at Nanking. After executing a number of imperial princes, he was dethroned by his rebellious uncle Yung Lo and forced to seek refuge in a monastery as a Buddhist monk.

Yung Lo (1402–1424)

Nicknamed the "Black Dragon" and designated the prince of Yen, Yung Lo was the fourth son of Hung Wu, the first emperor. Forceful, cruel, restless, and brilliant, he planned and constructed the Forbidden City, or the Great Within, and rebuilt the city of Peking, which had been destroyed during the overthrow of the Mongol dynasty in 1368. The first

Ming sovereign to occupy the Forbidden City, he died in Mongolia before his great work was completed.

Hung Hsi (1424–1425)

Hung Hsi, a son of Yung Lo, succeeded his able father in 1424; he died after an undistinguished reign that lasted for about a year.

Hsuan Te (1425–1435)

Hsuan Te was the first of a long line of pleasure-loving and extravagant rulers who lavished the revenues of the empire on the enrichment of the palaces in the Forbidden City.

CHENG T'UNG (1435–1449)
T'ien Shun (1457–1464)

The sixth and eighth emperor of the Ming dynasty, he ruled first as Cheng T'ung until 1449, when he was dethroned by his brother, and again as T'ien Shun after he in turn dethroned the seventh emperor.

Ching T'ai (1449–1457)

Ching T'ai overthrew his predecessor and brother, Cheng T'ung, enthroned himself for eight years, and was in turn overthrown by the same brother.

T'ien Shun (1457–1464)

See description of Cheng T'ung above.

Ch'eng Hua (1464–1487)

The undistinguished rule of this emperor was characterized by a sybaritic and extravagant existence.

Hung Chih (1487–1505)

The son of Ch'eng Hua, Hung Chih, added nothing but creeping decay to the dynasty by his extravagance and indifference to affairs of state.

Cheng Te (1505–1521)

Cheng Te's early energies were soon diverted to a completely licentious life, which earned him the reputation of the worst libertine of his line and eventually caused his death.

Chia Ching (1521–1566)

The twelfth Ming emperor, Chia Ching, inherited the pleasure-loving instincts of his father, Cheng Te, and his long reign was characterized by luxury and pleasure on a grand scale.

Lung Ch'ing (1566–1572)

Following his father's pattern of wasteful indulgence, Lung Ch'ing's short reign was marked by a continuation of extravagance and pleasure.

Wan Li (1572–1619)

Known as the Porcelain Emperor, Wan Li reached new heights in sybaritism. However, his absorbing interest in the arts, particularly the creation of fine porcelain, resulted in a great legacy to the world.

T'ai Ch'ang (1620)

T'ai Ch'ang, a son of Wan Li, reigned for less than one year. His early death ended a life completely lacking in distinction.

T'ien Chi (1620–1627)

Known as the Carpenter Emperor, T'ien Chi, son of T'ai Ch'ang, as-cended the throne at the age of fifteen. Indifferent to his royal duties, which he delegated to a pair of scoundrels—his chief eunuch and his old wet nurse—his only interest was in carpentry, at which he spent most of his time.

Ch'ung Cheng (1627–1644)

The seventeenth and last Ming emperor, Ch'ung Cheng, brother of the Carpenter Emperor, inherited over two hundred years of indifference and luxurious extravagance, which helped to bring about the rebellion that overthrew his dynasty. With the rebels in control of Peking and about to seize the palace, he hanged himself on Coal Hill.

CH'ING, OR MANCHU, DYNASTY (1644–1912)
Shun Chih (1644–1662)

Since Shun Chih was a child of eight years when he ascended the throne of China, the empire was directed by his forceful and able uncle, Prince Jui, who served as the regent until his nephew's majority. Surprisingly well educated for a Manchu of his time, Shun Chih died at the age of twenty-six.

K'ang Hsi (1662–1723)

Perhaps the greatest emperor of the Manchu dynasty, K'ang Hsi as-cended the throne at the age of eight. His grandmother guided his early years, and four regents governed until his majority at the age of fifteen. Highly erudite, open-minded, and energetic, he was both an able ad-ministrator and a capable military commander who personally led suc-cessful campaigns against outside enemies and internal rebels—thereby saving the empire for his dynasty.

Yung Cheng (1723–1736)

Though politically capable and an able administrator, Yung Cheng was far overshadowed by his great father and by the brilliant son who succeeded him.

Ch'ien Lung (1736–1796)

The son of Yung Cheng and the fourth Manchu emperor, he reigned for sixty years—after which he abdicated and lived for three more years. He was a lover of the arts, a builder, and a military leader who expanded Manchu power to its greatest extent. His reign was brilliant, although its final years marked the beginning of decline.

Chia Ch'ing (1796–1821)

Chia Ch'ing's long wait for the throne left him with a meanness of spirit that manifested itself in stinginess and avarice.

Tao Kuang (1821–1851)

Tao Kuang was a forceful and capable ruler who was constantly troubled by rebellion and war. Personally courageous, he was the last Manchu sovereign with any claim to greatness.

Hsien Feng (1851–1862)

Hsien Feng, the son of Tao Kuang, was a dissolute weakling whose reign was marked by misfortune and ineptitude. He died of diseases incurred by his licentious manner of living. His empress, Tz'u An, had no children, but one of his concubines (later known as Tz'u Hsi) had one son, who became the next emperor.

T'ung Chih (1862–1875)

When T'ung Chih, the son of Hsien Feng, took the throne, his mother, Tz'u Hsi, and his father's empress Tz'u An, were named as co-regents and co-empress dowagers. His short life was one of licentiousness, during which Tz'u Hsi exercised all real power.

Kuang Hsu (1875–1908)

The ninth emperor of the Manchu dynasty was the nephew of the Empress Dowager Tz'u Hsi—the child of her sister and an imperial prince. He was four years old when named emperor by his power-mad aunt. After attaining his majority, he attempted to institute much-needed reforms in the government, but was completely thwarted by Tz'u Hsi. He spent the last ten years of his life as a prisoner.

Hsuan T'ung (1908–1912)

Better known in the Western world as P'u Yi, the boy-emperor, Hsuan T'ung was the last Manchu emperor. He was the son of an imperial prince and the daughter of Tz'u Hsi's lover. Only two years old when he became sovereign, he "reigned" under his mother's regency from 1908 to 1912. After the republic was established, P'u Yi was allowed to remain in residence in the Forbidden City until 1924. From 1931 to 1945 he was Emperor of the Japanese puppet state of Manchukuo. Overwhelmed by revolution, wars, and rapidly changing times, he died in 1966, the last of his dynasty and the last emperor of China.

PART 1
Ten Thousand Yesterdays

THE SPIRIT OF THE PALACE-CITY

THE DREAM OF THE FOUNDERS

THE PLAN

THE SYMBOLS

THE GLORY AND THE TWILIGHT

THE SPIRIT OF THE PALACE-CITY

A semisacred myth during nearly five and a half centuries, the massive palace-city of the emperors of China now stands a brooding memorial to a past so grand in concept and dignity that it staggers the imagination of today's chaotic world. Used now, during the day for bureaucrats' offices and for stiff, crude official receptions, its vast, open square often swarms with China's masses, waving red banners and chanting slogans —a new generation that knows little and cares less about the history of the great palace that houses the men who decide the nation's destiny. The lusty youths are too deeply engrossed in their own affairs, hopes, ambitions, and frustrations to dwell overmuch on their country's past.

But, perhaps, when night has fallen over Peking—darkly and stormily, with a sharp wind that rattles the windows, races wildly down the narrow alleys, and whistles through the weeping willows—the ghosts of a brilliant, colorful, and often cruel past revisit the stately halls and gardens. If so, there would be gathered together in the palace's shadows the spirits of all east Asia's history: gorgeously robed kings, princes, nobles, and chieftains, riding lavishly caparisoned camels and swift horses; beautiful empresses, queens, and favored concubines, glittering with jewels and gowned in gleaming satins sewn all over with gold, silver, and precious gems; Dalai Lamas who had fought the snowy, wintry blasts of faraway Tibet to make the journey; abbots from distant Kumbum with its soaring temples roofed in gold tiles; ambassadors and emissaries from every Asian country and even Europe—some to do obeisance and offer tribute of fabulous worth, some to nurse the false pretension that their sovereigns were the equal of the Son of Heaven; brilliant scholars and statesmen in sober robes; artists and writers; poets and craftsmen; great generals and admirals whose haughty bluster would wither under the hot brilliance of the Golden Throne; generations of eunuchs, scheming and plotting to achieve power; Catholic priests; bedizened viceroys, governors, and officials who offered the treasures of the world to their lord; and finally, the vast horde of humble ones crowding in upon the heels of the mighty, shyly bowing in gracious politeness, hesitating lest they be refused admittance to this conclave of ghostly spirits—countless guards, maidservants, tradesmen, and palace children who had been poisoned lest they become rivals for power, old men honored for their longevity, mothers stretching their necks this way and that to see their daughters, whose only sin—that of beauty—had made them concubines and, thus, prisoners for life. Hundreds upon thousands of spirits—the great, colorful panoply of the past. The ones who had achieved China's greatness and the ones who had caused its downfall—all there together, looking sadly about. Was this the empire's punishment, long overdue, for the sins of greed, avarice, corruption, cruelty, ambition? Was this the score that had to be settled sooner or later for the follies of the past and the equally senseless follies of the present?

Then, with the rising of the sun, perhaps the spirits slip one by one out of the palace, as softly as a summer breeze. Some may pause briefly to survey the still-slumbering city, innocent and peaceful under the somber gray nacre of dawn. Others may linger long enough to watch windows light, to listen to the tramp of soldiers on guard before the palace gates, to see the city come to life with people, to hear little children, hurriedly dressing for school, begin their noisy, endless chant of Chairman Mao's philosophy; then, these spirits skim across the rooftops to take shelter wherever spirits dwell.

The enormous, walled palace-city within the vast, walled fortress-capital of Peking was truly the Great Within, the inner core of an enlightened Middle Kingdom to which the world beyond was barbarian and tributary. The Forbidden City, as the palace is commonly known, was a reserved place surrounded by high, purplish-red walls and soaring towers. It was built as a center of withdrawal, befitting the life of an emperor, the priest-king who, alone among all his myriad subjects, had the sole right and duty to address Heaven, from which came all blessings, including his own mandate to rule. This lofty concept, the relationship between Heaven, the emperor, the people, and the earth—all embodied in the person of the Supreme Lord of China—noble in theory, if not always in practice, remains one of the most exalted dreams of man to bridge the span between the unknown beyond the skies and the creatures who inhabit the earth.

The palace rests like an enameled medallion in the heart of Peking. From its Dragon Throne twenty-four successive Sons of Heaven, as the emperors were called, ruled the eighteen provinces of China and the tributary states situated in the north, the south, and the hinterland of western Asia. The very life of the vast empire pulsed and throbbed in tune with the palace-city. The eyes of all men turned in its direction for an ordered existence and for the inspiration they needed to carry on their lives. The mere thought of its image lifted them above the daily round of their activities, gave them a sense of security, turned their minds toward greater horizons, and kept alive their dreams of fortune, preferment, power, and wealth. Every peasant, no matter how lowly, knew that with a smile from Heaven he, too, could attain that sublime pinnacle from which his master faced both gods and men with equanimity.

The Forbidden City became the center of culture, the arts, poetry, history, and science. All that was outstanding, important, and fine sooner or later found its way to the imperial court. For centuries it attracted scholars, poets, painters, craftsmen, and artisans with the finest of their works, as well as the most priceless jewels and all the riches of a great empire. High-minded men served the Sons of Heaven with great dignity and selfless loyalty; and bold schemers plotted in the shadows of guardian towers to gain riches and power. Princes and eunuchs, nobles and commoners, loyal soldiers and base traitors, all struggled to gain imperial favors from the one who sat upon the Dragon Throne. Though a sophisticated, worldly place, the palace retained an unworldly, spiritual atmosphere that at times transcended all its activities. It crawled with wives, concubines, ladies in waiting, scores of children, thousands of maidservants and eunuchs, and countless imperial guards on the walls and towers. But the emperor saw no one from outside the gates except through an almost visible curtain of awe that characterized a formal audience. Then, of course, he was surrounded by scores of officials and attendants.

The blood and sweat, the lives and dreams of two hundred thousand slave laborers, craftsmen and artisans, stonemasons, bricklayers, and tilemakers were poured into the construction and embellishment of this earthly focal point where Heaven and the emperor became one in the eyes of all lesser beings. The carefully ordered rows of courts and halls that they laboriously built became a glittering yet gloomy stage for each man chosen to live out his life as a semidivine sovereign. He was so exalted and so set apart from other men, not even his own brothers were allowed to remain overnight within his closely guarded walls.

So strict was this rule that any man found within the palace enclosure after the gates were slammed shut at nightfall could be subjected to torture or put to death. Punishment might be by the "slicing process" (also known as the "Death by a Thousand Cuts") or decapitation by the guards and eunuchs. Or, on the whim of a thoroughly vicious eunuch, a leaden-faced, terrorized victim was led screaming to an open courtyard where he was bound with rawhide thongs and left on the stone paving to squirm under the broiling hot sun of the next day. The intense heat would dry and tighten the bonds, and the dampness of night would loosen them. This ensured a long, drawn-out torture, and to the delight of the eunuchs, the air would be rent with agonized screams before the last gasp of pain signaled death. More often than not, however, a trespasser was so roughly castrated he could, and often did, die of shock and loss of blood. If he survived, he was doomed to the life of a eunuch unable to carry on his family line. Nor could he appear after death before his ancestors; having an incomplete body, his spirit would also be incomplete and therefore unworthy.

Many tens of thousands lived out their lives within the palace walls. Year after year its paving stones grew smooth and shiny under the padding of their soft-soled shoes. But during the slow and measured passage of the centuries, only a rare few left more than a shallow imprint of their presence. Most of these were emperors. Some were great men, outstanding in character and achievements, and endowed with the ability to rule wisely. Too many were weak, of no mind at all, guilty of scandalous behavior and corruption, indulging in the luxury of depravity, forfeiting the esteem of their subjects. And, as always, death came as remorselessly to the highest and most glorious as it did to the lowliest slave. In its five hundred years as the center of the Chinese universe, the stones and tiles of the Forbidden City embraced the uneasy souls of more than a quarter of a million people who died within its crenelated walls: some by illness, some by the silken cord of enforced suicide, some by the rot of old age, some by torture, poison, or the dagger.

Small wonder, then, that when the flocks of black crows come soaring over the shadowed courts each evening as the light begins to ebb, an aura of brooding mystery drops like a sable cloak to enfold the golden roofs and towers of the Great Within. Strangely enough, time seems to stand still then. All of the accumulations of centuries are like one endless day, with no definite place to mark the merging of one century into another. The wings of the black crows whir in the sharp breeze, as they have for countless decades. The weeping willows still whisper sibilantly over the palace moat. Trees bud, leaves fall, as they have always done, and again there is heard the flirtatious sigh of trailing stems caressing the ruffled water. The twentieth century, moving, chaotic, pushing into the future, has a million sounds peculiarly its own, including the violent detonations of nuclear bombs—a full circle back to the original Chinese fireworks. But under the modern, raucous cacophony the sounds of the past are never quite silenced—not in a land where spirits live on, having dominated men's hopes and fears since time immemorial. If one listens, the footsteps of long ago, padding across the wide, stone courtyards, can be heard. One can hear, too, the measured tread of sentries at the parapets, the tumult of ancient pomp, pageantry, and gilded ceremony. Was it all yesterday—or aeons ago—those searing loves, the vicious hatreds, and cruel jealousies? So many sounds echoing through the flickering shadows of the past: the tormented cries of wretched souls writhing under remembered tortures; the muted, persuasive tones of those fawning for preferment, as men have always fawned for gain; the sharp keening over past griefs; the shrieks of horror, terror, and agony; the stroke of padded sticks on bronze drums; the delicate staccato of jade lightly tapping jade; the click and swish of painted fans beating the air; the thin laughter of a concubine and an emperor's gasp of satisfaction; the tinkle of porcelain cups against paper-thin saucers; a soft wail that swirls like something alive and diaphanous around the lacquered pillars—to die in a whisper on a marble terrace; the crackling of fireworks—and the endless, endless padding of lightly soled feet moving to their final destiny.

The arrival of the Jesuits in 1600 provided the Western world with the first accepted eyewitness accounts of the Ming dynasty court. Not since Marco Polo's descriptions of the Mongol court of nearly three hundred years earlier had Europe received anything other than vague, hearsay reports of the richness and power of the Chinese emperors. Later, Russian, Dutch, papal, and British embassies and missions richly embroidered the exotic tales. In more recent times the few writers who enjoyed the privilege of association with the imperial Manchu family have left detailed accounts of its colorful ways.

The symbolic and dignified etiquette of the Ming dynasty court was little changed by the alien Manchus who succeeded them. Life in the palace belonged to a pattern of culture that reached far back into the dim antiquity of China's past. The formality of all rites had been crystallized by the great sages, who believed that manners and a certain musical cadence were the essentials of all human relationships. A type of stylized conduct that had little in common with Occidental conventions pervaded life in the Forbidden City. The emphasis was on manners for their own sake, rather than on genuine courtesy.

To Occidental eyes, aware of the royal palaces of Europe in which entire courts had been housed under one roof, the Purple Protected City of the Sons of Heaven presented an incredibly confusing mass of symbolic decoration and alien architecture. It contains more than a thousand separate buildings—no one has ever known exactly how many—standing singly or in groups within their own walled courts: vast halls, small pavilions, living quarters, offices, storehouses, schoolrooms, and barracks. Many are roofed with imperial golden-yellow tiles said to be impregnated with a chemical substance found by primitive happenstance that prevents birds from lighting on and soiling the smooth surfaces. Others have green tiled roofs, the color allotted to nobles and important official buildings. Those with black tiles were for the military. A few have blue roofs, to symbolize mourning; and the remainder a dull, plebeian gray. Nonetheless, each structure bore a poetic name and had an appointed place in the intricate mosaic of palace life.

Imprisoned in white marble and colorful walls, the lore of nearly forty centuries of Chinese history and culture has often been lost in the secrecy that veils a remote past. Legends struggle to reveal the chilly bones of fact; and like most legends, they are tossed off with a smile, a shrug of indifferent shoulders, and are relegated to the shadows of Oriental mystery. Like the aura that envelops a long slumbering battlefield, the palace has a composite soul of its own—the sum total of all those who lived and perished within its walls.

THE DREAM OF THE FOUNDERS

The Forbidden City was conceived in a dream and created in the relentless ambition of two men—tutor and pupil. They were totally unlike, and yet, basically, they shared the same philosophy and the same, deep, absorbing love of beauty.

The tutor was a mystic—a Buddhist monk—who had renounced the world. He awakened one night from a dream of such clarity and beauty that he leaped from his bed and paced around his room in utter confusion. He was not sure he had even been asleep. He remembered quite well lying prone, his eyes wide open, staring into a strange darkness that had suddenly and inexplicably filled with so much shining beauty that he had had to lower his lids lest it blind him. He had dreamed of a glorious celestial city, more beautiful than Khanbalig, the once magnificent Tatar capital, greater than any city known to Asia—a huge and fitting residence for the emperor of China and the Son of Heaven. The monk's dream—as much prophecy as vision—stayed with him in the years to come.

The other man—his pupil—was the earthly founder of the Forbidden City: the bold, headstrong third monarch of the Ming dynasty, known to history as the Emperor Yung Lo.

The little that is known of the mystic monk casts only a flickering glow on life in a China liberated by its own people from the yoke of the Mongols in the fourteenth century. During that era Buddhism was highly esteemed. The first sovereign of the Ming dynasty had been himself a Buddhist priest; but for all his religiosity, he had also been a fiercely able leader who had driven the Mongols beyond the Great Wall. Then, in 1368, he had claimed the Dragon Throne for himself as the Emperor Hung Wu.

Portraits of the third Ming emperor, Yung Lo, show a brooding, swarthy man, in the prime of life, heavy in build and stance, the black eyes brimming with vitality. The lavish gold embroidery of his imposing red robes of state not only increase his bulk but underscore a relentless, dynamic ambition. He was born in 1360, the fourth son of the Emperor Hung Wu. His mother was a lady in waiting named Weng. Promoted to secondary empress at the birth of Yung Lo, she was a scheming, forceful woman who was constantly involved in plots and intrigues for the advantage of her son. Having sired twenty-three sons, the Emperor Hung Wu had been warned by a soothsayer that, despite his own plans, his fourth son would some day mount the Dragon Throne. It was, therefore, natural that the imperial father eyed this arrogant and contentious youth, who had been aptly nicknamed the Black Dragon, with considerable suspicion and anxiety.

The mystic monk had been appointed the lad's guardian and tutor when he was a mere boy. Though a dreamer, the monk was also a brilliant scholar and therefore fitted into the unique position reserved for men of the highest merit and integrity. In a civilization that had always venerated knowledge and the special bond between master and pupil, the monk—for all his visions—seemed an ideal selection. As time went on, and ambition flowed as hotly in the lad's blood as it did in his mother's, the imperial father counted on the monk to have a salutary effect on his son—settle him down, quiet him. But when the heir apparent, Yung Lo's oldest brother, died unexpectedly, the aging sovereign quickly named his grandson Chien Wen—the son of the dead prince—to succeed him.

Yung Lo was fifteen years old then, and the Empress Weng was enraged that her son had not been chosen. She conspired with other members of the court to murder the new heir and elevate Yung Lo to the throne; but the plot was discovered. Yung Lo was arrested and imprisoned for seven years. In 1390, in recognition of his good behavior, the emperor appointed him with Prince Kang of Chin to lead an expedition to the north against restless Tatar tribes. Then in 1393, after the capture of Peking, then called Pei P'ing-fu, the emperor designated his obstreperous fourth son as prince of Yen and placed him in command of all the northern armies. When he assumed his new post and title, Yung Lo was thirty-three years old, and still at his side was the mystic monk who was destined to influence much of his later life.

Early in his reign Emperor Hung Wu had established his capital at Nanking on the Yangtze River. Peking, called Khanbalig by the Mongols, had become a place of little importance. Nonetheless, this ruined city of the north had a long and colorful past. Starting as a fortified outpost named Chi about 1200 B.C., it was little more than a crude barrier against marauding tribes. With the passing of the centuries it slowly developed as a center for the caravan trade, became a walled town, and then the fortress-capital of the kingdom of Yen. In 221 B.C. it was completely destroyed. When rebuilt, it became known as the city of Yu-chou and remained intact until A.D. 986. It was destroyed by the Liaos, who built their capital on the same site in 1013, first calling it Nanching and then Yenching. After this short-lived dynasty was overthrown by the Chin Tatars, the city, renamed Chung-tu, was strong enough to impede, but not stop, the advance of the Mongol hordes in the thirteenth century.

When the troops of Genghis Khan finally captured the city, it was completely demolished and, in the words of contemporary accounts, given over to "three days of glorious slaughter." A new capital, called Khanbalig, was built by Kublai Khan in 1264 on the ashes and broken stones of the old city. The capital of the Mongol, or Yuan, dynasty was largely north of the site of the present walls as constructed by the Ming emperors. The dynasty of the alien Mongols lasted little more than a hundred years, its strength dissipated by riotous living, and the once-victorious troops sapped by corruption. The empire, which covered all eastern Eurasia, collapsed before the whirlwind of the Chinese rebellion that led to the enthronement of the Ming dynasty in 1368. Today the walls built by Kublai Khan can barely be traced, and with the exception of the circular banquet hall, or Western Palace, few relics of the Tatar masters remain.

As if to blot out all memories of the hated Mongols, the Chinese armies had laid waste the wildly barbarous splendor of Khanbalig with ruthless swords. All that remained of the lacquered pavilions of the palace, once curtained with sable, was one hall, where Yung Lo and his monk-tutor made their quarters. As far as the eye could see, the ancient city lay in dismal ruins, and drought clung like a curse over the countryside beyond. The old gardens were neglected and dry; meandering lakes no more than mud-caked wastes. The streets were full of holes and dust; the houses dust and holes. The markets were deserted. The caravans now trekked to the south.

However, Yung Lo, the ambitious Black Dragon, was not discouraged by his dilapidated palace and the appalling condition of the provincial capital. Despite the scars and sorrows of the land, he learned to like the vigorous climate and the healthy dryness, the clear northern sunshine,

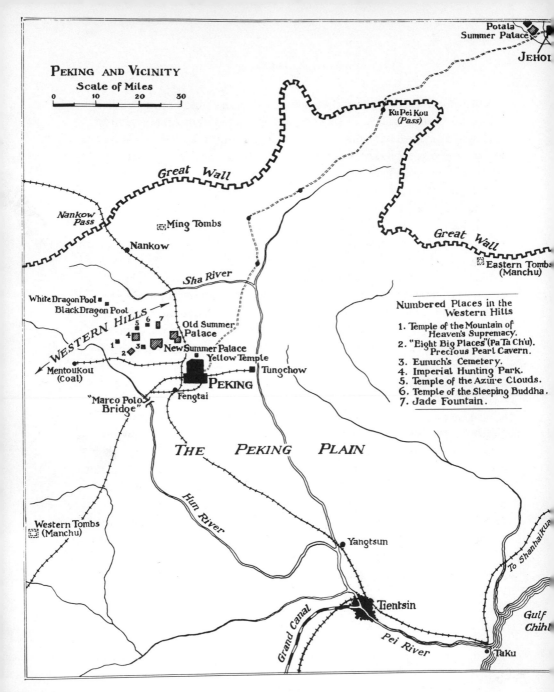

The city of Peking and vicinity.

and the dust-laden winds from the Gobi desert. He felt akin not only to the people, but to the site of their ravaged city, resting on a plain so wide and sweeping that the sky seemed like an inverted blue bowl—the very dome of Heaven. Far to the northwest rose the rugged hills that formed the base of the Great Wall. Beyond lived the restless tribes who still raided the lands their forefathers had so recently dominated. Yung Lo held them in check and, in so doing, learned to respect the men of the north. Their crude, comfortless, mud-walled villages, nestling beside networks of meandering, willow-bordered roads and canals, seemed to underscore the stamina and courage of the people. As great hunts in the distant hills became the means of training his growing armies, the whole terrain became even dearer to him. The judgment of the Tatar conquerors to place their capital here in the north of the Chinese empire had been, he decided, wise indeed. And as the days piled one on top of the other, each hour and all of his tireless energy was used in building up his personal power.

Just when Yung Lo's spiritual guardian, the monk, told him of his vision is not known; but it is likely that the future emperor listened with excitement, black eyes narrowing in thought and concentration. No doubt as the monk described in detail his "dream," Yung Lo was able to see it all: an imperial city embodying in architectural harmonies the ideals and principles of the Chinese conception of true greatness—a place of shining beauty, scores of palaces in orderly procession, vast courtyards guarded by massive walls, a great surrounding moat covered with lotus blooms, the flower of Buddha, and the towering gates—aloof and hidden from the eyes of all men, open to the heavens, the sun, the moon, and the stars.

Yung Lo once again looked to a future day when he might ascend the throne, no longer as the mere governor of a province, but as the emperor and sole ruler of a vast domain who would have the power to build the monk's dream and make it a shimmering reality. The mystic carefully pointed out that apart from the worldly advantages of such a display of might and wealth, the palace-city would proclaim the close relationship between the Lord of Heaven, who ruled above, and the Son of Heaven, who ruled on earth. The Heavenly One, the monk said, dwelt in the Purple Protected Enclosure, a constellation of fifteen celestial bodies clustering about the Star of the Red Myrtle, as the polar star was known. Below, his earthly deputy would inhabit a Purple Protected City, which should become the center of the terrestrial world as its celestial model was the center of all the galaxies above. Confucius had written: "A virtuous ruler is like the pole star that keeps its place while all other stars do homage to it." (Three hundred and fifty years later the Emperor Ch'ien Lung was to write to King George III of England: "My capital is the hub and center around which all nations of the world revolve.")

It was this son-to-father relationship with Heaven that gave all the sovereigns of China their semidivine character and sanctified filial piety beyond all other virtues. As son and heir to Heaven, the emperor, alone among all men, had the right to worship the Supreme Ruler in the sky. Heaven's blessing on his prospering fortunes was the mandate to rule. It was his duty to make direct and seasonal reports of his stewardship. As a priest-king, the emperor should dwell aloof and apart, "in harmony with the universe, obeying the laws of space and direction."

When national calamities indicated a lapse of virtue, or when successful rebellions or invasions occurred, these were the signals that Heaven had withdrawn its mandate from the sovereign. Alone, among all the peoples of the earth, the philosophy of the Chinese accepted the right of the masses to rebel when Heaven withdrew their monarch's right to rule.

For years Yung Lo, still prince of Yen, had been wise in the restraint of his words and deeds, but he was also restless and impatient. Much of his burning energy was used on the training of his army, a pursuit fully approved of by his troubled father, the Emperor Hung Wu. The Tatars still lingered resentfully on the Mongolian plains and once again were mobilizing strength. Far to the west the awesome star of Tamerlane had begun to flame ominously. In the north, however, all was well. Not only were Yung Lo's troops a bulwark of protection for the feudal Ming empire, but the kingdom of Korea once again began to pay its annual tribute. This was testimony to the ability of Yung Lo; and two years after the suppression of a Mongolian uprising, in 1398, he was given supreme authority over all civil and military affairs as governor of the vast and lawless territory known as Yen, which extended to Korea and the Yellow Sea.

Emperor Hung Wu, though vastly proud of Yung Lo, had little peace of mind. In addition to Tatars on the Mongolian plains and the threat of Tamerlane, a more imminent threat to the stability of his throne was his own grasping sons. He found it expedient, therefore, to dispatch the twenty-two imperial princes with all speed to a safe distance from Nanking, all sufficiently separated from one another to prevent them from combining forces. Thus, when Hung Wu died in 1398, all the scheming, ambitious princes were absent from Nanking and unable to attend the hasty enthronement of the emperor's grandson, Chien Wen, the appointed heir. The new, young sovereign, to ensure his position, quickly seized those of his uncles whom he could and had them executed. This folly, ill-timed since Tamerlane was reported to be preparing an expedition against China to match his Indian conquests, was also a mockery of Heaven's mandate to rule.

Though Yung Lo was ordered by the new sovereign to report to Nanchang, he flatly refused, nor would he relinquish his posts in the north. Instead, he rose in revolt and marched rapidly southward, capturing city after city enroute. Chien Wen tried desperately to prevent the rebellious northern army from crossing the Yangtze River, but his fleet of awkward-looking sailing junks surrendered. Thus the route to Nan king was open, and after a fiery seige, the capital city fell to Yung Lo's troops. The young ruler's palaces were put to the torch, and as the roaring flames began to consume them, he fled in panic, mingling with the horde of refugees to escape his uncle Yung Lo's wrath. Shortly thereafter he became a Buddhist monk and a seldom-mentioned legend. Heaven had disowned its erring son only four years after he had ascended the Dragon Throne.

Proclaiming himself emperor, Yung Lo soon justified his nickname of Black Dragon by the pitiless slaughter of his nephew's ministers and their families to the last child. Nanking cringed in horror under his cruel hand. He hated the city and in return was heartily hated by the people. But he governed well and forcefully, sent missions to Java, Sumatra, Siam, and Ceylon, defeated the Tatars on several expeditions, repulsed a Japanese invasion of southern Manchuria, and promulgated a penal code. He remained in Nanking until 1421, consolidating his empire and accumulating wealth to rebuild Peking. By the time his control was firm, Tamerlane had been dead for sixteen years. Yung Lo was ready at last to return north and carry out the mystic monk's dream. Thereafter his new capital was no longer known as Pei P'ing-fu, but as Pei-ching, or Peking, signifying "northern capital," as distinct from Nanking, which means "southern capital."

As did most Chinese emperors, Yung Lo experienced difficulties with his own ambitious and scheming sons. His second son, Kao Hsu—the prince of Han—was an expert archer and a bold cavalry leader who had been of great assistance to his father during the rebellion. He aspired, therefore, to succeed to the throne. But in 1404, when another son, Hung Hsi, was appointed heir apparent, the disappointed Kao Hsu resorted to vicious political attacks on his more fortunate brother and his supporters. In 1417 Yung Lo discovered that Kao Hsu, as restless as ever and even more obstreperous, had started an uprising in Nanking. Enraged, Yung Lo forthwith banished him to Shantung province.

The Forbidden City was still unfinished when Yung Lo died in Mongolia in 1424 while on a combined military and hunting expedition. His body was brought back to China and buried in an impressive tomb in the Western Hills. With his father dead, Kao Hsu brooded. He felt he had been cheated of the throne. His anger, fury, and ambition came to a head in 1426, when he raised the standard of rebellion against his nephew, Emperor Hsuan Te, who had acceded to the throne the year before. But unlike his father, Kao Hsu did not succeed. The rebellion was suppressed, and he was obliged to surrender to his nephew, who was merciless. Kao Hsu was dragged to Peking in chains, placed in a huge cauldron, and roasted to death. To commemorate this somewhat brutal execution and to serve as a warning to the overly ambitious, a brick structure surmounted by an iron pagoda was built to display the charred bones of the prince.

The successors of Yung Lo continued the task of completing the Great Within, lavishing the revenues of their empire on the endless changes of plan. In time it engrossed their entire interest and became far more important than their subjects. Lulled by its luxury, they turned their heads from the omens of Heaven's displeasure: the droughts, floods, famines, and the daring raids of Manchurian tribes. Though several of the Ming emperors were gifted men, even brilliant, most were erratic in their rule and sybaritic in their tastes.

The final deluge of destruction fell on the Emperor Ch'ung Cheng in April, 1644. It was Li Tzu-ch'eng's rebellion that gave the dying Ming dynasty its *coup de grace,* and a Chinese general, Wu San-kuei, who opened the gates to invasion and conquest. The Emperor Ch'ung Cheng was a man of good intentions; but he had come too late to save his line from the poisonous fruit of its own sins, and China was delivered to the alien Manchu dynasty. With one faithful eunuch trailing in his wake, this last of the elegant Ming rulers made his way through the north gate of his beloved palace, climbed the slope of Coal Hill—a place of supposed protection for his family—and hanged himself from the branch of a sophora tree. Later, the first Manchu sovereign encircled the tree's trunk with a heavy iron chain, a permanent stigma and punishment for the tree that was guilty of being an accessory in the death of an emperor. Ever since, this sophora has been known by the people of Peking as the Guilty Sophora.

Li Tzu-ch'eng's cause was just. Rebellions had blazed like wildfire in many quarters of the empire, and he was one of many who had risen up against extortionate taxes and unscrupulous officials. Li was a daring leader. But his armies were no more than an undisciplined mob that swept from city to city, pillaging, spreading chaos, and at last engulfing Peking itself.

Almost as soon as he had taken Peking, Li had to face the invading Manchus, and he lost a fierce and decisive battle near Shanhaikuan. Returning in defeat to the city, he hastily made himself emperor, and then, with all the loot he could lay his hands on, disappeared forever, followed by the remnants of his army.

When the Manchu armies triumphantly entered Peking, their leaders stared aghast at the destruction the rebel Li had wrought in so short a time. But the great palace-city of the Ming dynasty was not irreparably damaged. In time the new masters rebuilt the Forbidden City, wisely copying and restoring what they had not the genius to improve. Since they respected the inspiration of the founders, the Forbidden City is still a reflection of the vision of the mystic monk and a monument to the driving energy of the Emperor Yung Lo.

THE PLAN

The site and arrangement of the palaces, secluded by the Imperial City, which in turn was enclosed by the Tatar City of Peking, was decreed by both tradition and the most careful geomantic calculations. All accumulated observations on the adjustment of man to his surround-

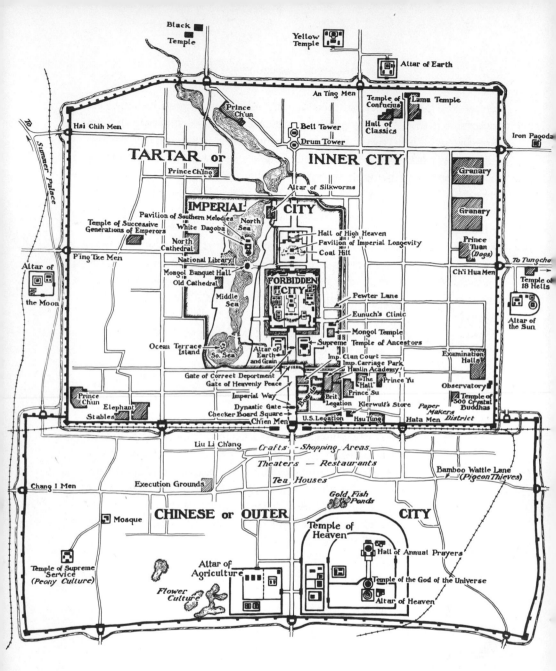

Peking at the time of the Boxer Uprising in 1900. This map includes all principal streets, buildings, and locations mentioned in the book. It also includes the National Library, which was not erected until 1925.

ings and to his fellow men were tangible forces in each undertaking of imperial China. Everything in life, either physical or spiritual, was in some manner subject to these influences and deeply concerned with the cardinal points. These were five in number, and they were esteemed in the following order: first, the center; then south; followed by east and west; and finally north.

From the most ancient times a fear of the north and its bad omens pervaded the thoughts of the Chinese people. Along their northern borders stretched endless desert barriers of scorching summer heat and bitter winter cold. In the far northwest rose the high escarpments of unscaled mountains that separated the Middle Kingdom from the outside world of unlettered barbarians. From these darkly mysterious regions of outlandish people and terrifying rumors came smothering dust storms, freezing winters, and invading armies of Tatars and Manchus (in more recent times Japanese and Russians).

With staggering toil and countless deaths the early princes of the states of Yen, Chao, and Ch'in had slowly built the barriers that later became known as the Great Wall when linked together by the first emperor of China, Ch'in Shih Huang Ti, in 221 B.C. Once completed, the wall was a system of defense in depth which extended from Shanhaikuan on the sea at the Manchurian border to Chia Yu Kuan in Kansu province, a winding obstacle of masonry some fifteen hundred miles long. With the reinforcing segments included, the entire length was about twenty-five hundred miles. Its height varied from twenty to thirty feet; its width at the base, fifteen to twenty-five feet. Pierced by few gates, its length was strengthened by thousands of watchtowers, from which a system of smoke signals could be sent to warn of impending attack. Its bulk consisted of heavily tamped earth and rubble, faced with brick and stone. From its western terminus a more primitive extension of packed earth extended for another six or seven hundred miles.

Ancient records indicate that at least one million slaves and prisoners were employed in its construction. So many of them died of exhaustion and semistarvation on their colossal task that for centuries it was called "the longest cemetery in the world"—for their bodies were imbedded in the rubble and masonry as the quickest means of disposal. For over two thousand years the Great Wall was manned by troops, who, from the parapets, shouted their defiance, fought off scaling ladders, and hurled arrows down into the ranks of attackers. (In recent times some of the more distant guardrooms have surrendered ghostly reminders of these men and their lonely vigils—spears, bows, and arrows, shields, and coats of mail, all of them too small to fit the average Chinese soldier of today.)

The south, on the contrary, provided warm sunshine, welcome rains, security and a sense of well-being. There was a teeming population in the south. Rich cities sent caravans of tribute and taxes to Peking, as well as silk and grain up the Grand Canal on slow-moving junks. Bordering the south were other rich lands that beckoned with wealth and ever-needed food. Their people were ripe to be taken as tributaries, and so they were —Tonkin, Annam (Vietnam), Laos, Cambodia, Cochin China, much of Thailand and the ancient kingdom of Ava (now in Burma).Beyond the southern seas were still other fertile lands to be colonized and exploited: the Philippines, Malaysia, and the jewel-like islands of the Indies.

Since the Chinese, for centuries, looked to the south as the place of good omen and smiling fortune, their cities, palaces, temples, and dwelling houses were always built to face in that direction. Their court-yards benefited from the life-giving warmth of the sun, and the outer gates opened toward the area of good things. Thus heads of families, looking to the future, invited only the best for their sons, grandsons, and all their descendants. But most important of all, the emperors sat on golden thrones that permitted them, as Sons of Heaven, to rest calm eyes on blue southern skies and assure harmony and prosperity for their people.

As reconstructed by the Emperor Yung Lo, Peking consisted of four separate walled cities, all contained within the outer battlements of over 22 miles in length, encompassing an area of about 26 square miles. The Inner City, later called the Tatar City by the Manchus, was roughly square in shape and about four miles by three and a half. Included within its limits was the Imperial City, which in turn enclosed the palaces of the Forbidden City. The adjoining Outer City, later called the Chinese City, was a rectangle of about five miles by two and a half. (After 1900 the Legation Quarter, in the southeast part of the Tatar City, became a fifth completely walled enclosure.) Surrounded by deep, wide moats, the parapeted walls of the Inner City were 40 feet high, 62 feet thick at the base, 34 feet wide at the top, and were strengthened every 60 yards by great bastions projecting 50 feet outward. The walls of the Outer City were 30 feet high, 25 feet thick at the base, and strongly buttressed every 200 yards. Sixteen gates, each protected by a powerful enceinte and surmounted by huge fortified towers, pierced the circuit of the walls.

The Great Within—as the Chinese called the Forbidden City—was laid out in the center of the city of Peking, its main gate facing south in a direct line with the main gate of the capital. The palaces were screened from the north by the only eminence in all Peking, an artificial hill shaped like a rest for a scholar's pens and brushes. It was built of earth supposedly left by the long-vanished khans in excavating to create lakes for their pleasure palaces. To the populace it was known as Coal Hill, because it was commonly believed to be a great pile of coal, surfaced with earth, that could be used for fuel in case of a long siege. More formally, it was known as the Protecting Hill of the Great Within.

The overall plan of the Forbidden City called for a rectangular enclosure about three quarters of a mile long and about half a mile wide, containing about two hundred and forty acres of ground. Surrounding the enclosure were over two and a quarter miles of ramparts, which were pierced by four towered gates and surmounted by fantastic towers at each corner. The great south and north gates were in the center of their respective walls; the less imposing east and west gates, to the south of center of their respective walls. All the main buildings faced south.

On each side of the south-north central core of buildings was a multitude of smaller palaces, living quarters, and offices. In their carefully secluded, separate courtyards, each was spaced and ordered in accordance with its appointed role in palace life. The main building of each group faced the southern skies, although there were a few exceptions—the most notable being a small hall in the northwestern section of the grounds that faced north. This hall was reserved for tactless ladies who needed discipline and for concubines no longer able to amuse the emperor. The open stages of the theaters also faced north, which permitted the imperial loge to face south, for the Son of Heaven, as he watched the dramas, could not compromise his dignity, even for amusement, by facing in any other direction.

Palace life in high Asia was on a grander, more magnificent scale than court life in Europe; and it was further complicated by the various roles of the Supreme Lord of China. As the ruler of the empire, he required throne halls, great halls for state occasions and lesser halls for daily audiences; as the Son of Heaven, the high priest of the land, a hall for ritual purification; as head of the imperial family, a shrine for the ancestral rites; as patron of three religions, temples of the three faiths of Buddhism, Lamaism, and Taoism. And, as the husband of many wives, he needed separate establishments for all his women, as well as palaces and school-rooms for his children. In addition, he had to provide accommodations for servants, the eunuch corps, maids, and, at the height of the Ming dynasty, as many as three thousand guards. During its greatest days the Forbidden City sheltered over ten thousand people.

Imperial dignity and the role of priest-king required isolation from the outside world. Thus everything needed by the emperor and the court was provided from within the palace precincts. If an empress desired a new robe, an order was delivered by her eunuchs to the Household Department, and thence to the storehouses, where bolts of the finest silk, specially woven for the palace or sent as tribute, were kept. If an empress dowager, the most important of all ladies, fancied a special brand of tea, an order was relayed to the tea storehouse through the Household Department. All the needs of the imperial family, including spices for the cooks, medicines for the sick, toys and schoolbooks for the children, were thus satisfied by the same, indirect channels. There were gardens for the emperor's relaxation, and others for the palace ladies. There were librar-ies, offices for the state secretariat, a printing plant, two theaters, and a mourning palace.

Two walled enclosures stood on either side of the Forbidden City itself: the Supreme Temple of the Ancestors on the east, and the Altar of Earth and Grain, now called Central Park, on the west. Thus, auspi-cious influences from these directions were shed on the halls and courts, just as Coal Hill provided shelter from the ill-omened north. The palace-city was linked to the empire by a ceremonious approach consisting of a broad, straight road, paved with massive blocks of stone, that widened out at intervals into the open courts guarded by imposing gates. This imperial highway progressed from the far outer gate of the Chinese City through Ch'ien Men—the great Front Gate of the Tatar City—through the lesser Dynastic Gate, then the Meridian Gate of the palace itself, and finally into the enormous first court of the Great Within.

When important embassies were to be received by the emperor, or if semibarbarous northern chieftains were to be impressed into a state of submission, it was the custom to spread golden sand over the entire three miles of straight road from the southern entrance of the Chinese City through all the massive succession of gates to the throne hall itself. After passing through the teeming city—all crowded with brilliantly uni-formed guards, courtiers, and officials—and finally, into the dimness of the many-pillared Hall of Audience that glittered with the robes and symbols of princes and nobles, the most haughty and arrogant of emissaries was certain to feel very humble indeed.

Across the first vast courtyard stood a lower gate that opened into an imposing Court of Honor, behind which began the procession of state throne halls on their high marble terraces. The first group—the Three Great Throne Halls—was purely ceremonial. The second, also consisting of three separate halls prefaced by a formal gate, contained the most important official buildings of the palace; no stranger could set foot beyond their guardian portal without special permission. Even the emperor passed this point only on state occasions and in formal procession. To the east and west of this series of throne halls were the residential palaces of the imperial family, to which only the most privileged visitors and relatives were invited, occasionally, to attend theatricals or family conclaves.

When the Emperor Yung Lo finally left Nanking, with the building of the Forbidden City foremost in his mind, he placed three master architects in charge: Hsu Tai of the imperial Construction Department, Yuan An, a eunuch of the Nanking palace staff, and Feng Chiao, a builder of high repute. Since education at that time paid little heed to the exact sciences, the three performed their labors with only the simplest of mathematical formulas. For guides, they had, in addition to tradition itself, a manual of official regulations governing the construction of palaces and a venerable book, *Method of Architecture.* The latter treatise, produced in 1103 by the scholar Li Chieh, used ample illustrations covering all the details of building the Chinese dignified as architecture. It ignored the utilitarian stone and brick construction of substructures, storehouses, ramparts, and floors. But the handsome details for balustrades, cornices, rainspouts, bridges, and panels were described and illustrated with great care. It also contained rules for the erection of the timber frames of buildings and carpenters' rules for fashioning doors, windows, coffered ceilings, and a system of complicated beams and brackets that supported the weight of tile roofs.

Most of the principles of Chinese architecture seem to have been established during the Shang dynasty, which ended in 1122 B.C. Unlike the builders of medieval Europe, the Chinese usually spread their structure as if to blend with the earth on which they rested. It was not considered prudent to dig deep into the ground or to construct high toward the sky. Either extreme might disturb the spirits who dwelt below or drifted above, and all people were wary of encroaching on their domains. Since the spirits of the air moved only in straight lines and never higher than a hundred feet above the earth a height limit of ninety-nine feet was placed on all structures except the pagodas at certain temples. As an example of this practice, the tower surmounting the Great Front Gate of Peking was ninety-nine feet high; thus it could not obstruct the passage of good spirits from the south into the capital. (It should be mentioned that the old Chinese measure, called a *ch'ih*, corresponds closely to the English measure of one foot).

For centuries the typical Chinese building, whether a palace hall, a peasant's hut, or a temple, was a rectangular, one-story, porched structure with a pitched roof, built on a platform of beaten earth, brick, or stone. This basic form was at times elaborated on with square, circular, or octagonal variations used in pleasure pavilions and shrines designed for ritual purposes. But the general pattern prevailed and was sufficiently adaptable to permit an addition of several stories when desired.

Exposed pillars of wood set in shallow stone sockets, like a cup in a saucer, and surmounted and locked by longitudinal, or transverse, cross-beams, supported the cantilevers, purlins, and rafters that framed the roof. As in a modern, steel-framed skyscraper, both inner and outer walls were essentially screens or curtains that had no structural significance. Since interior walls, doors, and windows either connected pillars or were placed between them, space within any building could be rearranged with ease. Pillars were painted or lacquered, the crossbeams enlivened with symbolic designs or pictures, and the exposed frame of the roof embellished with a forest of brackets, which, in early times, played a functional part in bearing a large share of the weight.

The greatest halls were dignified with a hip roof and a lower, shed roof protruding over a pillared veranda, or porch. The hipped joints at the corners of the eaves and the eaves themselves swept gracefully up to the ridgepole in a gentle curve that projected beyond the roof line. Much has been conjectured as to the origin of this characteristic roof form of China. One theory is that the pattern was derived from the concave tent roofs of nomadic ancestors; others believe that since gutters were never used, the design was meant to throw the water of heavy rains clear of the building, this protecting its walls and foundations. Less important structures contented themselves with a pitched roof finished off at each end with a simple gable.

The roofs of the Forbidden City were resplendent with glazed, colored tiles, and their supporting timbers were painted in brilliant shades. Enclosed by great flat tiles, the ridgepoles were decorated at each end with mythical fish-tailed creatures charged with the duty of warding off fires and other calamities, while processions of smaller animals were shown marching up the curve of the eaves. As was the case with most Chinese art forms, this fanciful adornment of the eaves was rooted in ancient history. In 283 B.C. Prince Min of the state of Ch'i, a cruel tyrant, was defeated in battle, captured, strung up to the corner of a roof ridge, and left hanging in the hot sun until he died. As a constant reminder of his infamy and his subsequent punishment, the people placed his effigy, mounted on a hen, on the roofs of their houses. To prevent him from escaping over the top of the roof, fierce creatures were fastened to the ends of the ridge-pole. At the time of the Emperor Yung Lo's reign other figures were being added to restrain the hen and her rider: a dragon, a phoenix, lion, unicorn, a horse, and finally the great fish-tailed figure at the top.

Early dynasties had built palaces of surprising size and fantastic beauty. For example, Ch'in Shih Huang Ti, Ch'in dynasty emperor and builder of the Great Wall, constructed an imperial palace of gigantic proportions, in keeping with his reputation as the greatest builder of all time. Seven hundred thousand prisoners of war and criminals slaved to complete it under the lashes of overseers' whips. One terrace was so vast that ten thousand persons could assemble on it, while banners fifty feet long could be hung from its balustrades without touching the ground.

The Han dynasty (206 B.C.–A.D. 264) set a higher, more elegant standard for its palaces. Throne halls were supported by pillars inlaid with jade, and cornices were decorated with gold and semiprecious stones. Elaborately carved marble balustrades and terraces were an important feature, too. Since the art of tilemaking was little understood, the floors of the Han structures were of beaten earth painted in brilliant colors.

The T'ang dynasty (618–906) laid aside the traditional earthbound concepts and raised multistoried buildings, sometimes joined by flying bridges. Chinese architecture is usually considered to have reached its apogee during this brilliant era of its history. The succeeding Sung dynasty followed the same pattern of extravagance, but later added a delicacy and poetic fancy that suggests the decadence of its reign.

The Mongol rule (1260–1368), known as the Yuan dynasty, accepted the

Chinese model for state halls, but in their living palaces they indulged themselves in a mixture of all the styles of construction used in their far-flung empire. They employed stone extensively, and sometimes added fabric roofs as reminders of their own felt-covered yurts, or tents. But their crude innovations and designs left little permanent effect on traditional Chinese architecture.

Two hundred thousand workmen toiled for over forty years on the great task of building Yung Lo's palace-city. With no cranes or other machines, the labor of hauling massive blocks of stone and mighty timbers became a matter of impressing more men and mules and using miles of ropes. No effort was spared, nor any amount of treasure. Forced labor —slaves and prisoners—built the Forbidden City; crushing taxes paid for it. Faraway jungles supplied the finest woods; the quarries in distant hills the finest marbles. Whole villages of brickmakers supplied bricks for the masons. Thousands of potters fashioned the glazed tiles for the mountains of roofs. Artisans and craftsmen from all the provinces gathered in Peking to carve, lacquer, and paint the panels, beams, ceilings, and pillars of the innumerable halls.

However, Yung Lo suffered one great disappointment. Although he had always operated on the greatest and most expensive scale, only three copies of his twenty-three-thousand-volume library were printed from hand-cut, wooden blocks. This operation proved to be too costly even for him.

Although the plan of the Great Within fell heir to all past ages and conformed to classical conventions, Emperor Yung Lo, influenced by his monk-tutor's dream, was able to bequeath to posterity the imprint of his own superb taste and the spirit of the period in his palace-city. His architects contrived a subtle elegance, a certain sinuous strength, an airy grace that suggests the exquisite porcelains of his dynasty. Restraint and refinement, the keynotes of Ming culture, dominated both thought and result.

To achieve this aesthetic beauty, only the finest materials were employed. Precious *persea nanmu*, a fragrant, southern wood—seasoned and impervious to time—was transported from distant Yunnan and Kweichow provinces for the pillars. Stone of the best quality came from Feng Shang; variegated marbles from Hsuchow, specially made bricks from Ling Ching and Soochow. In contrast to the gaudy reds, greens, and glaring yellow used by the Mongols, the Ming builders enhanced the beauty of their halls with softer tones of faded bronze, purplish red, greenish blue, golden yellow, and turquoise.

The builders had scarcely completed their ambitious work when the three Great Throne Halls and many of the separate palaces were destroyed by fire. Two more state halls went up in flames during the Feast of Lanterns in honor of the new year. Rebuilt in 1516, they were twice more destroyed and twice rebuilt before the end of the Ming dynasty. Earthquakes in 1624, 1666, 1679, 1680—when parts of the palace-city burned—and 1830 caused heavy damage to the Great Within. In 1731 a severe tremor—the worst in Chinese history—was so powerful that not only was much of Peking destroyed, but over a hundred thousand people perished under crumbling walls. Numerous fires occurred during the Ming and Manchu dynasties, many of which were the work of greedy eunuchs who thus covered up their thefts of imperial possessions. But after each disaster, the ruined halls and palaces were rebuilt according to their original plan and former beauty.

THE SYMBOLS

Despite the challenging vision of Yung Lo and his tutor, and the talent of the three architects, tradition dominated the entire creation of the Forbidden City like a watchful and jealous matriarch. Motifs were deep with ancient meaning. Symbols of imperial power were repeated in tireless variation. Carved marble waves and clouds enhanced the dignity of the Son of Heaven. A thousand lucky symbols were included to ensure Heaven's blessing and protection: characters for long life and happiness, bats, cranes, butterflies, flowers, fruit, birds, beasts, bamboo, pines, tortoises, and deer.

The mystic lore of numbers was incorporated with great consistency throughout the palaces. Five marble bridges spanned the stream that swept in a wide bow across the great courts; five flights of marble steps ascended to the throne dais. The huge Meridian Gate had five tunneled sally ports. There were two groups of state halls, each consisting of three buildings. Ornaments occurred in pairs. But to Chinese eyes a pair did not necessarily mean identity. A man and wife—not twins—conveyed the ancient conception of yin and yang, of opposites denoting the complementary aspects of life. Each number had its own, separate lore: *one* was considered unlucky, *ten* the perfect number, *four* a double pair; *eight* was associated with Buddhism, *seven* was the number of the heart and virtue; and there were *six* boards of government.

Heraldry, coats of arms, and family crests, as known in the West, did not exist in China. Instead, there was the dragon. The Supreme Lord was head of a dragon empire of four classes of subjects—nobles, officials, the military, and the people—of many princely kin, and numerous personal descendants. The imperial dragon family wore yellow; and the four classes in order of rank, blue, red, white, and black.

The five-clawed dragon was the personal symbol of the emperor; and it was emblazoned on all his possessions. The image of this fabulous monster was repeated endlessly in great halls, on ceilings, and on encaustic tile plaques, to proclaim the power of its imperial master over all things under Heaven. Nobles of whatever rank were permitted to use a four-clawed dragon as a symbol. Certain great temples were authorized the use of the five-clawed dragon, such as the Lama Temple in Peking, since an emperor had been born within its palatial halls.

The origin of the dragon and the myths that surround its existence have long been hidden in the mists of Chinese antiquity. It is possible that the *alligator sinensis* of the Yangtze Valley and the crocodile of southern China were the real ancestors of the fantastic creatures that evolved through the centuries in Chinese legend. A dragon of pure blood could be recognized by nine distinguishing features; horns of a stag, head of a camel, eyes of a demon, coils of a serpent, scales of a fish, feet of a vulture, claws of a tiger, ears like a bull, and the viscera of a tortoise. His horns were as sensitive as the antennae of a snail; and no sound escaped his ears. He had three weaknesses: his greatest bliss was to lay coiled in a thicket of bamboo; arsenic was an elixir to him; and swallow's flesh was the choicest of all dainties. A wise man who had dined on swallows never tempted the dragon by riding afterward in a boat.

Since "dragon bones" were believed to cure many ills, they were highly valued in ancient China. Their cure-all reputation presented a challenge to Western medical scientists in the twentieth century, who wanted to expose the myth. Analysis of the bones showed them to be relics—some fossilized—of many varieties of animal, both prehistoric and modern.

At court and throughout the empire, the spring festival was celebrated in honor of these creatures, and the dragon king was saluted on his official birthday in the ninth month of the year. But, mystical or not, the dragon was expected to perform certain duties for the people, particularly that of bringing rain in long periods of drought. If, after due prayers and sacrifices at his shrine in a local temple, the dragon still failed to quench the parched earth, the villagers believed his image should be punished and defiled. Gilded effigies were then dragged from the altars, hurled with curses into the village offal pits, and spat on by their indignant "worshipers." When the rains finally did come, the dragon figure would be hauled from the filth, thoroughly cleaned, and again established in the temple, restored to the good graces of his simple-minded votaries.

The dragon gods, who dwelled in the depths of the Black Dragon Pool and the neighboring White Dragon Pool,—located about twelve miles northwest of Peking—were expected to expand their influence to include much wider areas of the empire and, on occasion, were visited by the emperor in person. If prayers and offerings to the black dragon caused bubbles in the waters of the pool or a mist to float on its surface, rain was certain to relieve the worst drought. But if no bubbles or mist appeared, a visit to the shrine of the white dragon was mandatory, since it was firmly believed that the smell of burning incense at his shrine would not fail to bring a welcome downpour to the parched fields.

The phoenix was regarded as the symbol of the empress and the entire imperial family. Known as the *feng*, the male of this mythical bird-creature usually accompanied the dragon. While the latter was the lord of all the waters—oceans, rivers, rain, clouds, and mists—the phoenix was associated with the sun and fire. Since the phoenix represented the active principle of creation, it was believed to exert great influence on fertility. According to ancient detailed accounts, it had the head of a hen, the eyes of a man, the neck of a serpent, the viscera of a locust, the brow of a swallow, the back of a tortoise, the plumage of a love pheasant, and a long, fish-shaped tail consisting of twelve or thirteen plumes (the number depending on the number of months in the calendar). Combining all five of the Chinese primary colors, its plumage was brilliant—in contrast to the darkness of the dragon. At the last "recorded" appearance of a phoenix, one was seen scratching at the grave of the Emperor Hung

Wu's father near his native home in Anhui province. The village has been known ever since as Feng Huang Fu, or Place of the Yellow Phoenix.

The finest carvings of imperial dragons in the Forbidden City were on the marble panels that were placed on an incline between the center flights of steps leading to the great gates and halls. Tradition decreed that no human foot should ever tread on these panels. They were the stairways over which only the spirits passed, lightly and silently, to take their part in the ceremonies of the Great Within. The yellow chair of the emperor was borne *over* the panels, as his bearers trod the narrow steps on either side. As the Son of Heaven, he had the right to mingle with the invisible spirits, but even he could not set foot upon their pathways.

Among the most curious of the imperial symbols were the round, marble sundial and the square grain measure, which were placed at the east and west ends of the terraces before several important throne halls. Atop a swastika-carved pedestal, the grain measure has the appearance of a miniature dovecot, the rooflet of which is merely a cover for a square box with four open sides. Since the origin of the measure remains a mystery, the architects probably placed it where it stood in obedience to tradition. Some have claimed it represented justice and the sovereign as a lawgiver; others that it was an imperial letter box into which petitions and complaints might be placed. Most have considered it a stylized form of grain measure, which, when filled to the brim with wheat or rice, was meant as an offering to the emperor in his capacity as First Farmer of the Land. This was an act of national gratitude for his having plowed the "first furrow" in the preceding spring, thus setting an example for all growers of grain. It was also regarded as a symbol of a safely harvested crop.

The special grain measure on the Terrace of the Palace of Cloudless Heaven contained a rare bronze cube known as the Wang Mang Foot. Created by Wang Mang, a usurper during the Han dynasty, it was the established standard of linear and cubic measure for the empire. Though of great importance and often mentioned in Chinese records, it disappeared for several centuries and was not found until Feng Yu-hsiang, called the Christian General, drove the last emperor of the Manchu dynasty from the Forbidden City in 1924.

The marble sundial, a companion piece to the grain measure on the terraces of several important buildings, set on a circular base and supported by four square pillars, lay in a carved crescent that was inclined at an angle of thirty degrees toward the south. The form of the base suggested completion and imperial virtue. Virtue for its own sake was highly regarded. A good man, by reason of his goodness, was always a most respected member of any community in China. Therefore, it was suitable that the emperor be constantly reminded that his virtue should shine at all times like the sun at high noon.

As the earliest time-measuring device, the sundial represented an important imperial obligation: regulating time for the empire. This was done each year by the issuance of a lunar calendar. To an agricultural people like the Chinese, the procession of the equinoxes and the phases of the moon were all-important, and the imperial almanac informed them when they might expect an early autumn, a late frost, rain, floods, or drought.

Also of importance was the astrological information contained in the almanac, which acted as a guide for all human conduct, indicating lucky days for marriage, for burying the dead, for building, buying, selling— even for bathing—as well as the solutions for the countless problems that beset the daily life of the people. Astrology had gone hand in hand with astronomy since men first recognized that heavenly bodies moved in cycles. Centuries of study had engendered the conviction that life might be reduced to a formula by accurate observation and deduction. The bible of this school of thought was the Confucian *Book of Changes;* but as a manual for the patterns of existence, it became so involved that only the most learned could make anything out of it. The vast majority depended on the almanac, which contained digests from the complete work.

In the days of the Mongol khans the almanac had been prepared by Arabs, who were prominent in many capacities at the court, since they were the most noted mathematicians of that period. During the Ming regime, as contact with Mohammedan countries became less and less frequent, the Chinese, who replaced the Arabs, grew careless in the accuracy of their observations and in their calculations of celestial bodies. When the imperial Board of Astronomy miscalculated the dates of the equinoxes, its mistakes created a serious situation, for these dates coincided with the Great Sacrifices to Heaven. As a result, if the emperor carried out his sacred duties on days that were obviously incorrect, he would appear ridiculous in the eyes of his people.

At this time the early Jesuit missionaries who came to China were among the most brilliant scientists of the period. When word of their talents reached the court, the Emperor Wan Li lost no time in summoning them to Peking and commanded them to correct the calendar. They set about their task with alacrity, for this was a heaven-sent opportunity to contact the intellectual classes and court circles, whom they regarded as their best field for missionary efforts.

Chief among these Jesuits and the first to reach Peking was Matteo Ricci, who in his native Italy had been a pupil of the celebrated Christopher Clavius, one of the greatest mathematicians of his time. Before Ricci's death in 1610, this cultivated and courageous man succeeded in making several illustrious converts at the imperial court. But he and later priest-astronomers were so hampered by obstinate, distrustful officials of the Board of Astronomy that little real progress was accomplished toward improving the all-important calendar.

It was not until after the Manchu conquest that Adam Schall, a Belgian priest and a highly capable mathematician, was able to correct the accumulated errors. His pupil, the young Emperor Shun Chih, so respected and loved Schall that he called him *maffa*, the Manchu term for "father." Naturally, such a close friendship aroused jealousy at court. After the sovereign's early death, Schall, who had grown old and ill, was dismissed and thrown into prison, where he was chained to a pillar and starved. Eventually, he was sentenced to death by the slicing process. This barbarous punishment was administered by trained experts who progressively cut off small pieces of flesh from the condemned man; or loosened with a sharp knife strips of skin, which were slowly torn from his body. Under countless repetitions the screaming victim might last for days before he succumbed. The efficiency of the skilled anatomists who performed this torture was judged by the length of time they were able to prolong life in the hapless prisoner.

On the day in 1666 that Adam Schall's inhuman sentence was announced, a great earthquake shook Peking. A courageous Manchu dignitary, taking advantage of the terror and confusion created by the heaving convulsions of the ground—for such calamities indicated the displeasure of Heaven—hurried to the grandmother of the emperor. She was a strong-minded Tatar woman. Her determination and good sense had safeguarded her son, and later her grandson, through the first two critical decades of Manchu rule. When the dignitary showed her the order for Schall's execution and asked if she meant to set her seal to the death warrant of her dead son's tutor, the redoubtable old lady was outraged.

She threw the document to the floor, trampled on it, and in forceful terms expressed her opinion of the responsible officials. Thus Schall was saved and shortly thereafter released. But broken and weakened by his terrible ordeal, he died four months later on August 5, 1666, at the age of seventy-five.

Other cruelties in China—and the Far East—had reached refinements that would have won the envy of the Spanish Inquisition. It was fairly commonplace for a magistrate to hand down vicious sentences to prisoners found guilty of any crimes, even petty ones: finger- or toe-nails pulled out, branding, crippling by breaking bones, a hand cut off, eyes gouged out, or blinding with a sharp iron rod. Indeed, as late as the first quarter of the twentieth century rich ex-nobles in Peking blinded their most accomplished Mongolian minstrels so as to prevent them from running away or returning to their distant homes. Poison in various forms was used to do away with a rival, an enemy, an unfaithful woman, or a brother in line to inherit land and titles. Death after prolonged pain, the source of which could not be traced, became a fine art. One method consisted of sharpening a small sliver of bamboo, rolling it into a tiny coil, and binding it with easily digested grass or gut string. This was then placed in an article of food known to be a favorite of the intended victim. When swallowed, the binding soon dissolved, and the coiled bamboo sliver straightened out like a released spring, its sharp points piercing the lining of the stomach or the intestines and causing a slow and agonizing death. In a comparable method, finely chopped tiger or cat whiskers were placed in food; their numerous infinitesimal barbs would catch in the digestive tract and cause painful sores or infections that were impossible to treat.

After Adam Schall's death, it again became obvious that the almanac was becoming inaccurate and that the people had lost all respect for it. Eventually, their complaints reached the ears of the young Emperor K'ang Hsi. Though only thirteen years old at the time, K'ang Hsi fully understood the importance of the calendar and promptly ordered a thorough investigation into its defects. He soon learned that during his father's reign calculations for the almanac had been entrusted to foreigners, some of whom were still living unobtrusively in Peking. When he sent messengers out into the city to inqire if these strangers were aware of errors in the almanac, Father Ferdinand Verbiest, the deceased Schall's devoted assistant, replied that it contained many glaring mistakes—the worst being that it credited the coming year with having thirteen lunar months, whereas it actually had but twelve. K'ang Hsi at once summoned the Jesuit to audience and repeated his question. Again, Verbiest asserted that the almanac was manifestly incorrect and offered to prove his claim.

"I will calculate on the terrace," he said, "the proportion of shadow cast by the style for any hour Your Majesty suggests. By the length of the shadow, I can determine the height of the sun. From that I can tell its position in the zodiac. Then Your Majesty can judge for yourself if this is the same location as that marked in the calendar."

The head of the Board of Astronomy, Schall's old and bitter enemy, tried to save face and circumvent the priest by ridiculing his strange religion. Then he added irately that it was beneath imperial dignity to seek knowledge from outlandish foreigners. The young sovereign turned in fury on the bearded old incompetent. How dared *he* open his mouth —*he* who had pretended to search the empire for competent assistants —*he* who had known all along that at his door were the very men who had remedied the situation in the past!

Next day, on the wide terrace of the throne hall, Verbiest—wearing Manchu dress, his hair tied back in a long braid—waited to demonstate to the Emperor K'ang Hsi just how far wrong the Chinese officials had been. Gathered about him and his simple apparatus—a shaft placed vertically in the ground to create a shadow that could be measured—were the youthful sovereign and his attendants. It was a bitterly cold day. All were bundled in winter brocade robes lined with fur and continually stamped their thick, felt-soled boots on the frost-parched stones to warm their feet. Finally the experiment was over. Verbiest succeeded in his demonstration! A man of great tact and charm, from then on he had no trouble in catching the interest of the Son of Heaven in other curiosities of European learning. A short time later he was appointed the young man's teacher.

However, as so often happens in the Far East, what had seemed a clearcut victory ended in compromise. The preparation of astronomical data was thenceforth entrusted to the foreign priests, but the fixing of days for fasts and feasts, of lucky and unlucky days, was left to their Chinese colleagues. It was a wise arrangement. Jesuit intelligence could never have rationalized its conscience in such an atmosphere of hocus-pocus, and the peculiar logic of astrology would have baffled even their enlightened minds. But long after the last days of imperial dynasties, the general populace continued to demand information from the almanac. In 1922, the date and hour of the boy-emperor's wedding was carefully fixed by the Astrologers Royal—and again, how mistaken were their calculations! As late as the middle 1940's, though the Western calendar had long since been adopted, peasants still sowed their crops, reaped their harvests, and celebrated the rebirth of the year in accordance with the lunar calendar. Though no longer stamped with official blessing, it remained to them an inspired guide from the heavens.

THE GLORY AND THE TWILIGHT

Under Ch'ien Lung, the fourth emperor of the Manchu dynasty, who reigned from 1736 to 1796 and died in 1799, life in the Forbidden City was as brilliant and the palaces almost as beautiful as during the most opulent days of the Ming dynasty. During Ch'ien Lung's sixty-year rule, Yung Lo, the founder of the Great Within, must have looked down from the world of spirits on his dream city, his heart rejoicing. The Forbidden City—the core of all Asia—sparkled in the sunlight of Ch'ien Lung's splendor, as it sheltered that great man as its master. A generous lord who enjoyed magnificence, he gilded and painted, built and rebuilt, and begrudged nothing to his palace-city, which was his home and that of his family for nearly ninety years before he inherited the Dragon Throne. China had become so much home to the Manchus that each day the hills and plains and forests of their native land seemed a little more remote. Manchuria, beyond the Wall, slowly became the "Great Outside" while the palace became more and more the "Great Within."

Compared to the Ming rulers, and in particular to the extravagant Wan Li, the Manchus were economical in rebuilding the ruined palaces they had found when they entered Peking in 1644. With them, utility supplanted fantasy and elegance. Pine-wood pillars from Manchuria replaced the costly, perfumed *persea nanmu* ones from the south. Conventional one-story pavilions were substituted for many two-storied buildings. Some of the great gardens and lakes vanished or were changed

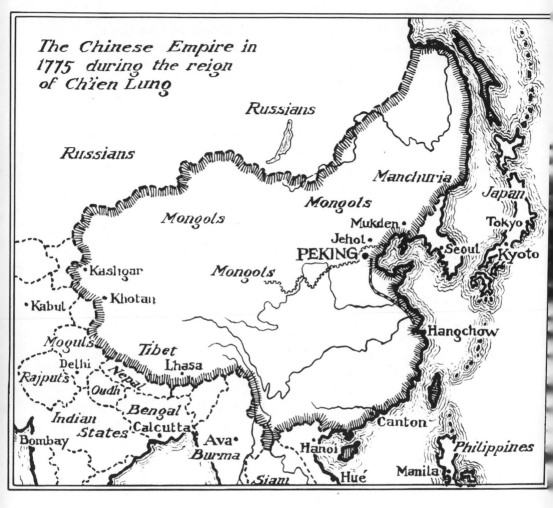

The Chinese Empire at its greatest extent, in 1775 during the reign of the Emperor Ch'ien Lung.

beyond recognition. Under the first of the Manchus, Shun Chih, reconstruction was devoted to barest essentials; under the second, K'ang Hsi, to the requisites of the monarchy; under the third, Yung Cheng, to utility and comfort. But during the long reign of Ch'ien Lung—from 1736 to 1796—luxury and elegance once more blossomed throughout the courts. His most noteworthy additions to the Forbidden City were the great library in the southeast section and the huge retirement palace in the northeast. In addition, many of the halls of state and residential palaces were renovated or redecorated, and shrines and temples to the gods were embellished or enlarged by the monarch's lavish hand.

A remarkable individual, Ch'ien Lung's popularity with the Chinese was both merited and sincere. A tall, imposing man, he had a ready wit and a gay and spacious personality that soon was felt throughout the empire. They were all convinced that he would be a great emperor, and this was further confirmed by his large, heavy ear lobes, an indication, according to the soothsayers, of a brilliant destiny. They liked to compare him to their own beloved T'ai Tsung of the T'ang dynasty who had been such a man a thousand years before. It was natural, therefore, that rumor and gossip claimed he was not of the imperial Manchu clan, but actually the child of a high Chinese official. However, the desire was probably father to the often-repeated tale of his birth.

According to the story, the true child of the heir apparent and future third emperor, Yung Cheng, was born sickly and deformed. At the same moment a robust, healthy son was born to a high Chinese dignitary of the court. Disappointed, and mindful of the need to continue a strong dynastic line, Yung Cheng ordered the babies switched under the pall of utmost secrecy, and thus the son of a Chinese official later became the Manchu Emperor Ch'ien Lung. So ran the popular and generally accepted gossip in Peking for over two hundred years. There is no way to prove the tale or to refute it; such things have happened before in Oriental history. If true, there is no record of what became of the sickly infant; and against the story stands the fact that there were other sons and nephews eligible for accession to the throne, so a switch of babies to ensure a strong dynastic succession was never necessary in the first place.

When Ch'ien Lung was born—in what was then a palace in the northeast quarter of the Tatar City, which later became the great Lama Temple—he was the fourth son. His father was one of many brothers, all of whom had sons of their own. Endowed with the best qualities of both the Chinese and Manchu peoples, Ch'ien Lung's life was characterized by a largeness of spirit, which placed him among the true aristocracy of the earth; and his reign was among the most outstanding in Chinese history. He was fortunate at the time of his accession. The fires of ambition, which had burned so fiercely in the descendants of Genghis Khan and Tamerlane, and which had scourged all Asia and parts of Europe, were flickering out. Sungaria had defied the earlier Manchu emperors for nearly a hundred years, but it was now subjugated. Tibet and Chinese Turkistan were conquered, and other military successes carried Ch'ien Lung's power to the borders of Persia, India, and Turkey. Burma, Annam, and Korea paid him tribute. In fact, during his reign the Manchu empire reached its greatest territorial extent.

In administration Ch'ien Lung was equally successful. He owed much to an efficient organization of the state as well as to his personal popularity. His state progresses, extraordinarily expensive as they were, made him familiar to his subjects, who could see for themselves that their emperor was a man worthy of respect and a fulfillment of their conception of how a great sovereign should look and act. The pomp and splendors of the court flattered their national vanity. The handsome show gave them some return for the money they had paid in taxes. But, extravagant as he was, Ch'ien Lung remitted the land tax four times during his reign, spent vast sums on conservation in the provinces bordering the Yellow River, and carefully regulated the currency for the benefit of the entire empire. In the markets the people sang a contented little jingle:

> Oh, the cash of Ch'ien Lung!
> May it be the sign of the emperor's long life!
> Oh, the cash of Ch'ien Lung!
> May he live for millions of years!

The conscientious fulfillment of his ritual obligations toward Heaven, ancestors, and the gods made the people feel that he was an emperor upon whom Heaven and earth looked with approval. As a scholar, he never neglected an opportunity to honor Confucian and other classical learning, a practice that earned him the respect of the literary classes. His edicts and his conversation were couched in such scholarly language that they evoked a constant chorus of sycophantic admiration. A passable poet, a fine calligrapher, and a man not without literary vanities, he left many examples of his work on silk and paper scrolls, tablets of jade and ivory, garden stones, and even rocky cliffs. During his reign the support he lavished on all the arts, crafts, and culture in general brought them to a greatness that has never since been surpassed.

In private life Ch'ien Lung distinguished himself as a hearty lover of romance who showered his limitless virility on scores—perhaps hundreds—of agreeable ladies. To his mother he was a devoted son; to his three empresses an affectionate husband. From his sons he won a wholesome and obedient respect—an achievement not always obtained by the heads of any imperial family. He was an excellent judge of horses, and he appreciated a good dinner, augmented by frequent cups of wine, almost as much as a compliant female. Incognito adventures to the teahouses, theaters, and bookshops in the Outer Chinese City held a special zest for him. His sayings and doings, usually exaggerated by gossip, were a delight to the common people and gave them easy hearts.

The first fifty years of his reign passed, each one more glorious than its predecessor, each adding to the splendor of the Forbidden City and the magnificent garden palaces—one near the Western Hills, the other near Jehol in Inner Mongolia. Vast sums of money flowed in from the prosperous treasuries of the provinces. Envoys with huge caravans came from the tributary princes, bringing elephants from Annam to lend majesty to great processions, golden Buddhas from Nepal, fine carpets from Tibet, jades from Burma, fine porcelains and brocades to decorate the throne halls and the temples. The Jesuit Giovanni Benedetto Castiglione, regarded by the Chinese as one of their greatest artists (his Chinese name was Lang Shih-ning) painted Ch'ien Lung's favorite white falcon and presented the painting, with an appropriate inscription, on his birthday. On another, his mother gave him a black and gold lacquer snuff bottle, delicately emblazoned with the imperial dragon. His doves and pigeons, and the flowers of his gardens, were copied endlessly on exquisite porcelains. The antlers of stags he had slain were entwined to make a fanciful throne chair on which he liked to sit. To keep his fingers supple, he inscribed walnuts and water chestnuts with designs of his own creation. He loved every trifling souvenir of the passing years. No detail was beneath his notice, nor was any item ever rejected for lack of interest.

Ch'ien Lung considered his highest officials as mere clerks for the transmission of his orders. He watched the chamberlains of the Household Department with the eye of a careful housekeeper, making quick mental inventories and calculations, fully aware that the cost of food in the imperial kitchens was far too high. He had a habit of inspecting his palace-cities with a regularity that was highly distasteful to the peculating staffs.

The sixth and last decade of Ch'ien Lung's reign lapped the land in the indolent warmth of a late summer afternoon. As the Manchu sun crossed its zenith, triumph and power softened to luxury and ease. The well-knit armies of the conquest became hordes of dubiously organized, ill-trained, ill-paid levies. But for the aging emperor time seemed to stand still. His heart and his zest for life were still strong. He continued to enjoy the homage of the great embassies who visited his court. They, in turn, were deeply impressed by China's Son of Heaven and his fabulous palaces. On the sixtieth anniversary of his accession, Ch'ien Lung abdicated. Filial piety and good taste demanded that his reign should not exceed the length of that of his illustrious grandfather, the Emperor K'ang Hsi.

Chia Ch'ing, his son and successor, was a a man of mediocre ability and smallness of spirit that at times bordered on downright stinginess. Perhaps he had served too long as an apprentice to his father, and since the old emperor's abdication was more of form than fact, he, as the new ruler, had to suffer three more years of dutiful subservience. With the great sovereign's death in 1799, the rich, warm light of popularity and splendor that had long surrounded the throne began to fade. It was as if a wind had uncovered rotten places, and in their malodorous aroma, discontent sprang up. In 1813 open rebellion broke out and, for a day and night, menaced the Great Within. But the Manchus were not yet ready to depart the scene of history.

The dynasty hung on for over a hundred years after the death of Ch'ien Lung. But its tenure was marked by defeat after defeat, one humiliating treaty after another, the loss of ancient lands, the thud of heavy boots of foreign armies, the roar of cannon from alien ships, the rise of strange commercial cities along its shores, and arrival of a peculiar new religion that preached meekness and faith instead of the grandeur of empire and its oneness with Heaven. With each blow against their ancient power, it became more and more clear that the Manchus had lost the Mandate of Heaven.

But the brooding walls and towers of the Great Within still stand as haughty reminders of former greatness; still await some sign from the Heaven that might announce a future mandate; and still shelter the silent spirits who come each evening to shed their tears for a world that is no more.

PART 2
The Approaches to the Palaces

CH'IEN MEN, THE FRONT GATE OF PEKING

THE DYNASTIC GATE

THE GATE OF HEAVENLY PEACE

THE GATE OF CORRECT DEPORTMENT

CH'IEN MEN, THE FRONT GATE OF PEKING

When Peking was the capital of the empire, all the gates of the city were heavily barred at sundown. A quarter of an hour before closing time, an iron gong was beaten outside each guardroom. At first slow, the tempo was gradually increased to create a continuous resonant sound. As the vibrations died down, guards inside the gate tunnels shouted loud warnings for another five minutes. Finally, the heavy portals were closed and bolted with huge beams of wood. As night deepened, different quarters of the city were blocked off one from the other by gates across the main thoroughfares.

But on the first and fifteenth of the month, and on special occasions, the sleeping city was rudely disturbed at midnight by a harsh clang. All those who heard the clamor knew that the massive iron-studded gates of Ch'ien Men—with its two inner and two outer towers, connected by a double enceinte of walls—were being opened to allow officials who had been spending the evening at haunts of amusement or who lived in the Outer City to enter for a predawn audience at the palace.

The opening of the gates was conducted with a rough confusion of ceremony. The watchman, beating a loud cadence with his bamboo clappers, directed the straining efforts of the special gate crew. It was his duty to see that the gates were opened at the proper hour as recorded by the clepsydra, or water clock, in the guardhouse, and to make certain no unauthorized persons slipped in with the crowd. Some officials rode through in blue-hooded carts drawn by sleek mules or square-headed, shaggy ponies; others sat in green sedan chairs. These were accompanied by outriders, extra bearers, and retinues of servants carrying round, white lanterns of buffalo horn, on which their masters' names and titles were inscribed in red characters. After the last group had gone through, it was the watchman's duty to bar the gates until dawn, when the ordinary traffic of the city was once again allowed to pass in and out.

At no time, day or night, was the center tunnel of the great Front Gate opened to the multitude. That was reserved for the emperor alone; it was

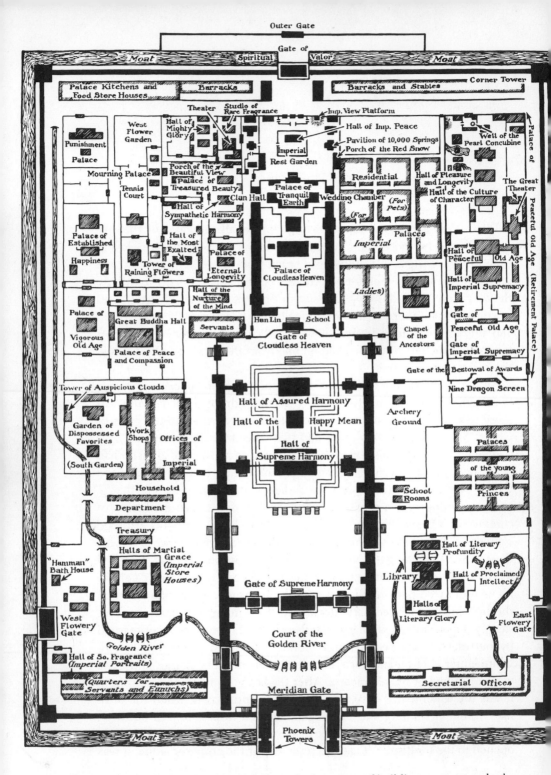

The Forbidden City. This map includes only the names of buildings, courts, and other locations mentioned in the book.

in a direct line with the main gates and halls of the Forbidden City. Another reservation was that no corpse, not even that of the sovereign, was permitted to pass through it. The dead were taboo.

The great Front Gate was considered a political barometer for the city of Peking. When trouble brewed, an ominous quiet descended on its stone-paved court, guns and troops appeared, and the populace raced helter-skelter for the safety of their shuttered homes and shops. But when all was peaceful, every form of conveyance known at the time, human and animal, pushed through. In recent years lurching trucks, darting bicycles, rickshaws, and automobiles, with their incessant bells and raucous horns, have been a part of the scene.

But the traffic of imperial days was even more cacophonous—herds of swine; flocks of sheep whose fat tails were smeared with red paint to indicate that they were destined for slaughter; shaggy, two-humped camels tied nose to tail, spitting disdainfully on pedestrians and half choking them in clouds of dust; Mongols in clumsy, felt-lined boots, their ungainly sheepskin robes caked with grease and dirt; silk-robed scholars carrying bird cages on long bamboo poles, gingerly mincing their way through the din to the bookshops of the Liu Li Ch'ang district of the Outer City; little, iron-tired passenger carts—the common conveyance before rickshaws—jockeying for position with heavy transport wagons. Torrents of foul expletives vied with the squeak of ungreased wheels and the groaning sing-song of men whose backs were bent under heavily loaded carrying poles. Mohammedan carters, their sweat- and wind-darkened faces crusted by months of sun and dust, whipped and shouted at motley teams of horses, mules, and oxen. And sublimely indifferent to anything but their own self-assumed rights were the young nobles, wealthy dandies, and their attendants. Astride long-tailed pacing ponies accoutered with silver-studded saddles, tassels, and richly embroidered saddle skirts, they rode haughtily toward the tunnels of the gate.

Though a formal progress could have begun at the distant southern entrance to the Chinese City, the great Front Gate was considered the first of the series of gates approaching the palaces. Its double-storied towers, roofed with green tiles, rose over fifty feet above the parapets of the high city walls. Massively built of brick and stone, the ramparts were so wide that two war chariots, galloping abreast at breakneck speed, could use it as a roadway and not interfere with massed troops defending the outer bastions.

Two small temples stood against the outer wall on each side of the gate; one dedicated to Kuan Yin, often called the goddess of mercy; the other to Kuan Yu, the god of war and patron saint of the Manchu dynasty. Kuan Yu was so popular that hundreds of temples were erected in his honor—ten in Peking alone. An historical figure and military hero, Kuan Yu was born in A.D. 162 and killed in combat in 219. Legend claims that his prowess in battle was so extraordinary all other commanders seemed mere amateurs. After his master's death, Kuan Yu's war horse, named the Red Hare, committed suicide by refusing to eat.

THE DYNASTIC GATE

The open square between the inner tower of the great Front Gate and the next entrance, the Dynastic Gate, was popularly known as the Checkerboard. Built by the Emperor Yung Lo and patterned on a Chinese checkerboard, this wide space was originally enclosed by a stone wall. The common people of the city soon nicknamed it the Pig Sty. In so doing, they confused the Ming family name of "Chu," meaning "pearl," with the Chinese word *chu* meaning "pig." After the fall of the Ming dynasty, a well-known jingle voiced the hope of the masses: "The pen is here, but not the pig. So long as the pen is here, the pig will come back."

The Dynastic Gate was set on a low platform. The roofs of its one-story tower were tiled in golden yellow, and therefore it was the first truly imperial entrance to the palace. At all times rigidly guarded, it was opened for lesser mortals only on the rarest of occasions. Commoners who attempted to cross its threshold were beaten with a hundred blows of the "bamboo rod of punishment," and the officer in charge of the gate was degraded. Death by strangulation was meted out to any stranger who succeeded in reaching the emperor's apartments while the gate was open.

Immediately facing the gate was a small space closed off by stone posts, which, more often than not, were off balance and awry. There, from sunrise to sunset, beggars and half-naked ragamuffins, safe from the disturbance of the traffic, gossiped, slept, scratched themselves, and picked vermin from their ragged clothes. Because of their unique vantage point, they were always acutely aware of everything that happened in the city. Only when the emperor was about to go forth in state were these idlers chased away. Then the posts were straightened to stand at attention and the paving stones cleared of tufts of grass sprouting between the crevices.

The people saw nothing of the imposing entourage surrounding the progresses of the Son of Heaven, for they were forbidden on pain of death to look upon their sovereign at such times. Usually the days for official exits were set forth in the almanac. Still, if the emperor had reason to use the Dynastic Gate at any time other than the carefully ordained occasions, the hectic preparations were a warning to the public. The first sign was the appearance of palace workmen spreading yellow sand over the paving of the Checkerboard so that chair bearers would not stumble as they ran rapidly over the rutted blocks.

Above the gate hung a large tablet, framed in carved and gilded wood, with the name of the reigning dynasty inscribed in bronze characters, two feet high. Under the pillared porch, which was always freshly painted before the emperor passed in state, were massive, red-lacquered doors embossed with rows of round, gilt knobs. According to legend, these knobs simulated a snail's shell and were copies of knobs designed by Lu Pan, the god of carpenters and builders. Long ago this man of simple wisdom had stated: "When danger threatens, the snail withdraws into his shell and securely closes the entrance. So should a man nightly close the doors of his house against his enemies."

From the Dynastic Gate stretched an impressive stone-paved avenue of great length. Screened by high red walls topped with yellow-tiled rooflets, its open squares and white marble bridges heralded imperial grandeur beyond. Father Matteo Ripa, one of the Jesuits attached to the court of the Emperor K'ang Hsi, described in his memoirs the ceremonial progress in 1720 of Count Ismailoff, the envoy of Czar Peter the Great. "The count," he wrote, "had a fine person and a noble expression of countenance" as he passed through the Dynastic Gate with "a retinue of ninety persons and the sound of trumpets, drums, and other instruments." Mounted on a horse presented by the Son of Heaven, the ambassador was flanked on one side by a dwarf, on the other by a giant. He rode in the midst of his entourage, "all with drawn swords and in splendid array." Though not the first Russian mission to arrive in Peking, it was the first to be treated with honor.

As a special mark of esteem, the Imperial Way was occasionally opened for a victorious general, with the bell and drum towers of the palace-city booming out a sonorous welcome. The pavements echoed to the sounds of martial pomp. Proud horsemen rode bridle to bridle, followed by regiment after regiment of marching foot soldiers, the sun glinting on their arms and the blazing colors of their uniforms. Others privileged to pass through the side arches of the Dynastic Gate were ambassadors, visiting foreign princes, and high religious dignitaries.

On the rarest of all occasions the Imperial Way was opened to honor an empress-bride, at which time even the central arches of the gates, reserved exclusively for the passage of the sovereign lord, stood wide to welcome her wedding chair. Her entrance into the palace-city, which was to be her home, and her prison, was accompanied by the padding feet of many chair bearers and the soft tinkle of ancient ceremonial music.

Just east of the formal approach to the next gate stood the Manchu Clan Court, a grim reminder that exemplary behavior was expected of the dynastic family. On orders from the throne, members of the imperial family were tried there by their equals in rank for crimes and violations of the laws of the clan. If found guilty, princes were either imprisoned in its Empty Chamber, a form of solitary confinement, or given the silken cord to commit suicide.

THE GATE OF HEAVENLY PEACE

Before reaching the Gate of Heavenly Peace, the Imperial Way broadened into a gigantic quadrangle. What the Red Square is now to Moscow, this vast court was to Peking. Once silent, secluded, and forbidden to the public, modern history has made it the rallying point for political meetings and parades. The people of the city first assembled there with the silent blessing of Sun Yat-sen, the father of the republic, whose brass portrait was buried beneath a stone slab nearby and enclosed by a rickety wooden fence. China's first president, Yuan Shih-k'ai, reviewed his troops there when he took office. Throughout the troubled years of attempted democracy, it was the scene of demonstrations, fights, and the shedding of blood. During the eight years of Japanese occupation that ended in 1945, electric signs and triumphal arches gloated over the invaders' victories. Later, students and revolutionists chanted their slogans in its vastness.

One of the many arms of the Golden River formed a moat on the north side of the huge paved square, facing the gate tower. Flowing from its source at the Jade Fountain fourteen miles away, this winding stream poured good "water" influences into the Great Within. Across it were five arched, white marble bridges with richly carved balustrades and panels that led to the five entrances in the massive wall below the tower. The center bridge was reserved for the emperor; the pair on either side for his splendid escorts.

A pair of huge, white marble lions and two white marble columns, commonly called the Pillars of Victory, guarded the center bridge. In the Ming period the lions were called the dogs of Fo, or of Buddha. Each of Buddha's divine attributes was endowed with a symbol; and his noblest, wisdom, was worthy of the noblest of beasts. With characteristic lack of modesty, the emperors adopted the symbolic lion-dogs as their own, for in the privacy of their household courts, they enjoyed the self-awarded title of the "Enlightened One," or Buddha. Moreover, the lion was the guardian beast of the north.

Two legends involve the Gate of Heavenly Peace and Li Tzu-ch'eng, who overthrew the decadent Ming dynasty in 1644. Riding toward the gate at the head of his rabble army, Li reined in his horse, and standing straight in his stirrups, raised his bow to shoot an arrow toward the topmost character in the gate's name panel, which meant "heaven." If he hit it, he believed that Heaven would grant him its mandate to ascend the throne. But he missed, and a great sigh—as if from one giant man —rose from his troops. Missing was obviously a bad omen; it meant he had been rejected, as, indeed, he had. The army rode on, not even looking up at the quivering arrow that was to leave a hole for all time. According to the second legend, as they were about to enter the gate, uncertain now and a little afraid, two huge lions sprang out to bar their entrance. Li again rose in his saddle, raised his bow, and as two arrows sped through the air, the animals fled. But as Li went out the gate in his headlong flight from Peking, he glanced back over his shoulder and saw to his amazement where there had been nothing there were now two stone lions flanking the entrance—and so they have remained as guardians ever since. A hole in the belly of one has dripped moisture for over three hundred years, supposedly marking the wound of Li's arrow.

Many important temples and palaces in China were protected by a pair of stone lions at their gates. The female, with a cub lying on its back under her right paw, from which it was supposed to suck milk, was always at the left side of the entrance. At the right was the male, with a ball, or globe, under his left forefoot. The ball was believed to contain milk, which could be squeezed out and drunk as a medicine by the sick. The depictions of Buddha in his aspect of god of medicine show him holding a symbolic globe in one hand.

The only monument to Li Tzu-ch'eng's short and violent rule was a brick carved with a flower in the wall of the tunnel of the Gate of Just Rule—one of the entrances in the west wall of the Tatar City through which Li had stormed to take the capital—and it had a symbolic meaning. In ancient times thieves were branded on the left arm for their first offense, on the right arm for the second, and on the left temple for the third. The Manchus ordered this flower carving to brand the gate for all time as a criminal, for having permitted a rebel to pass through its portals.

The Pillars of Victory, also called the Flowery Sign Posts, show Indian influence and are probably a Chinese version of those placed by the Buddhist Emperor Asoka throughout his empire between 250 and 232 B.C. The pillars of Peking were deeply and handsomely carved with the design of a coiled dragon writhing upward through layers of clouds. Cross pieces of irregular shape, richly etched with cloud motifs, were just below the capitals, which were surmounted by stylized lion figures. These pillars may have been sophisticated descendants of totem poles, a theory strengthened by the presence of the dragon on the shaft and the depiction of the beast on the capital.

If the mythical feline was a totem animal, it was probably not a lion, for China was never the habitat of that beast, not even in prehistoric times. It could, however, have represented the tiger, which is still found in northern Manchuria and the far south. And in China the tiger has always been a totem animal—with the dual aspects of protector and destroyer—and from time immemorial it has been credited with certain magical powers. Even today, despite Mao's fight against all superstitions, mothers threaten a naughty child with the warning: *Ma-hu lai!* ("The ghost-tiger will come!"). And, doubtless some still manage to safeguard their babies by embroidering tiger heads on the little shoes and caps. It was also the custom in many places to carve the outline of a tiger on grave tablets as a protection for the ancestors.

As a protector-destroyer, the tiger was commonly and somewhat humorously displayed in certain shops in Peking. Chinese who owned meat stores often hung out large pictures of pigs in order to insult the Mohammedans operating a similar establishment across a narrow lane or alley. But no Moslem, be he Chinese or bearded Turki, remained intimidated for long. He simply displayed a larger picture of the ferocious tiger bearing his fangs at the insolent pigs. All the world knew that tigers devoured pigs. So, defeated, the pork sellers would withdraw their jeering signs in embarrassed frustration, while the street crowds and beggars ridiculed their loss of face.

In the course of centuries primitive totem poles, no longer useful as tribal distinctions, evolved into symbols of authority and power. Thus, the old-fashioned yamen, or office of a provincial governor, was flanked by wooden pillars comparable to those before the Gate of Heavenly Peace. Some historians claim that these pillars were survivals of the Boards of Criticism and Detraction instituted by the legendary Perfect Emperor Yao. He placed before his palace gates such columns, to which the people could attach their opinions of the government and suggestions for improving it.

In ancient times a Drum of Remonstrance also stood outside the palace gates. It was beaten by a special official to solicit direct appeals for justice from the emperor. A happy reign was indicated by an old saying: "The Drum of Remonstrance is covered with moss." In the course of time the drum and bell were placed in towers and used as signals for alarm. The ancient function was later transferred to a bell and, in at least one case, was continued into the middle 1930's by the warlord governor of Shantung province, who established "grievance-airing bells" for the benefit of his people. It is doubtful, however, if many of their complaints survived the bureaucracy of the provincial government—which was responsible for their grievances in the first place.

In Peking the Drum and Bell Towers, directly north of the Great

Within, were originally constructed by the Mongols, but were rebuilt in both the Ming and Manchu dynasties. During the casting of the present great bell, the story goes, the foundrymaster failed repeatedly to achieve the required perfection. The Emperor Yung Lo, impatient to get on with the completion of his dream city, threatened to behead the foreman. The terrified man's daughter, frantic to save her father's life, slipped unseen into the building and, as the molten metal of another try was being poured, leaped into the mold to become a permanent part of the bell— which resulted in a perfect casting with a deep resonance. In an attempt to save her life, the foundrymaster succeeded only in grasping one of her shoes, and for over five hundred years, whenever the bell was struck, it has given forth a secondary sound of *hsieh*, the Chinese word for "shoe."

There were two pairs of Pillars of Victory at the Gate of Heavenly Peace—one inside and the other outside the entrance. The lions surmounting the inner Flowery Sign Posts were carved with tightly closed mouths, to impress upon those living within the palace that when a Son of Heaven left the grounds, silence should be observed regarding his activities. The lions on the outside had wideopen mouths, an invitation for one and all to report any malpractices by court officials during the emperor's absence. In order to advance themselves, most officials were only too eager to exaggerate the slightest irregularities of their rivals.

On one occasion the Emperor Yung Lo—weary of state affairs and tired to the bone with the vast responsibility of building a perfect celestial city—planned to depart on a hunting expedition and leave a trusted general in charge of the palace. So fearful was the general that an enemy might fabricate a story on his misconduct with the ladies of the court that he castrated himself before the emperor left the Forbidden City and concealed the severed testicles in the hollow of the emperor's saddle. On the monarch's return the general's worries turned out to be only too well founded. In reply to vicious accusations, he proved his innocence by producing the hidden parts from the emperor's saddle. Yung Lo was so impressed with such excessive loyalty that he appointed the general his chief eunuch and, after the eunuch's death, deified him as the patron saint of eunuchs, with a temple erected in his honor outside the city.

In the late Manchu period a guard of no more than ten men at any one time was stationed at the Gate of Heavenly Peace. The policy of displaying so few troops was based on the sovereign's desire for symbols of prosperity, creation, virtue, and all good things requiring no military force to command respect. The great sages of China had always abhorred the sword. The soldier, in their minds, was a destroyer. An old proverb states: "From good iron come plowshares; from bad iron, swords." Since virtue was the only armor suited to the palaces, the Ming emperors never wore military dress in the great throne halls. The warrior Manchus continued this tradition as a politic gesture of respect to a civilization far more ancient than their own. In time the idea became so firmly imbedded in their consciousness, that it seemed natural.

When van Braam in 1794 conducted an embassy from the Dutch East India Company to the court of Ch'ien Lung, he was impressed by the unmilitary appearance of the palace-city. His account stated: "Neither upon this occasion, nor at any of the ceremonies at which the Emperor was present, did I ever see a military guard. . . . Anyone would naturally expect to find a small army in the imperial residence, but he will see nothing like it   This Court is then the only one, even in Asia, where the chief of the nation is not protected by a formidable military guard."

Though a careful observer, van Braam could have seen only a limited portion of the palace-city. Had he seen it all, he would have been aware of a large number of troops deployed at all inner and outer gates. He was correct in noting the lack of military ostentation, but the emperor and the sanctity of his home were always heavily guarded.

THE GATE OF CORRECT DEPORTMENT

Proceeding past the Gate of Heavenly Peace, the Imperial Way stretched across another stone-paved court, flanked by high red walls, to the Gate of Correct Deportment. This gate was a conventional structure of no marked individuality and of little historic interest. But its tunneled entrances opened on to the last formal approach to the palaces, which terminated at the gigantic Wu Men, or Meridian Gate.

Ch'ien Men, the great front gate to the city of Peking. The central portal, visible here, was reserved for the Emperor's use alone. In the foreground is a memorial arch called a *p'ai-lou*. This type of arch was erected to commemorate important events and men and women distinguished in the service of their country. (*Library of Congress*).

Ch'ien Men in 1934, taken from the south. The outer gate, formerly connected by an enceinte to the walls of the Tartar City (running across the center of the photo), is in the foreground. The high tower surmounting the city wall was part of the defense system. Beyond the high tower is the low Dynastic Gate and the Imperial Way. The flat square in the center is the U.S. Marine Guard drill field. To its right are the U.S. Marine barracks and the American Embassy compound. At the extreme right outside the Tartar City walls is the railway station. The large building above the gate towers is the Grand Hotel de Pékin.

The Imperial Way, from the south. In the left foreground is the Gate of Heavenly Peace, then the Gate of Correct Deportment, the Meridian Gate, the Court of the Golden River, and the Gate of Supreme Harmony (at top center). To the left is the Altar of Earth and Grain. To the right is the Supreme Temple of Ancestors.

The Meridian Gate and the ceremonial court in which the great "elephant ceremonies," reviews, and military receptions were held. This photo, taken in 1901, shows U.S. infantry lined up in honor of the German minister, Count Waldersee, following the defeat of the "Boxers". U.S. Minister Edward H. Conger and his family appear in foreground. *(Library of Congress)*.

The Supreme Temple of Ancestors (taken from the south) in its park of cypresses just outside the walls of the Forbidden City. In the upper left is a corner of the Forbidden City showing the outer wall, the moat, the southeast Corner Tower, and the tower of the East Flowery Gate. A part of the city of Peking is shown at the top and upper right. *(Photo by Hartung, Peking).*

The terrace on top of the walls of the Meridian Gate, the main entrance to the Forbidden City. In the center is the west Phoenix Tower; at the right, the southeast corner of the main gate tower. *(Photo by Benjamin March, Peking).*

The Court of the Golden River, the first court leading to the Three Great Throne Halls, in winter. In the foreground is the Golden River with its five marble bridges; to the left, just outside the photograph, is the Gate of Supreme Harmony.

The Hall of Supreme Harmony, the principal throne hall of the palace, in winter. It is the largest building in the Forbidden City.

The imperial "dragon" throne in the Palace of Cloudless Heaven in the Forbidden City. There were a number of similar thrones in other halls. The characters above the throne say "Honorable and great Ching [Manchu] Dynasty." *(Library of Congress).*

An aerial view of the Hall of Annual Prayers (commonly called the Temple of Heaven) in the 700-acre park of the Temple of Heaven. Photo taken from the southwest.

The Hall of Annual Prayers which, with the Altar of Heaven, was the site of the supreme sacrifice to Heaven at the New Year.

A gate tower on the east wall of Peking. All sixteen of the city gates were surmounted by similar towers. The city moat is in the foreground. (Note fisherman and net). *(Library of Congress).*

The gate of Cloudless Heaven. Similar guardian stone lions—one male, the other female—were placed before most important palace and temple gates. *(Library of Congress).*

The main gate to the Supreme Temple of Ancestors just outside the Forbidden City. *(Photo by the author.)*

A Tibetan-style temple in the ground of the Potala of Jehol about 140 miles northeast of Peking. Like the original Potala in Lhasa, this building enclosed an open court in which stands a temple-hall whose double-tiered roofs and decorations are encased with gold leaf. *(Photo by the author).*

The marble, "camel-back" bridge in the park of the New Summer Palace about 12 miles northwest of Peking.

The Great Pagoda at the New Summer Palace.

The "Marble Boat" beside a marble quay on the lake in the New Summer Palace, about 12 miles northwest of Peking.

The main entrance to the New Summer Palace.

The Imperial Loge of the Great Theater in the Palace of Peaceful Old Age. The three-tiered stage of the theater is outside this photograph to the right. The long, low structure in the right foreground contained the stalls, or boxes, in which noble guests were seated. *(Photograph of a painting by the author)*.

The Phoenix Chair (wedding chair) of an empress-bride on the terrace before the Palace of Cloudless Heaven. Photograph taken in 1903.

A Peking cart, 1901. Coal hill in background. A corner tower on the palace wall shows over the top of the cart. *(Library of Congress)*.

The Emperor Tao Kuang, who reigned from 1821 to 1851, wearing a jade thumb ring and carrying the Tatar (Manchu) bow, and archery equipment. *(Photograph of a painting by the author).*

Manchu noble of high rank and bride in wedding robes, 1901. Courtyard is in prince's palace in Peking.

A corner tower and the outer wall of the Forbidden City. There are four identical towers, one at teach corner. Though fanciful in appearance, each housed a guard room. The wooden bridge in the foreground is modern.

The principal hall of the Supreme Temple of Ancestors outside the Forbidden City. The Manchus never permitted any Chinese to enter this hall. *(Photo by the author)*.

The Empress Dowager Tz'u An, the co-Empress Dowager with Tz'u Hsi from 1861 to 1881, in formal court robes. *(Photograph of a painting by the author from the Empress' official "ancestor portrait")*.

The Empress Dowager Tz'u Hsi in formal audience robes in 1903. Note the pearl cape, high Manchu shoes and the Manchu headdresses. From left to right, the other ladies are: Chin Fei, the principal concubine of the Emperor Kuang Hsu; Princess Shou Chan (adopted by the Dowager as an imperial princess), later Madame Dan Pa-cho'ao, a lady-in-waiting; Princess Der Ling (also adopted as an imperial princess), later Mrs. White, a lady-in-waiting; Madame Yu Keng, wife of the Minister to Paris and mother of the two ladies-in-waiting (being Chinese, she did not wear the Manchu headdress); and Empress Lung Yu, the first consort of the Emperor Kuang Hsu.

The "Boy Emperor" Hsuan T'ung (P'u Yi) in 1903, less than a year after his accession to the Dragon Throne at the age of two.

Ancestor tablets on their throne chair in the Supreme Temple of Ancestors. *(Photo by Benjamin March, Peking).*

The alcoved bed of the Empress Dowager Tz'u Hsi in the Hall of the Culture of Character, a residential palace in the Palace of Peaceful Old Age, the Forbidden City. Above the bed is the Empress Dowager's private oratory. *(Photography of a painting by the author).*

PART 3
The Guardian Walls

THE MERIDIAN GATE

The Meridan Gate, the gate of the sun at high noon, was the solar symbol of the height and brilliance of imperial power. The first gentle rays of the morning sun touched the tile roofs of the towers, sparkled there throughout the day, and faded only when the shining, orange disk slipped behind the ramparts of the distant Western Hills.

Dazzled by the Meridian Gate as they emerged from the shady tunnel of the Gate of Correct Deportment, the colorful retinue of Russia's Count Ismailoff stopped in their tracks to stare in awe. A member of the entourage recorded in his journal: "I felt inclined to shout aloud at the first view of that mighty building and suffered an intense exaltation at the grandeur of it. . . . the entrance to the Kremlin, with its single doorway surmounted by Our Lady of Kazan in her little shrine, is puny compared to this!"

The rebel Li Tzu-ch'eng, fleeing before the victorious Manchus in 1644, had burned the gate, and it was one of the first buildings to be restored by the new dynasty. Rising to a height of some forty feet, the massive masonry of the substructure formed three sides of a vast quadrangular court. The central wall of the gates was surmounted by a great tower crowned with double roofs of imperial yellow tiles, standing above a balustraded, white marble terrace. Four twin-tiered Phoenix Towers, linked by huge galleries and connected to the main tower, rose over the mighty shoulders of the base. Three tunneled entrances pierced the thirty-five-foot-thick wall beneath the central tower, and two smaller entrances curved within the masonry of the embracing arms.

A break was left in the center of the marble balustrade for the golden chair of the emperor so that he could use the terrace as an outdoor throne room. From this spot, high above the great courtyard and the spectacular tableau of his subjects, he reviewed his army at the close of victorious campaigns and watched the distribution of the almanac to vassal princes at the New Year.

On other solemn occasions the heavy, brass-studded, red doors of the main gateway were thrown open for the ceremonial progress of the emperor. At such times the huge "bell of goings-out and comings-in," and the great drum in the opposite Phoenix Tower, were struck at regular intervals. Their sonorous vibrations fell with heavy solemnity upon the silent capital. Thus the people knew that their sovereign was leaving the Great Within to perform traditional rites for their benefit at the Temple of Heaven, the Altar of Earth, the Great Hall of Ancestors, or the Altar of Earth and Grain. The average illiterate Chinese did not understand these higher cults and did not pretend to try. They were content that the emperor acted as their mediator with Heaven and Earth, leaving them free to burn incense at the shrines of lesser deities of their own choice. It was at these times that the ruler was in truth a priest-king who had prepared himself by fasting, meditation, and abstention from all pleasures. When he proceeded on a sacrificial progress, the streets were cleared, a hush lay over the city, and only awed whispers were exchanged as all awaited the blessing of Heaven or the gift of fertility from the Earth.

The majesty of the Meridian Gate and its forecourt were a fitting background for the unrivaled display of pageantry of these ceremonial exits from the palace-city. Tribute elephants from Annam lined each side of the sovereign's route outside the gate. They were gorgeously caparisoned, with priceless porcelain vases ornamenting their heads and backs, each beast attended by servants and trainers. With trunks locked, they stood in a powerful double phalanx, closing the path to anyone but the emperor. Then, trumpets blared from the marble balustrade, the great bell and drum were struck, and the doors of the central gate swung slowly open. The enormous, golden sedan chair with its hundred and twenty bearers—sometimes the emperor was carried in an elephant chariot—moved slowly through the tunnel of the gates. The state elephants at once unlocked their trunks, stepped back to clear the route, and then raised their trunks high in a lofty salute to the Supreme Lord.

Like court officials, each elephant was granted a title of nobility in an imperial rescript, at the reading of which the beast knelt respectfully and appeared to listen. If one of the huge animals was punished for having offended His Majesty at a ceremony—perhaps by trampling an attendant, crushing the life out of a guard, or merely failing in the performance of some duty—it was reduced in rank. If a duke, it was probably lowered to a count. When a whipping was ordered, the great beast was securely chained. Since it could not do otherwise, it docilely accepted the punishment. Or sometimes two reliable, older elephants, using their trunks, forced the culprit to its knees and held it in place as a keeper flogged it. Then, prodded by trainers, the animal would perform an elaborate bow to the emperor in "thanks" for the generous correction, as was required of all officials when penalized. Like human courtiers, the elephants were expected to understand and respect both etiquette and ceremony. Once the sedan chair of the emperor had passed through their ranks outside the Meridian Gate, these obedient "elephant-officials" filed with ponderous dignity into their proper places in the long and splendid cortege.

In addition to drawing the special chariot of the emperor and participating in his ceremonial exits, the huge, pampered beasts were also present when officials or embassies entered or left the palace by way of the Meridian Gate. On those occasions three pairs of elegantly equipped animals, waiting in the quadrangle before the entrance, knelt at the sounding of the great bell, which presaged the opening of the gates for the arrival of the great men and their retinues. When all had entered, the six elephants rose, formed facing pairs, and interlocked trunks to bar the way.

Great stables in the southwest corner of the Tatar City housed these ennobled pachyderms in incredible luxury. Built in 1495, the Elephant Quarters occupied an area of over twenty acres and contained forty-eight stalls, each thirty-six by eighteen feet, with walls six feet thick. A wide, deep trench edged each compartment to provide the Annamite keepers a place to jump for their lives when the animals became unruly. Dozens of trainers and attendants served them and watched over their health. But since many of those men were avaricious and often pocketed the cash intended to buy food for their charges, the hungry elephants would rampage and strike out murderously with their trunks when rations were scanty.

When an elephant died, the event was reported instantly to the emperor, who at once decreed a period of mourning. But there was no mourning among the overseers. Being the sons of a practical race, they hacked the huge carcass into chunks and sold the meat to the poor—an unlawful means of profiteering. However, it was perfectly lawful for the keepers to sell the much-prized elephant dung to the ladies of Peking, who used it as a shampoo, believing firmly it would impart a brilliant gloss to their hair!

Known in China since 2205 B.C., elephants were fully trained for use in imperial ceremonies as early as the T'ang dynasty (618–906). During the Ming and Manchu periods they were sent to Peking as tribute from the kingdoms of Ava and Annam. In Mongolia the temple artists and craftsmen devised a semimythical figure of a horse-elephant, a strange creature that embodied the speed of the one as it galloped over the barren steppes and the power and majesty of the other.

Not only did the emperors grant high rank to the state elephants, but some bestowed patents of nobility on other objects of their admiration. Ch'ien Lung conferred the rank of "duke" on what he considered an exceptionally beautiful tree. As late as 1936 the tree still stood a few miles outside of Peking, somewhat gnarled and less beautiful, but nonetheless a duke.

The Jesuit Gabriel de Magalhaens, a distant kinsman of the Portuguese navigator Magellan, lived for many years at the court of K'ang Hsi. He wrote the following account of an imperial procession to the Temple of Heaven:

> Heading the procession are twenty-four men carrying huge painted drums which they sound solemnly at intervals, and twenty-four trumpeters carrying instruments three feet long and ornamented with golden cirles and tuned to the note of the drums; twenty-four men carrying long, red-lacquered poles topped with bunches of gilded leaves; a hundred halberdiers with lances shaped like crescents; a hundred bearers of gilded maces; four hundred bearers of richly carved and decorated lanterns; four hundred bearers of torches made of scented wood which burned with a brilliant perfumed flame; two hundred lancers, their weapons trimmed with brilliant strips of silk or the tails of leopards, wolves and other wild animals; twenty-four bearers with banners with the fifty-six constellations, into which the Chinese formerly divided all the stars of the heavens, painted upon them; two hundred bearers of fans mounted on huge poles gilded and painted with the sun and the moon, dragons and animals; twenty-four bearers of ceremonial umbrellas with deep flounces richly

embroidered; a group of men carrying the "eight utensils" which the Emperor ordinarily uses—a golden basin, a pitcher, a silken napkin, etc.; ten horses white as snow with saddles and bridles set with pearls and precious stones; another hundred lancers and Court chamberlains forming an escort around the chair of the Emperor.

After His Majesty, followed the princes of the blood and the highest dignitaries of the land, superbly gowned and walking in procession according to their rank. Then came five hundred young nobles, equally richly dressed, and a thousand Eunuchs of the Presence wearing red gowns embroidered with flowers and gold and silver stars and hats with long straight black plumes. A yellow chair to be used within the temple enclosure, smaller than the great state chair, two large elephant chariots, a big chariot drawn by eight horses, a chariot drawn by four, all these vehicles, likewise the elephants and their leaders, the horses and their grooms are richly caparisoned and every chair and chariot is followed by a captain with fifty soldiers. Finally, came two thousand literary officials, and two thousand military officials in robes of ceremony, in silken coats aflame like rainbows. These bring up the rear of the mighty cortege.

On the day before the winter solstice the emperor rode in an elephant chariot to the sacred enclosure in the Chinese City, accompanied by an entourage of about two thousand officials and attendants. On arrival at the west gate he walked to the Temple of the God of the Universe and prostrated himself before the tablets. Then he returned to the Hall of Abstinence in the Great Within, where he spent the night in fasting and meditation.

Two hours before daylight, he proceeded in a great solemn progress (as described by Magalhaens) to the south gate of the inner enclosure. There he waited in a yellow silk tent until the sacred tablets had been invited to emerge from their shrine and all officials had taken their proper places for the ceremony. Then, as loud peals of music shattered the silence, the emperor ascended the top terrace of the Altar of Heaven and called upon the God of the Universe to look down upon its earthly link to all mankind. He then made nine prostrations and offered gifts of silk and jade. The great gathering of awe-stricken officials was so still in that moment that only the swaying branches of the ancient cypresses could be heard. All eyes were lifted to the high, white marble altar under a dome of blue sky, where the kneeling Son of Heaven communed with the One God, alone and out of sight. This supreme deity, without form or image of any kind, reflected the enlightened doctrine of monotheism that Heaven and God in the Great Beyond were one with the Son of Heaven on earth. This belief acknowledged no hell and promised no heaven, other than that of a pure heart. Though superstitions ran rampant throughout the land, it accepted none and ignored the demigods and devils that filled the temples.

When the service finally was concluded, the "round blue gem"—probably a fine, polished piece of blue Peking glass which symbolized heaven on earth—was returned in solemn state to the Temple of the God of the Universe, from which it had been brought. Having descended from the high altar, the emperor waited respectfully in the yellow tent until the sacred tablets had been placed in their shrine, after which he returned to the palace.

The Temple and Altar of Heaven were located in a seven-hundred-acre walled enclosure outside the Tatar City. A ninety-foot-high, circular structure of three stories, each story roofed with deep-blue tiles, the temple was actually the Hall of Annual Prayers. Originally it had not been intended as a place of worship to Heaven, but to make supplications for a good harvest. In 1889, as a rebuke to a sacrilegious centipede that had dared to crawl to the topmost golden sphere, it was struck by lightning and burned down. The rebuilding began at once when the American shipping magnate Robert Dollar provided the main pillars for its circular colonnade with a shipment of great logs of Oregon fir. At the opposite end of the parklike enclosure stood the three white marble terraces of the Altar of Heaven, representing Heaven, Earth, and Man in descending order of importance. Between these two principal structures stood the significantly named Temple of the God of the Universe.

THE MOAT AND THE WALLS

"The strength of a wall," Genghis Khan pronounced, "is neither greater nor less than the courage of the men who defend it."

His words might well have been heeded by the later Ming and Manchu emperors, and applied to the spectacular walls their ancestors had built for the protection of their palace-city. From the fall of the Ming dynasty in 1644 to the Boxer Uprising, which ended with the Allied relief of Peking, it had never been necessary to defend the Great Within. In 1900 terrifying stories of "cloudy ladders," the "fire that flies," and the "fire that could be exploded in bamboo tubes" struck fear into the hearts of the palace guards, who were too cowardly to fight. Once the walls of the Tatar City fell to the Allied Relief Expedition, the guards scurried like rats in hopeless panic and disappeared into the warrens of the city until the trouble was over.

The crenelated walls of the Forbidden City, painted a purplish-red color, formed a solid defensive rampart twenty-two feet high. The two and a quarter miles of parapets were broken by four gates and four rather elegant watchtowers—one at each corner. The three-tiered roofs of the towers had an air of lightness and refinement that characterized the Ming dynasty construction known as the nine beams and eighteen pillars.

Surrounding the entire fortified rectangle was a broad moat, lined with massive blocks of stone, its still, deep waters like a bronze mirror grown green with age. Gliding lazily in its depths were great numbers of ancient carp—some still tabbed with iron rings dating from the Ming dynasty could be seen as late as the 1930's. In midsummer a carpet of lotus leaves, pierced by the uplifted pink blossoms of countless sweet-smelling flowers, covered the glistening, dark surface of the moats. Under the hot July sun the long stems of lotus buds pushed through the leaves as if reaching for strength toward the Lord of Light. And at dawn, under the sun's first light, the petals began to open with a soft, murmurous sound. Poets and philosophers, priests and the sincerely pious, were on hand then, knotted in groups along the parapet, to watch the graceful buds below unfold and reveal the golden heart of the blossoms. To all true believers of the Buddha, the lotus blossoms—the flower of the Enlightened One—symbolized the rebirth of the soul in the core of these heaven-blessed flowers. Like Buddha's sacred teaching, the lotus rises from the mud and slime to open the purity of its pink or white fulfillment in the clear light of a summer day.

In imperial days, the blossoming season over, the huge, round leaves were a perquisite of the palace guards, who sold them to provision shops for wrapping food. The pods were also gathered, and the fat, round seeds, believed to cool the blood on excessively hot days, were often served in restaurants as a delicate relish before meals. Since most ailments were rather blandly diagnosed as an excess of hot vapors or cold vapors, the green seeds were sometimes used as a medicinal remedy. As the blossom was a symbol of feminine beauty, the crushed and broken bound feet of Chinese women were referred to as "golden lotus flowers" or "lily feet."

At the spring festival, in a ceremony dating from A.D. 733, lotus leaves bearing lighted candles were set afloat on lakes and large ponds. In memory of those who had died in defense of their country and to remind the heroic dead that their grateful homeland had not forgotten them, large boats of paper, sixty to a hundred feet long, with crews of paper men and scores of lighted candles, were launched on the lakes of the nearby Sea Palaces. After appropriately simple ceremonies, the "ghost boats" were set afire so that the "spirit soldiers" could return to their world of shadows, guided by the flicker of countless lights dancing on the surface of the water.

To guard the walls, gates, and watchtowers, the Ming emperors employed a specially trained corps of gorgeously arrayed eunuchs. But the Manchus, originally hardy warriors themselves, preferred their own well-disciplined troops and used them during the long period when the dynasty was at the height of its vigor. These guards were drawn from the eight Banner organizations into which the clans were divided and in which every Manchu was an hereditary member. However, certain designated units admitted both Mongols and Chinese who had assisted the Manchus in their conquest. The organization of a Banner consisted of a unified division of troops corresponding in a very rough way to a mixed cavalry brigade of both horse and foot soldiers. Though without supporting troops, it could be expanded readily by levies of individuals or the attachment of complete tactical units.

There were three superior and five inferior Banners, each distinguished by the color of its triangular standard. The banners of the three superior divisions were yellow bordered with red, solid yellow and solid white. Those of the inferior were white bordered with red, solid red, red bordered with white, solid blue, and blue bordered with red. The colors represented the elements; and since the elements opposed and neutralized each other, the banners were deployed with full regard for this relationship. Thus, theoretically at least, the safety of the empire and the throne was assured, not only against invaders, but also against mutinies or army coups.

In order to impose their rule, the Manchus stationed Banner garrisons at all strategic points throughout China. As an example, such a garrison was sent on permanent assignment to the distant province of Yunnan on the borders of Burma, Thailand, and what is now Vietnam. Since few of the troops were accompanied by wives, men of the Banner intermingled freely with the more primitive natives—immigrant Chinese, Lolos, Shans and, other tribespeople. Eventually, the infusion of Manchus and north China blood made the cultured dialect of Peking and its environs far more common in Yunnan than it was in the long-established and highly developed Yangtze valley and coastal regions.

Under the early Manchu emperors the Banners were a true fighting force whose spirit and valor were maintained by hard campaigns and constant training. The Emperors K'ang Hsi and Ch'ien Lung accompanied most of their military expeditions into battle. Their palace guards were the elite of the entire army. But by 1821, when Tao Kuang acceded to the throne, the Manchu armies had become hopelessly demoralized by graft and bribery, vitiated by years of comparative idleness, and forgetful that the populace still regarded them as hated aliens. Even the palace guards had degenerated to scarcely more than lazy pensioners. A few decades later the Empress Dowager Tz'u Hsi, that last strong ruler of imperial China, complained bitterly of the lack of military discipline and commanded that a modern force be organized and equipped. Some of the troops were then uniformed in semi-European style and armed with rifles, which, with bayonets fixed, made excellent carrying poles for cages of singing birds. Though Chinese gentlemen commonly aired their caged larks and thrushes at the ends of light bamboo poles, the picture

of a mob of illiterate soldiers, in semi-modern uniform, aping this dilet-
tante custom was one that outraged their commander. Mirroring the
decline of the reigning house, this body of so-called troops became, in a
very short time, as worthless as its long-gowned predecessors.

Long before the throne had lost all real communication with the army,
a position in the household troops was a comfortable sinecure, and appointments in the guards were much sought after. Favorites among the
officers were allowed to hold three commissions at the same time—one
in their own Banner, a second in the outer guards, and a third in the inner
guards—which made chances for promotion and graft almost equal to
those enjoyed by the court eunuchs.

During the last hundred years of the Manchu regime, about a thousand
outer guards were stationed at the gates of the ceremonial section of the
palace-city, and about three hundred inner guards constituted the personal bodyguard of the emperor. The inner guards were on duty at all
the gates that controlled entrance and exit to the inner courts, and also
stood watch over the palace walls in four-man details. Other assignments
might include acting as messengers or as caretakers of unoccupied palaces—both duties could be highly lucrative. When the Manchu dynasty
was at the height of its power, the duties of the imperial guard were
arduous. The entire force was divided into four reliefs, three on rotating
duty during each twenty-four hours, while the fourth was off duty. Their
watches as sentinels were only about two hours in length. Never more
than two hundred and fifty outer guards were on duty at any one time,
and only about seventy-five inner guards protected His Majesty and the
privacy of the residential palaces. When the emperor left the Forbidden
City, his personal bodyguard accompanied him, leaving no more than a
handful of men behind.

Originally, the guards wore the uniform of the Manchu army, consisting of short jackets and loose trousers. But later they were promoted to
the long, plum-colored official gown over an inner robe of a different
color; high boots of black velvet or other cloth; round hats topped by a
button indicating rank; and a fierce-looking four-footed beast embroidered in a square on the breast and back of the outer gown. All the officers
held court rank, and the senior usually received the highest of decorations, the riding cape. Though known as the Yellow Jacket, generally it
was the same color as the banner of the recipient, if he was not directly
attached to the court. Troops were armed only with a short sword and

bows and arrows, supplemented by fans for summer, and for rainy weather umbrellas and oil paper covers for their hats.

This set a pattern that continued for many years. The supposedly modernized army of the Empress Dowager Tz'u Hsi was also equipped with oilpaper parasols, as well as fans. To Western eyes the sight of dirty, poorly clad troops marching, each man holding a raised parasol or waving a paper fan, appears ridiculous. But ridiculous or not, neither Chinese nor Manchu soldiers like to get wet, not even for much-needed baths. Indeed, so strong was this distaste that they were not expected to fight when it rained. Had they been so ordered, they would either have noisily refused outright or simply sat down on their haunches, sulking. Not until the Japanese and Communist armies forced raging battles that wiped out these delicate sensibilities, did Chinese troops fight in wet weather or at night.

Only partly supplied by wagon trains or horse-drawn carts, Manchu troops (and the later Republican armies) were compelled to live off the country through which they passed like the scourge of an enemy invasion. Regardless of pleas for mercy, peasants and villagers were forced to disgorge their scanty hoards of rice, pork, and vegetables to feed the rapacious soldiers. When moving through barren country, the troops were usually half starved. According to an ancient and often-repeated story, when an imperial army was defeated during a rebellion and compelled to retire into Szechuan province, the men were forced to subsist largely on a common local form of moss, or lichen, which proved to be nourishing—probably because of high vitamin and mineral content. Since then, this silvery-colored moss, when boiled and sweetened, has been considered a "healthy" dessert with which to end a heavy or overly rich meal.

Compelled to be resourceful in order to augment their meager diet in forward combat areas during the early part of World War II, Chinese troops in Yunnan province scoured the countryside through which they marched for dogs. After being caught, the dogs were firmly leashed and marched jauntily beside the men until food became scarce. Then they ended in the cooking pots. Shockingly, the official ration of a Chinese soldier at that time consisted of twenty-two ounces of rice and one eighth ounce of salt per day—and nothing else. In some instances unwilling recruits were marched hundreds of miles to their division areas on this scanty ration. To prevent their escape, it was not uncommon to see these half-starved peasant lads tied neck to neck with coarse rope. Weakened by hunger and exhaustion, many died on the way. The more fortunate escaped and vanished into the neighboring hills. In 1945 the head of the Chinese Red Cross estimated that ninety per cent of the forcibly impressed recruits failed to reach the forward division training or combat areas. Treated with such callous neglect, it was not surprising that only a few years later entire divisions defected from Chiang Kai-shek and his harassed regime.

In the time of the Manchus the favored guards of the Inner Courts of the Forbidden City were drawn from the three superior Banners and usually included some of the lower-ranking imperial cousins. Though they were required to attend the sovereign when he held audience, this function was actually conducted by a minister of the Presence or a grand chamberlain, normally a prince or a very high official. During the reign of the Empress Dowager Tz'u Hsi, (1862-1908) this important post, which carried with it a tremendous influence on all the affairs of the land, was filled by a eunuch.

Several powerful figures rose from the palace guard during the Manchu regime, the most notorious being Ho Shen, who flourished in the later years of the reign of Emperor Ch'ien Lung (1736-1796). Originally a sergeant, Ho Shen was not even remotely connected to the imperial clan. He attracted the attention of the aging emperor by quoting from the *Four Books*—the emperor's own compilation of all the works of antiquity—as he ran alongside the imperial sedan chair, and he was ordered to attend an audience after their return to the palace.

Thus, Ho Shen was launched on his colorful and corrupt career. Of humble origin, but educated and of handsome appearance, he quickly became a person of consequence at court and ultimately rose to the position of grand councilor. Toward some he displayed a manner of great charm and graciousness; toward others his arrogance was insupportable. He was particularly resented by the heir apparent, Chia Ch'ing, who had a long and unforgiving memory, and a streak of avarice equal to that of Ho Shen himself. When Chia Ch'ing ascended the throne at his father's abdication, he was forced to endure the upstart's ever-increasing depredations as long as the old emperor was still alive. Meanwhile, as Controller General of two government boards, Ho Shen had unlimited opportunities to raid the imperial treasury and revenues. His enemies, bitter with envy, gossiped that the luxury of his palace rivaled that of the Forbidden

City. They whispered it about, one to another, that his immense wealth was greater than that of any other official in the empire. To top it all, when his son managed to marry an imperial princess, letters patent granting him nobility were decreed by the throne.

When the old sovereign finally died, Chia Ch'ing's first act was to dismiss the corrupt favorite and confiscate his entire wealth. Ho Shen's envious accusers had not been exaggerating. To begin with, he owned seventy-five pawnshops and thirteen curio stores. Such commercial activities were highly profitable in the Orient, but forbidden by imperial house law to the nobility to which Ho Shen had been elevated by Ch'ien Lung. Gold bars worth nearly forty million American dollars (at today's value) and thirty thousand pieces of jewelry, were found hidden in his garden. He owned two storehouses filled with white jade, and two more containing the finest silk, nearly eighty thousand fox and sable garments, and thousands of gold and silver objects. A great pearl, said to have belonged to Kublai Khan and to have been sent as tribute to the Emperor Ch'ien Lung, was found—and eventually became one of the favorite treasures of the Empress Dowager Tz'u Hsi.

To cover his gloating satisfaction in unmasking the scoundrel, Chia Ch'ing issued a series of unctuous memorials and took great delight in inventorying the hoard, most of which had been stolen from the imperial storehouses. At last Ho Shen was sentenced to commit suicide by hanging; he received the silken cord with dignity and died with courage. His last act was to give the traditional "thanks" to the new emperor for permitting him the privilege of suicide rather than letting him die like a common criminal at a public execution.

He had a point there. Common criminals met their fate at the Execution Grounds, an area that doubled as a vegetable market, in the western section of the Chinese City. Their sentences were usually carried out at daybreak in the presence of a number of supervising officials. The chief executioner's instruments consisted of five, long-handled, broad-bladed swords, each of which had its own name and was credited with having its own personality. The weapons were also supposed to be able to sing at night of the bloody deeds they had perpetrated.

After being forced to listen to a reading of the imperial decree, each prisoner bowed and acknowledged the justice of his punishment, thus absolving all the officials from any responsibility for his impending demise. He was then turned over to the chief executioner, known as the

Devil's Hand, and compelled to kneel on the ground. As an assistant held his head in a convenient position by means of a cord, the headsman lifted the great sword. Then, with a loud blood-curdling shout, and one flashing downward stroke, the victim's head was severed. Since no one but the emperor could issue the order for an execution, which might be delayed because of his illness or absence from Peking, as many as fifty or sixty unfortunates could be lined up at one time to meet death. As each head fell with a great spurt and splatter of blood, the dense crowd of spectators went wild with excitement. The skill and dexterity of the Devil's Hand was much admired and underscored in repeated yells of approval.

To prevent the outraged ghosts of the decapitated victims from returning to seek revenge, the Execution Ground was surrounded by a "spirit barrier" with three permanently closed entrances—the "Tiger Guarded Bridge," the portal of the "spirit general," and a heavy iron gate. A fourth gate was left open to allow all violently departed spirits to find their way in peace to the Western Paradise.

Another member of the imperial bodyguard who reached the highest rank and whose grandson became an emperor was Duke Jung Lu, a cousin and staunch supporter of the Empress Dowager Tz'u Hsi, of which more follows later.

The last intriguing member of the guards was Chang Hsun. He was called the kingmaker because of his efforts in 1917 to restore Jung Lu's grandson—P'u Yi, the boy-emperor—to the throne he had lost with the establishment of the Republic five years earlier. According to Peking gossip, Chang Hsun attracted the attention of the empress dowager as she was taking an evening stroll along the wall of the palace. His good looks and handsome figure struck her fancy and lingered warmly in her thoughts. Then she acted. In a matter of days he was appointed to command the entire palace guard and became known as the "white-skinned favorite."

Actually, Chang Hsun was a middle aged man of forty-eight at the time of his appointment in 1902. He had had a long career of assignments in the empire and had received a number of important awards from the throne. Also, he had been ordered by the viceroy of Chihli to accompany the empress dowager and the empress when they returned to Peking over a year and a half after their panicked flight from the Allied Relief Force in 1900. Seventeen years later, on July 2, 1917, when the Manchu court was but a shadow of its former grandeur, the impulsive old loyalist attempted to restore the monarchy by a *coup d'état.* It failed miserably. What had been intended as repayment of an old debt of gratitude, accomplished no more than embarrassment and discomfort to the remnants of the imperial family. Five years later Chang Hsun died in Tientsin. He was buried with great pomp and was granted a form of posthumous canonization, with the title of "loyal and brave," by the powerless boy-emperor, P'u Yi.

PART 4
The Three Great Throne Halls

THE APPROACHES:
The Court of the Golden River
The Gate of Supreme Harmony

THE HALL OF SUPREME HARMONY

THE HALL OF THE HAPPY MEAN

THE HALL OF ASSURED HARMONY

The Court of The Golden River

"When the snow lies deep on the roofs of the Dragon King," the spacious Court of the Golden River, just beyond the Meridian Gate, is white and silent under the somber expanse of the twilight sky. Against its pallid glow, great flocks of crows are etched in inky blackness on their homeward flight to the dark cypresses of the Supreme Temple of the Ancestors. For years their evening assemblies were a reminder to all men of an ancient prophecy: "The day the crows fail to return, the reigning dynasty will lose the Mandate of Heaven to rule the empire." But, inasmuch as they have not failed to return in nearly six decades since the fall of the last emperor — through an early Republic, an abortive restoration, warlord regimes, a dictatorship, a Japanese occupation, and finally Communist rule—the politics of their nightly parliaments seem highly adaptable.

In effect, the Court of the Golden River is an atrium "roofed" only by the sky. Its four sides are enclosed by high, red walls, colonnaded porches of low buildings, and pierced by four gates. Far to the east and west the towers above the outer entrances to the palaces loom like high cliffs against which the myriad roofs of lesser halls, pavilions, and waiting rooms seem to create an architectural sea of breaking waves and shining yellow ripples.

On ordinary days, apart from the guards and sweepers, the nearly deserted paving stones waited silently for the entrance or exit of the imperial presence. Undulating from east to west, the quiet waters of the Golden River curved within a marble-lined canal shaped like an archer's bow. Aimed directly toward the entrance gates, the bow, ready to be drawn, symbolized defense and ensured both protection and good fortune for the palace beyond. Turbulent streams, like China's three great rivers, were known to have swept good luck into the sea; but this little canal flowed sedately across the entire width of the court that faces the

Gate of Supreme Harmony. Its five gracefully arched and balustraded white marble bridges were popularly known as the Five Arrows. In designing them, the architects relied on the ancient sages and introduced the spirit of the Five Elements (earth, wood, iron, water and fire), the Five Virtues, the Five Classics, the Five Colors, and the Five Spheres. In short, they invoked the highly lucky number of five—and five times five to the fifth degree.

The serenity of the court derives from the proportions of complementary forces, equal in power but opposite in nature: on the south the towering height and massive weight of the Meridian Gate; on the north the lightness and grace of the Gate of Supreme Harmony; on the east and west two identical, twin gates. All were linked together by walls and buildings to form a perfectly contrived balance.

The Gate of Supreme Harmony

Supported by a low marble terrace, the Gate of Supreme Harmony is one of the few to have escaped destruction in the frequent fires that swept through the Forbidden City. An original Ming dynasty structure, it was repaired many times, the last in 1890. After the burning of the great halls and gates by the rebel Li Tzu-ch'eng in 1644, it was almost the only building suitable for the enthronement of the first Manchu emperor of China, Shun Chih, who became the Son of Heaven at the age of eight.

An enthronement in imperial China was the equivalent of a coronation in Europe and entailed the most careful preparations. But for little Shun Chih's elevation to the throne the scanty revenues of the fledgling court were far too insufficient to provide an elaborate display. At that time the Manchus controlled only a few of the provinces of the Ming empire. They could not afford any extravagance.

The selection of Shun Chih as the first Manchu emperor in that dangerous early period of the conquest was made with sound reasoning. A ruler could name as his heir any one of his sons, any kinsman of a younger generation, or, through adoption, one of no blood relationship. Though only four years old at the time of his father's death, Shun Chih's sturdy little body appealed to the warrior Manchus who admired strong physiques. Moreover, his mother's dowry was impressive. She was Lady Bochito, a princess of the powerful and newly allied Korchin tribe of Tatars; she outranked all other ladies who had borne sons to T'ai Tsung, and was the custodian of the Great Seal of Genghis Khan. So Shun Chih was chosen, despite the fact that he had six half brothers—one of whom was thirty—and fifteen princely uncles. One of the uncles, Prince Jui— often referred to by his Manchu title, the Dorgun Ama Wang—was wisely selected to be regent.

The alliance between Prince Jui and Shun Chih's mother made it inevitable that court gossip would suspect the regent was the sovereign's real father. But since Manchu women had always been accorded a surprising amount of freedom compared to Chinese women, the resentment of their close association was as much jealousy of Prince Jui and envy of Lady Bochito's power as it was of moral indignation.

Without Prince Jui behind the Dragon Throne, the young emperor could not have ruled China, even with his powerful mother. Prince Jui controlled the clans and the army, and he could have overthrown his nephew at any time. Indeed, on one occasion he was invited by plotters to usurp the throne. He refused, and instead managed to subdue the large brood of ambitious princes and whip them into a solid wall of loyalty behind the young sovereign. Prince Jui used his military genius to organize the empire and proved himself to be a worthy son of the great Nurhachu. It was he who had cunningly made a traitor of the Chinese General Wu San-kuei at the Great Wall, and he who commanded Wu's army along with his own against the rebel Li Tzu-ch'eng. Once Peking had fallen, he forced the humiliating queue on General Wu and kept a watchful eye on him lest he turn traitor again. Early in his regency Prince Jui stated that "an empire founded on horseback cannot be governed from horseback," recognizing that his inexperienced people would find it almost impossible to control a land where they were considered barbarians. So he set about to correct that Chinese opinion. The Manchus were of mixed Tatar and Tungusic origin; the great khans were their remote ancestors. These two facts gave their descendants a right, albeit a shadowy one, to occupy China. The Chinese were also constantly reminded that the Ming dynasty had lost the Mandate of Heaven and most of north China *before* the Manchu invasion.

Prince Jui's first decree as regent forbade any further looting in Peking. Next, he provided a decent burial for the last Ming emperor, Ch'ung Cheng, and proclaimed three days of national mourning, both in his memory and the empress'. He extended a hand of conciliation to all Chinese who would accept it. Those who would not, he struck down with a clenched fist. Officials who had remained at their posts during the troubles were retained and rewarded. His proclamation was brief: "Those who served their former masters faithfully, let them also serve me faithfully."

Since the Manchus had more or less adopted the Ming system of government in their own capital at Mukden, few fundamental changes were necessary in Peking. The six administrative boards of the former dynasty—Law, Order, Justice, War, Revenue, and Civil Rites—were retained. The heads of the six boards became a cabinet of secretaries who advised the regent, and this cabinet rapidly emerged as the most powerful executive body in the empire. In Mukden board members had been little more than exalted clerks and scribes. Civil administration had been comparatively rudimentary, each clan organization solving most of its own problems and enforcing individual laws and discipline over the clansmen. These laws, of course, did not apply to the Chinese who lived under a legal system, which they had devised over many centuries and which was revised by each succeeding emperor. When appointments were made, both a Manchu and a Chinese served in each high office, the former always having precedence over the Chinese colleague.

It was Prince Jui who coped successfully with the knotty problem of the language barrier by putting thousands of interpreters, clerks, and scribes to work on the new decrees issued in both Manchu and Chinese. Prince Jui knew only too well that the comparatively simple script of the conquerors was regarded with contempt by the more cultivated and sophisticated Chinese. But if it delighted the Chinese to look down their noses at him and his hardy warriors, he returned the insult by indulging in a bit of contempt too: he thought their complicated characters and elegant refinements were both feminine and effete and that they typified a people who had neither the time, disposition, nor stamina to defend their own land—and so had lost it.

While Prince Jui directed affairs of state, Shun Chih's mother undertook the emperor's upbringing and made of her son the most idealistic of Manchu rulers. His physical and moral welfare were guarded with far-sighted vigilance, as evidenced by an iron pillar that she had placed at the entrance of the palace with the inscription: "If any females with bound feet dare to pass this gate, let them be summarily beheaded!"

Determined that her son should not become fascinated by Chinese ladies with "lily feet," she instituted the dynastic house law, which forbade a Chinese consort for an emperor. Leery of eunuchs, she urged the initiation of laws designed to keep them within bounds. Their official rank was abolished, and not until the latter part of the Manchu period did they once again become a menace.

It was Prince Jui who insisted that the queue for all male Chinese and bound feet for all Chinese females become obligatory. Though the binding of feet was an ancient, but not always practiced, custom among the upper classes, it had never been adopted by the great mass of Chinese women. In time, this painful custom became so accepted that it was continued for years after it ceased to be required by law.

As the southern and central provinces were wrested from the Ming princes and their adherents, they were parceled out as fiefs to the more important Chinese who had helped the Manchus in the conquest of their native land. General Wu San-kuei was richly rewarded with the great province of Yunnan.

In 1650 a hunting accident in Mongolia ended the life of Prince Jui at the age of only thirty-nine. Still seething with envy, his enemies pounced on him in death and questioned his loyalty. Unable to refute their charges from the grave, Jui was publicly disgraced and his name stricken from the imperial clan register. (Not until a hundred years later was he reinstated by the Emperor Ch'ien Lung.)

In his early youth, except for the time devoted to studies, Shun Chih lived much the same as any other Manchu princeling of his age. Though sports were his chief amusement, he was alert mentally, avidly interested in the great victories of the clans, and he took his regal responsibilities with great seriousness. In addition to the study of his native language, his education included the complete curriculum of a Chinese scholar. Because of his stern mother, the court was highly proper, though its manners were still tinged with the rough freedom of the northern plains. Compared to life in the palace under the pleasure-loving Ming emperors, the youthful Shun Chih's court was decidedly dull.

Most important of all, coming of age for Shun Chih meant that a suitable, healthy bride had to be found to provide him with descendants to carry on the imperial line. For his first wife, his mother selected a lady of the Korchin tribe: Borichichin. In accordance with the custom, she was several years Shun Chih's senior. But it was not a happy selection. The girl was unmannered and ill-tempered; and in no time she and her young lord were quarreling. Disgusted and enraged, Shun Chih's mother demoted Borichichin to a concubine of the third rank. At fifteen he took a second empress. This one bore him a son, who was later to become one of the greatest emperors of his line—K'ang Hsi.

Then, to his mother's horror, the youthful Shun Chih fell deeply in love with a concubine, the Lady Tung. He spoke of her as "the mistress of my happiness . . . at hearing whose voice the Son of Heaven rejoices." A girl of rare good sense and sympathetic understanding, she unselfishly sacrificed herself for his welfare. Though Shun Chih was delighted with her virtues, the court was annoyed. She was a nuisance and a priggish busybody! They bitterly resented her attention to affairs of state and considered her insistence that Shun Chih read each character of the edicts submitted to him to be meddlesome. But no matter how they carped and complained, her influence remained complete.

In the autumn of Shun Chih's twenty-third year, Lady Tung died suddenly. Whether or not she was poisoned—which is more than probable—is not known. But her death rocked the young emperor to his depths. He spent hours each day composing epitaphs to her memory, or seeking solace with Buddhist priests. "His grief for her loss," an astonished chronicler wrote, "seems to have been perfectly genuine, whereby he is greatly distinguished among imperial husbands who generally rejoice at the deaths of their consorts."

But Shun Chih's bitter grief was brief. He and Lady Tung were not separated for long. Before the winter ended, Shun Chih, too, was dead. The state annals claim that the emperor died of smallpox, the disease most dreaded by the Manchus. The northern warriors were dangerously susceptible to the frequent epidemics of the Chinese. A serious outbreak of smallpox in their ranks could have weakened them and destroyed their still precarious hold on the empire.

Though the enthronement of little Shun Chih had been almost parsimonious in character, the ceremonies of his many successors were gorgeous and stately. These functions took place within a few days after the death of an emperor, during which brief interval the court postponed wearing the official white of mourning. Many dignitaries, heads of departments of the imperial household, and eunuch chamberlains were bowed down with a grief born of fear rather than sorrow. New brooms swept clean, and new imperial brooms could be efficiently brisk. The enthronement ceremonies were the responsibility of the Board of Rites, whereas the late emperor's funeral details were handled by the Household Department.

The chamberlains of the imperial wardrobe provided a magnificent robe for the new emperor, of golden yellow, the symbolic color of the throne and of the earth. It was cut like the ordinary court costume, but more lavishly embroidered. The lower long skirt had a rich border of waves and spray, beneath a design of mountains. The upper robe was embroidered with clouds against which the Dragon King posed in gold-threaded splendor. Surrounding the dragon king were eight of his royal dragon kin, four on each side; these symbolized the highest rank of five-clawed dragons that could grant all wishes to the virtuous. Twelve additional objects prescribed by the *Book of Rites* were interspersed among the clouds of heaven, the rocks of earth, and the waves of the sea.

The Perfect Emperor Yao had long ago declared: "I wish to see the emblematic figures of the ancients—the sun, the moon, the stars, the mountains, the dragon and the flaming fowl depicted on the upper garment; the temple cups, the aquatic grass, the flames, the grains of rice, the hatchet and the symbol of distinction embroidered on the lower garment. I wish to see all these displayed with the five colors, so as to form the official robe."

Instead of a crown, His Majesty wore the usual shallow, bowl-shaped hat, surmounted by a spiked gold ornament—in contrast to the round button of rank worn by nobles and officials. From the base of the ornament to the edge of the brim, where a huge pearl was set, hung a thick fringe of red silk.

Very early on the day selected by the Board of Astronomy, members of the imperial family and high officials gathered together in the court before the hall designated for the enthronement ceremony. They had risen shortly after midnight and, assisted by servants, had struggled into their elaborate robes. Long before the first light of day their sedan chairs and carts arrived at the palace. All Manchu ceremonies, even minor ones, began while the sky was still dark and ended as the last light of day faded in the western sky. "Lamps," the old saying ran, "are for use in the morning; not at night."

As princes and officials assembled for the enthronement, the president of the Board of Rites begged the new emperor to clothe himself in mourning. This done, the president accompanied him to the hall where the late ruler lay in state. There the heir announced to his deceased predecessor that he would accept the imperial decree that named him sovereign of the empire. Only his close imperial relatives were present, watching in silent awe as he knelt and prostrated himself before the great coffin in the solemn nine-fold *k'o-t'ou,* or kowtow, an elaborate obeisance, in which the performer knelt and touched his forehead to the ground nine times.

Then the heir returned to his private quarters and arrayed himself in the Dragon Robes of state. Clothed in this bedazzling glory, he rode in the massive golden chariot to the throne hall of his mother, who had already been created empress dowager. Seated in her magnificent robes on her chair of state, she accepted his formal *k'o-t'ou;* and from that moment until her death she remained the first lady of the empire, a rarefied position few empresses lived long enough to enjoy.

The new sovereign then seated himself in the great sedan chair of state and was carried to the site chosen for the ceremony, where the assembled throng of princes and dignitaries waited silently. When he arrived, the president of the Board of Rites prostrated himself before the new emperor and made the official pronouncement: "Ascend the throne!" At that moment the entire assemblage bowed in deep obeisance.

The emperor then mounted the high dais of the Dragon Throne and seated himself with the gravest formality, turning his face toward the south, one of his titles being "The Face that is Turned Toward the South." The assembled princes and officials knelt and bowed again, thus signifying their official approval of the enthronement. The ceremony over, the court went into a three-year mourning period for the late emperor, during which time only white was worn and no gaiety permitted.

One of the first acts of the new sovereign was to attach the Great Seal of Lawfully Transmitted Authority to a decree announcing his succession. This was proclaimed with suitable ceremony throughout the land. But it was not an occasion for festivity. There were no teeming crowds, no fireworks, no processions in the streets. The people stood, listened, bowed in deep respect to their new emperor, and then went about their usual business.

Next, it was customary for the new sovereign to issue a second decree. As an example the following, proclaimed by the Emperor Tao Kuang (1821-1851), indicates what a Manchu sovereign wished his subjects to believe:

Our Ta Ch'ing [Manchu] Dynasty has received the most substantial signs of Heaven's kind care. Our ancestors, Tai Su and T'ai Tsung, began to lay the vast foundation; and Shun Chih became the sole monarch of China. Our sacred ancestors, K'ang Hsi, the Emperor Yung Cheng, the glory of his age, and Ch'ien Lung, the eminent in honor, all abounded in virtue, were divine in martial prowess, consolidated the glory of the empire and molded the whole to peaceful harmony.

His late Majesty, who has now gone on the great journey, governed all under Heaven's canopy for twenty-five years, exercising the greatest caution and industry. During neither evening nor morning was he ever idle. He assiduously aimed at the best possible rule, and hence his government was excellent and illustrious. The Court and the country felt the deepest reverence, and the stillness of profound awe. A benevolent heart and a benevolent administration were universally diffused in China proper, as well as beyond it. Order and tranquillity prevailed, and the tens of thousands of common people were happy. But in the midst of a hope that his glorious reign would be long protracted and the help of Heaven would be received for many years, unexpectedly, the Dragon Charioteer [the Emperor] became a guest on high.

My sacred and indulgent father had, in the year that he began to rule, silently settled that the Divine Utensil [the Throne] should devolve on my contemptible person. I, knowing the feebleness of my virtue, at first felt much afraid that I should not be competent to the office. But on reflecting that the sages and his late Majesty had all laid the duty on me— and Heaven's Throne should not be long vacant—I have done violence to my feelings and forced myself to pause in my heartfelt grief that I may with reverence obey the unalterable decree. On the 27th day of the 8th Moon [October 3], I propose devoutly to announce the event to Heaven, to Earth, to my Ancestors and to the Gods of the Land and of the Grain; and shall then sit down on the Imperial Throne. Let the next year be the first of Tao Kuang.

I look upward and hope to be able to continue former excellences. I lay my hand on my heart with feelings of respect and cautious awe. When a monarch addresses himself to the empire, he ought to confer benefits on his kindred and extensively bestow gracious favors. Whatever is proper to be done on this occasion is stated below.

Then followed twenty-two paragraphs listing gifts to be conferred on nobles and officers and promotions to be made; suspended dignitaries to be restored to their full pay and honors, sacrifices to be made to Confucius and the emperors of earlier dynasties, pardons to be extended to criminals; banished convicts to be recalled; debts on taxes in arrears to be forgiven; and donations to be bestowed on the aged. It concluded:

> Lo, now! On succeeding to the Throne, I shall exercise myself to give repose to the millions of my people. Assist me to sustain the burden laid on my shoulders! With veneration I receive the charge of Heaven's great concern. Ye kings and statesmen, great and small, civil and military, everyone to be faithful, devoted and aid in supporting this vast affair that our family dominion may be preserved for hundreds and tens of thousands of years in never ending tranquillity and glory! Promulgate this to all under Heaven. Cause everyone to hear it!

For Shun Chih's enthronement the guardrooms at each end of the central building of the Gate of Supreme Harmony were refurbished, the red-lacquered pillars and open porch repainted, the white marble terrace and double-tiered roof of yellow tiles scoured to a freshness that sparkled in the clear northern sunlight. Though the debris and wreckage from the fires set by the rebel bandit Li had been cleared away in the two years since the Manchus entered the palace, adjacent roofs, walls, and pillars still stood in blackened ruins.

At the time this gate was the only building in this part of the Forbidden City that remained intact in the midst of the general dilapidation—its tunnels and brilliant colors pointed the way to despoiled courts and palaces beyond.

THE HALL OF SUPREME HARMONY

The brass-studded panels of the Gate of Supreme Harmony open to reveal the first and largest of the great throne halls—the Hall of Supreme Harmony. Across the two-hundred-yard-wide Court of Honor, it rises above three tiers of white marble terraces—an imposing palace of red-lacquered walls and pillars, with soaring yellow-tiled roofs. Reserved for only the greatest of ceremonies, it was there that the sacred dignity of the emperor—sitting on the awesome Dragon Throne and shielded by a canopy from the eyes of his most powerful subjects—touched the zenith of solemnity.

The very name of this hall was impressive. In the *Book of Changes,* Confucius alludes to "supreme harmony" as an all-embracing, transcendental harmony between Heaven and Earth. When the hall was rebuilt during the reign of the Emperor K'ang Hsi (1662-1723), its name implied a promise by the Manchu dynasty to respect the ideals and principles of good government as prescribed by China's most honored sage. Revered to the point of slavish acceptance, the narrow ultraconservatism of Confucius, unfortunately, contributed more than any other factor toward shutting off all original thought and impeding any normal social progress in the "celestial" empire.

An austere and majestic dignity characterizes the Hall of Supreme Harmony. It was literally at the center of the imperial universe and loomed high above the empty expanse of its vast forecourt. Seven gates linked by red walls, low galleries serving as waiting rooms, corner pavilions, and lesser, two-storied halls, all formed a closed perimeter of undulating roof lines that screened out the world.

Called the Dragon Pavement, the three tiers of marble terraces were mounted by three flights of five stairways. The center one was the deeply carved "spirit stairway," sacred and untouched by human feet. Over its carved panel the imperial chair was borne on great state occasions. Flanking the "spirit stairway" were four other flights—two on the east side and two on the west; these were used by such dignitaries as might be permitted the supreme privilege of making personal obeisance to the emperor on days of high ceremony.

Eighteen huge, three-legged incense burners surmounted by peaked and fluted bronze covers were interspersed in groups from the level of the courtyard to the top terrace. Though usually believed to represent the eighteen provinces into which the Manchus divided the empire, they were probably no more than a double set of copies of the famous nine tripods of the Chou dynasty (1122 to 255 B.C.). On the upper terrace, against the walls of the building, stood the sun dial, the grain measure, two large cranes symbolizing longevity, and four enormous gilt-bronze bowls, which, when filled with oil and ignited, illuminated the side stairways used for predawn audiences.

A pair of great bronze tortoises, or the "sons of dragons who willingly bear weights" and symbolizing strength, completed the ornaments on the marble platforms before the Hall of Supreme Harmony. Replicas of these creatures were frequently placed in the grounds of temples and usually bore tall, inscribed stone tablets balanced upright on their backs. Their most worthy virtue was the power to restrain official greed and corruption, in which they more often than not failed. According to tradition, the scholar who passed first in the triannual examinations solemnly mounted the head of one of these tortoises, and, having just been granted the title of *Chuang Yuan* (meaning "optimum") by the Han Lin Academy and assured of a good official post, publicly pledged himself to be an honest servant of his emperor. (Established in A.D. 740, the Han Lin Academy was a combined Academy of Letters and College of Heralds, as well as the custodian of Emperor Yung Lo's twenty-three-thousand-volume encyclopedia.)

The throne hall itself was two hundred feet wide, a hundred feet deep, and a hundred and ten feet high. Its walls were three feet thick, and each pillar supporting the roof was the trunk of a single great tree. The gleaming yellow tiles of the mountainous hipped roof were set in a special mortar, which prevented wind-blown seeds from taking root. Surmounting the ends of the tile-encased ridgepole was a pair of dragon-headed finials. These terminated a procession of figures on the sweeping curves of the four eaves, led by Ming Wang, the wicked prince of the Chou dynasty, on his fairy hen.

The decoration of the great hall was planned in accordance with a proper conception of the Five Colors in harmonious order with the Five Elements, the Five Spheres, and the Five Directions. The dark paving of the courtyard represented black; the marble terrace, white; the frame and walls of the building, red; the glistening roof, yellow; the fifth and highest, the azure blue of the sky above. Small designs of deeper blue, green, white and gold, painted on the exposed crossbeams and ornamental flanges of the twelve pillars of the open porch, were mere accents; as were the gilt dragon handles, hinges of the doors, and the long gilt chains hanging from the top of the ridge as protection against lightning.

The present hall was constructed in 1690 under the supervision of a noted architect Liang Ch'in, of the palace Board of Reconstruction and Repairs. Father Gerbillon, one of the missionaries at the court of K'ang Hsi, wrote:

> This hall was burned down several years ago, and already, for some time, more than a million ounces of silver have been set aside to rebuild it, but the work has not yet been begun because so far no beams have been found as large as those of the original Ming Dynasty building, and they have to be brought a great distance.

Since then, this throne hall has been repaired many times. The most recent renovation was done between 1887 and 1889 for the marriage of the Emperor Kuang Hsu in February, 1889.

The Hall of Supreme Harmony was the setting for the great New Year reception and celebration. Other festivals—the spring; the midsummer, or Dragon Boat Festival; and the autumn, or Moon Feast—though celebrated in the Forbidden City until the Manchu dynasty was finally overthrown, were held in lesser courts or halls. But the New Year was the greatest celebration of all, and every individual in the empire shared in its excitement. It was not only the official birthday of the empire, but of every man, woman and child in the land, from the emperor down to the meanest beggar. In a sense it symbolized a reunion of the spirits of the living and the dead, of the different members of a family, and of the sovereign and his people. It signified the awakening of life and the stirring of the soil as the dark nights of winter dissipated before the light and warmth of the coming spring.

The day preceding the great New Year reception was a deeply religious time and rigidly solemn. The emperor, on the highest terrace of the Altar of Heaven, reported to the one God of the Universe and beseeched a blessing for his reign and subjects. This duty over, he received the thanks of the princes and dignitaries of state for having interceded with Heaven for their benefit, and each reassured him of allegiance. It was the duty of all imperial kinsmen, the nobility, and officials, as well as of all representatives of tributary regions, to assemble in the Forbidden City and pay their respects to their supreme sovereign.

While all this elaborate pre-New Year formality was taking place, the whole country was in a state of anticipation and dignified enthrallment. When the great day arrived, every child was taken to greet its grandparents. Every bride presented her infant son—his cheeks rubbed with rouge to simulate health—to her father and mother. Every student honored his teacher. Every friend called on his friends. Every servant saluted his master. Every debtor repaid his debts—if he could. Wishes for health, joy, and wealth for the coming year filled the cold air. Even the beggars huddled outside the Dynastic Gate were fed, for no one could go hungry at this joyous season.

The Manchus were wise in learning to live on ceremony and in observing all the New Year customs of the Chinese. Yet they also privately celebrated some of their own peculiar rites: As the year ended, the kitchen god was feasted; as the New Year dawned, ancestors were worshiped. They also adhered to another time-worn tradition: the emperor sent gifts to all of his family, his court, and his officials. Presents of silk and jewels went from the sovereign to his empress; gowns and furs to lesser ladies of the court; horses, bronzes, and furs to the princes of the imperial family; and inscriptions written with his own distinguished brush, food, and flowers to all he wished to honor. If the gift were flowers, it had to be a pair of growing plants in porcelain pots. Cut flowers were taboo. Sometimes the emperor sent twisted dwarf trees of plum and cherry that had been forced into early bloom; or miniature orange and lemon trees weighted with fruit; faintly scented peonies; "heavenly bamboo," brilliant with clusters of red berries. Lilies, or "water fairies," were often a gift from the sovereign. Even wisteria and magnolia offered their frail beauty for this first among all feasts.

When the imperial princes, nobles, and officials gathered for the New Year reception in the court before the Hall of Supreme Harmony, they came to offer thanks not only for favors received during the year, but also for the gifts they had just received.

Mongol princes and chiefs of tribes beyond the Great Wall were summoned in rotation once every three years. To entertain more than a third of these uncouth barbarians at one time was more than the refined and elegant court could endure. These primitive vassals gnawed on great chunks of meat, swilled down huge quantities of wine with a noisy smacking of lips, and snatched at the New Year presents with greasy, unwashed hands. Envoys from distant Tibet and Nepal were obliged to appear at court at fixed intervals, too. They started out on the arduous journey with costly caravans and often traveled a full year to reach Peking. By then their horses were lean and half starved, their camels worn out. The snow in the high passes of the Himalayas was so deep that their animals floundered up to their bellies in drifts; and retainers, half frozen themselves, dragged their masters over the clogged trails on priceless tribute carpets.

Tibetan travelers to Peking were not only beset by the horrendous dangers of nature—mile-high cliffs, icy winters, raging sand storms, and the droughts in almost endless deserts—but they also faced the barbarous greed of hostile tribesmen. As any caravan crossed the rugged mountains and wide steppes of their territories, the brigands lay in wait, always ready to kill and loot. Fortunately, the more superstitious they were, the more they feared the mysterious power of the Dalai Lama. In order to ensure a caravan's safety, each embassy that had to pass through unfriendly lands was armed with a prestigious Tibetan passport. These five-foot-long scrolls of gold satin were stamped with two seals: that of the Dalai Lama and the great, square imprint of the emperor—in Chinese characters as well as in Manchu, Mongolian, and Tibetan. A likeness of the Dalai Lama sitting on the rounded top of the world, was painted at the upper part of the document. At the bottom was an assortment of threatening devils and gods. The long text, usually written in Tibetan and Mongolian, contained a detailed and gory account of the horrors that would be visited upon any and all who failed to provide the bearer with food, shelter, water, fresh horses, and protection on demand—horrors that included fire and flood, thunder and lightning, disease and death, earthquake, and famine. Thus armed, the envoys began their monthslong trek with what sometimes proved to be a false sense of security against the dangers of travel.

After a few months at the capital, the resources of these unfortunate guests were often exhausted. On arrival they were presented a New Year gift of gold and silver ingots in accordance with their rank and station, but this imperial largesse by no means covered the costs of such a great journey. Arriving in state, most returned home in rags, forced to sell their own furs and carpets to pay their way. Not a few had to climb on foot over the stony Nankow Pass to the Great Wall, their bedraggled beasts too weak to carry them up that long, steep road. The emperors were not displeased with this state of affairs: impoverished princes could raise no rebellions.

Also present at the New Year festivities were the heads of the Eight Princely Families, descendants of senior nobles—often called the Iron-capped Princes—who had aided the Manchu imperial family most in the conquest of China and were therefore granted the right to retain their titles in perpetuity. Apart from these privileged few, Manchu law required that each succeeding generation of the ordinary nobility be dropped down one rank from that of the father. In such a descending scale, the son of a noble of the twelfth degree had no title at all, though possibly he was still a member of the imperial clan. Descendants of the founder of the dynasty always had the right to attend at court. The close kin of His Majesty—brothers, sons, uncles, nephews, and cousins—were divided into four ranks of senior and junior princes. There were also four ranks of dukes and four lower ranks roughly corresponding to those of European nobility. At the great New Year ceremony it was easy to tell who was who: strict laws regulated the color and value of all insignia of rank, each symbol indicating the exact position of all princes and nobles, and each of the nine ranks of civil and military officials.

The following description of prescribed insignia was written by a scholarly Englishman, S. Wells Williams during the reign of Tao Kuang (1821-1851), when the old court dress was rigidly adhered to by all those entitled to wear it:

> Civilians of the first rank wear a precious ruby or transparent red stone, a stork embroidered on the back and breast of the robe, and a girdle clasp of prehenite set in rubies. Military men differ in having a unicorn instead of a stork, their buttons and clasps being the same as civilians.
> Civilians of the second rank wear a red coral button, a robe

embroidered with a golden pheasant, and a gold girdle clasp set with rubies. The lion is emblazoned on the military.

Civilians of the third rank wear a sapphire and a one-eyed peacock feather, a robe with an embroidered peacock, and a clasp of worked gold. Military officers have an embroidered leopard instead of a peacock.

Civilians of the fourth rank are distinguished by a blue opaque stone, a crane on the breast, and a clasp of worked gold with a silver button. Military officers wear a tiger instead of a crane.

Civilians of the fifth rank are denoted by a crystal button, a silver pheasant, and a clasp of plain gold with a silver button. The bear is the escutcheon of military men.

Civilians of the sixth rank wear an opaque white shell button, a blue plume, an egret worked on the breast, and a mother-of-pearl clasp. Military men wear a 'pien,' or little tiger.

Civilians of the seventh rank have a plain gold button, a partridge on the breast, and a clasp of silver. A rhinoceros designates the military, as it does in the next rank.

The eighth rank wears a gold button, a quail on the breast and a clasp of clear horn.

The ninth rank is distinguished by a silver button, a sparrow on the breast, and a clasp of buffalo horn. Military men are marked by a sea horse embroidered on their robes.

No matter how closely a woman might be related to the imperial family, she was never allowed to appear at the New Year reception, or even to enter the Hall of Supreme Harmony and its great Court of Honor. In fact, her sex barred her from all ceremonies in either place.

All those attending the festival wore new robes, as new garments were traditional for both rich and poor on the first day of the year. The prescribed official dress was an ankle-length inner robe of satin or silk, with a stiff, turned-down collar attached to a sleeveless vest of plain blue silk. Buttoning down the center of the front, this garment varied from all other governmental apparel—which buttoned across the breast and down the right side. A somewhat shorter over-robe, or coat, of dark plum-colored brocade, had long sleeves with reversible cuffs, which were turned down to cover the hands in the presence of a superior. The cuffs, shaped like a horse's hoof, and the split in the front and rear seam of the over-robe recalled the times when the Manchus were constantly on horseback. Known as the parting wrapper, the ample folds of the outer coat were confined at the waist by a girdle, to which were attached embroidered chopstick and knife cases, a jewelled watch pocket, and similar personal articles. Full trousers, bound at the ankles with white bands, were worn under the robes. Court boots were of elegant black velvet or satin, with white kid or felt soles. In summer the headdress was a hat woven of finely split bamboo; in winter a porkpie type creation with a fur brim, the crown hidden by red silk fringe and surmounted by the round button of rank.

A little after midnight all the guests gathered together in the Court of Honor. There they were often kept waiting in the bitter cold, shivering in their fur-lined robes. Above them loomed the dark and frosty star-lit sky; below, the glaring flames of burning oil in the huge gilt bowls. Only the senior princes and highest officials were invited into nearby chill rooms for hot tea and refreshments; the vast majority of guests waited outside in the bitter cold of the courtyard, praying they would not turn into blocks of ice before the reception began. Had they been anywhere else but the Forbidden City, there would have been a continuous grumble of indignation—but not so here. They gazed upon hundreds of flickering lanterns—some of buffalo horn, others with panels of delicately painted silk and paper—and shivered. They watched rockets ripping and bursting through the darkness, and as elaborate decorative pieces crackled and glowed like multicolored phosphoresence, they hugged themselves within their robes. Each new aerial picture was announced by a crashing explosion of more giant crackers—they watched, waited, and shivered.

The entertainment seemed endless. The Jesuit Father Ripa, who saw many New Year festivals at the court of K'ang Hsi, wrote: "It may be affirmed without exaggeration that on the night when the old year terminates and the new year begins, there is more gunpowder consumed in China than throughout Europe during the whole twelve months."

At the appointed time, long before the first light of dawn, the court chamberlains marshaled the guests into eighteen double diagonal rows in the vast Court of Honor: civil officials on the east, military on the west, their positions marked by two lines of square paving stones. Each stone had a bronze plaque shaped like a miniature mountain inscribed in both Chinese and Manchu with the rank of the person who was to occupy it.

One of the letters of Father Ripa, who was present at a New Year ceremony, shows his amazement at the order, design, and choreography he witnessed. He wrote: "In this great multitude where nothing could be expected but confusion and disorder, everything is so admirably well regulated and performed in the most exact order, everyone knowing his place, there are no disputes about precedence."

Having been *crystallized* by centuries of tradition, the entire ritual of the ceremony was absolutely rigid. While the eunuchs in richly embroidered gowns hurried about, arranging the last details, the scarlet-robed court musicians took their places on the marble terrace before the doors of the hall. The music was traditional—similar to that played in the days of Confucius. With percussion instruments dominating the compositions chosen for the great ceremonies, the resulting sounds were as solemn as funeral dirges. This doleful cacophony was heightened by the sound of a light stick striking on twelve golden bells hanging in a gilded frame.

As the astrologers' auspicious moment approached, the long procession of the sovereign left the Inner Courts and, winding its way past lesser throne halls, neared the great Hall of Supreme Harmony. As the emperor's arrival grew imminent, it was announced with a piercing cry: "The Lord of Ten Thousand Years approaches!" Instead of passing through the orderly ranks of officials kneeling in the bitter cold, the chair of state was borne to a small rear entrance. When the yellow canopy came into view at the center doorway of the throne hall, the imperial princes and topmost officials strode with calm dignity to their assigned places on the icy terrace. As the emperor ascended the throne, hanging jade plaques were tapped by the court musicians and a long pole was beaten hard against a dome-shaped drum. Throughout the whole ceremony one musician, his face grave for the occasion, scraped back and forth on the iron mane of a wooden lion, creating a noise not unlike the explosions of tiny firecrackers. At this moment the whole assembly performed in unison the significant act of the entire ceremony—the nine-fold obeisance of congratulation. Finally, on the command to "return thanks for the imperial bounty," all those present again performed the nine-fold *k'o-t'ou*.

Now the emperor was on the throne, but he could be seen only by the chamberlains of the household and the four eunuchs of the Presence (who corresponded roughly to equerries in a European royal court). Carefully the canopy was raised to screen the chair of state from the view of even the nearby closest kin. The emperor did not show himself to his entire court at important ceremonies. He was too sacred to be the object of anyone's gaze. Later, when certain of the princes and nobles were permitted to enter the throne hall, they dared not raise their eyes to the Buddhalike face, for at this time their priest-king had ceased to be a human. Those permitted to enter the Presence were the few princes and officials who had been allowed on the terrace and the first two rows of the nine grades of dignitaries who were stationed in the courtyard below. They moved through a side door to make personal obeisance to their sovereign lord, each man holding in both hands a jade or jeweled *jui*, a curved scepter about eighteen inches long, one end of which formed a round disk, the other tapering into a curved finial, and the whole beautifully carved or inlaid. It was originally meant to serve as a token of respectful greetings, symbolizing "in accordance with wishes"—auspicious wishes for happiness, long life, and prosperity. Since no man dared look upon the face of his Supreme Lord at any ceremony or formal state occasion, the scepter was intended to rivet the gaze of the bearer on its perfection lest he be tempted to commit the unpardonable offense of looking at his emperor.

The vast majority of the guests, including some of those who had traveled thousands of miles to offer homage, did not even catch a glimpse of His Majesty. Indeed, many could scarcely hear the master of ceremonies telling them when to kneel, when to stand, and when to *k'o-t'ou*. Only the abrupt changes and spasmodic bursts of music made it possible for them to follow the ritual at all.

The interior of the great Hall of Supreme Harmony was solemn and imposing. It was penetratingly chill, too. Light filtered so delicately through the thick Korean paper in the lattices of the narrow doors and windows that the dark rose color of the walls and the lavish, gilded lacquer remained in shadows. In shadows, too, were the golden, lacelike carvings of the canopies over the doors leading to anterooms and the heavily carved dragons rising to cloudy heights about the pillars near the throne. Triple rows of huge pillars rose from the dark marble of the floor to join massive crossbeams and a multitude of brackets that framed the coffered ceiling. The blues and greens of the flat panels, emblazoned with a full-faced dragon rampant, invited the ghosts of past emperors to watch the activities of their descendants from this sacred place.

The ceiling in the center of the hall opened to form a recess, an interior cupola. It reached almost as high as the ridgepole and contained a golden dragon with enormous eyes capable of seeing in all directions from its deeply carved and gilded vault. This odd construction may have symbolized the Emperor's role as the Master of Time.

The focal point in this enormous room was the throne chair itself. It was without ostentation. Shielding the "precious seat" on its high dais was an elaborately carved and fretted screen of seven panels. The selection of the throne was important: if a son succeeded his father, he had to use his grandfather's chair of state. No other seats were permitted in any hall where the Son of Heaven had his official chair. All subjects were required either to stand or kneel in his august presence.

The furnishings of the Hall of Supreme Harmony were of heroic proportions: two gigantic mirrors in hardwood frames; huge pairs of cabinets made of precious woods; long tables of hard woods and lacquer, displaying treasures of bronze, jade, and porcelain worth a king's ransom. In winter open braziers filled with glowing charcoal blazed with a show of heat, but did little to cut the icy chill of the vast space. For ceremonies the hall was only dimly lit by elaborate lanterns on high stands or hanging from the ceiling beams. Each was a work of art—glass, horn, or painted silk. The glow of the braziers shone in the gilded lacquer, made the surface of the tall mirrors shine with silver, and touched with fiery brilliance the long folds of embroidered banners. The true light, however, was that of the Presence. Garbed in his gorgeous Dragon Robes and seated squarely on his golden Dragon Throne, the Supreme Lord was stiffly erect, his feet planted on the footstool of the earth. With his face veiled by the drifting blue fragrance of innumerable incense burners, he was, indeed, a demigod among earthly mortals; and to all his subjects a true son of the God of the Infinite Space that filled the heavens. The closing lines of the revered *Book of History* could serve as an epitaph to this annual apotheosis of each emperor: "The decline and fall of a state may arise from one man. The glory and tranquillity of a state may also arise from the goodness of one man."

When the light of a new dawn and a new year began to sweep away the darkness of the old, the musicians droned out a closing anthem. The golden canopy was withdrawn, and the Great Presence left the hall in the midst of his glittering cortege. He was borne at once to the palace of the empress dowager, to whom he paid his filial respects in her own throne hall. That done, he was free to lay aside his magnificent Dragon Robes and enjoy his share of the family revelry.

In 1933, five years after the capital was moved to Nanking, the Chinese government moved most of the remaining treasures of the Forbidden City to that Yangtze River city.

From 1933 to 1938, when the palace was open to visitors, some of its former priceless contents were still in the Forbidden City. The huge mirrors in heavily carved frames still flanked the throne in the Hall of Supreme Harmony. The iridescence of countless, tiny kingfisher feathers glistened like blue fire against the black lacquer of a pair of large panels. Ch'ien Lung's stag-horn throne was exhibited against one wall. But the most impressive sight, never displayed in this room during imperial rule, was the portraits of a thousand years of emperors staring down from the high red walls: elegant Sung rulers in white, rough and gaudy Mongols, refined Ming emperors in brilliant red, and Manchus in light blue and plum color. Here, indeed, was the story of all dynasties, Chinese or alien—a graphic revelation of decline. In each family line the face of the first emperor invariably was strong and crudely forceful. He was the one who had fought and scratched his way to power. The second, his son or heir, was most likely a strong man, educated, and determined to consolidate his father's gains. The third was apt to be refined and rather elegant, but still a leader of men. The fourth was refined, elegant, and with the delicate contours of weakness; and those who followed became increasingly weak until the last of each line seemed scarcely more than a dressed-up idiot nervously waiting for the roughneck who would oust him from the throne to found a new dynasty. One exception to this trend toward decadence was Emperor Ch'ien Lung (1736-1796) of the Manchus. His strong face combined the virtues, wisdom, strength, and refinement of the greatest rulers. This portrait lesson in history remained on display until after the Japanese occupation of 1937. And now? Who stares down from those solemn walls? Marx, Lenin, and Mao Tse-tung, perhaps? Others of the Communist hierarchy? Have they, too, started a new dynasty? Will they also topple as have all those who preceded them? Or, has the age of ruling dynasties passed forever into the limbo of dimming history—to be succeeded by a permanent dynasty of the people?

The spacious Dragon Pavement of three-tiered, white marble terraces extends to the rear of the Hall of Supreme Harmony to form a continuous substructure for the second and third great buildings of the group known as the Three Great Throne Halls. In his *History of China*, compiled from Jesuit accounts of the early eighteenth century, J.B. du Halde gave a brief description of its monumental character:

> The terrasses upon which these apartments are built contribute very much to give them that Air of Grandeur which strikes the eye; these terrasses are about fifteen foot high, cas'd with white marble adorned with Ballisters of pretty good workmanship, and opened only at the steps placed at each side, and in the middle and corners of the front. These terrasses, before the windows of the Apartments, make a broad plat-form, paved with marble which in their length from east to west always project seven or eight feet beyond the building.

THE HALL OF THE HAPPY MEAN

The second in the procession of three halls, the Hall of the Happy Mean was the smallest. Square in form, it was surrounded on all four sides by an open porch whose rounded pillars supported the wide eaves and pitched roof whose apex terminated in a golden, almost pearl-shaped orb. This structure was undoubtedly the architectural model for the superb Golden Pavilion of Jehol—the "most perfectly designed building"—which stood in a deep courtyard, half hidden by the towering walls of the vast Lamaist temple known as the Potala because it was patterned after the famous Potala temple-palace of Lhasa in Tibet. (The Chinese government building at the Chicago World's Fair of 1933 was a replica of the Golden Pavilion.)

Though originally consecrated to the peaceful pursuit of husbandry, the Hall of the Happy Mean was the scene of more than one violent event. When a rebel band, in an abortive attempt to overthrow the Manchu dynasty, broke into the Forbidden City, it was at this hall that the future Emperor Tao Kuang (1821-1851) confronted the intruders, and, before driving them off, left an arrow imbedded in the elaborate ceiling.

For many years it remained as a memento to the courage of that sovereign. Again, in 1898, the reform-minded Emperor Kuang Hsu was arrested at the doors of the Hall of the Happy Mean by command of his aunt, the Empress Dowager Tz'u Hsi, and dragged off to ten years of imprisonment in the Sea Palaces. An iron tablet bolted to one wall recalls the strong-willed Lady Bochito, the regent Prince Jui and their efforts to end the eunuch menace during the reign of her son Shun Chih, the first Manchu emperor. The tablet states that eunuchs would not be permitted to interfere in state affairs. But unfortunately, it was a marker with no lasting effect, since the latter half of the dynasty's rule was riddled with eunuch power and corruption.

Dedicated to the rites of agriculture, the Hall of the Happy Mean occasionally served as an antechamber for the far larger Hall of Supreme Harmony. From the days of the legendary Emperor Shen Nung, who first taught the people to till the soil, the ruler of China had been regarded as the First Farmer of the Empire. And, indeed, the plow was one of the symbols of his office.

At the beginning of the spring equinox many of the larger cities throughout the land staged gaily colored processions. They were led by governors or magistrates, who escorted a beribboned effigy of the spring ox to the city gates to welcome the burgeoning season. In Peking the spring rites were observed with all the dignified solemnity the court could devise. Preparations for this important event began soon after the New Year. Beasts were carefully chosen for the sacrifices, and venerable farmers, noted for their husbandry, were honored with a command from the emperor to assist him in his duties toward the gods of agriculture. Like any good farmer, the emperor cast an appraising eye on the instruments to be used in the ceremony: a plow, colored yellow as a symbol of the earth; a gilded grain basket for the seed; a yellow-handled whip for guiding the oxen; and the heavily spiked, wooden harrow—all assembled in the Hall of the Happy Mean.

For three days prior to the sacrifices the emperor prepared himself by fasting, abstinence, and meditation; and on the third evening he formally announced the observance to the ancestors. Before dawn of the great day, the imperial cortege left the Forbidden City through the Meridian Gate. Proceeding along the Imperial Way, it went through the Dynastic Gate, the great Front Gate, and finally reached the Altar of Agriculture in the Chinese City. After offering the sacrifice at the altar and asking for the blessing of Shen Nung, the sovereign moved to a nearby plot of land and sowed the five grains: wheat, large and small millet, rice, and beans—the commodities on which the empire depended for its life. He was assisted by three princes, nine presidents of various boards, and officials desig-nated to carry the boxes containing the seeds. After plowing several furrows, the emperor turned the implement over to the princes, officials, and farmers—in order of rank. The whole performance took place in complete silence.

While the Emperor Yung Cheng (1723-1736) was observing the usual three-year mourning period for the death of his father, he was forbidden by custom from performing any imperial rites, including those of the spring planting. According to du Halde's *History of China*, he therefore offered formal apologies to the ancestors for his inability to fulfill his obligations in person and promised "to conform himself every year thereafter to this ancient and laudable custom, having already published a few months since, an Instruction signed with a Red Pencil, that is to say with his own hand, to exhort the people to addict themselves to Husbandry without ceasing. At the end of the ceremony, the Imperial Prince who represented the Emperor presented the eighty-four farmers present, half of whom were old men, with four pieces of dyed cotton, which was given to each for Garments."

Du Halde adds:

> The Governor of Peking goes to visit this field which is cultivated with great care. He overlooks the furrows, and examines carefully if there are no extraordinary ears, such as they take to be good omens. For instance, he is greatly pleased if he finds on this occasion a stalk that bears thirteen ears.
>
> In the autumn, the same Governor goes to get in the Corn, and puts it in yellow sacks which is the Imperial Color, and these sacks are kept safe in a Magazine built for that purpose called the Imperial Magazine. This Corn is kept for the most solemn ceremonies. When the Emperor sacrifices to Heaven or Earth, he offers it as the Fruit of his Hand, and on certain days of the year, he presents it to his Ancestors as if they were still living.

Imperial interest in agriculture was sincere and genuine. When any provincial official was received in audience, the emperor always made careful inquiry regarding the crops in his district. Good farmers were occasionally singled out and rewarded with high ranks and privileges. Good weather was a matter of national concern. When badly needed rain came at last, a horde of grateful people—even city dwellers—called on their governor to compliment him. It was as if he had been instrumental in producing the deluge; and he accepted their homage without embarrassment. A season of good precipitation was a token of Heaven's blessing, of the abounding virtue of the sovereign, and, to a lesser degree, the virtue of the emperor's representative, the governor.

THE HALL OF ASSURED HARMONY

The last of the three great throne halls, the Hall of Assured Harmony, was dedicated to the temporal and military aspect of the ruler. It was there that he honored and feasted the scholars of his empire; and there that foreign envoys and tributary vassals were received.

To be a successful scholar in imperial days was to be a true aristocrat of Chinese society. Even a disappointed candidate in the examinations became a "fringe" member of the elect. Every family yearned for a son who by his learning could bring honor and enduring glory to its line. The tribute paid to the favored few by the emperor was of the utmost practical value, too. The administration of the government depended in large measure on the ability and honesty of its officials. Poets referred to them as the "willing horses" of His Majesty. All scholarly learning was of a distinctly utopian nature. Technical knowledge— artisans and craftsmen —denoted a mercenary spirit not really desirable in a devoted servant of the monarch. Statecraft was pre-eminent. That called for a broad base in the humanities, observation and judgment, and a thorough knowledge of the highly moral classics along with the ability to interpret them.

But to become a scholar was no easy matter. The examinations were difficult and required training, practice, nerves, and stamina. During the first century of the Manchu dynasty, all of the northern clansmen were exempt from the literary examinations, which was probably just as well since most could not have passed them anyway. All Chinese candidates for government office, however, were obliged to pass—as had been the custom since the early part of the fifteenth century. The highest of these tests were held every three years in the old Examination Halls, hard by the east wall of Peking. Other examinations of lesser importance—which had to be passed before qualifying for the triannual tests in Peking—were held once a year in the provincial capitals.

To pass highest in the Peking examinations was to become immortal. For over seven centuries, at the Temple of Confucius in the northeast section of the Tatar City, hundreds of stone tablets had accumulated, all inscribed with the names and addresses of successful candidates in the triannual examinations. No aspirant ever began to prepare for his intellectual future without visualizing his name in bold characters on one of these tablets; nor did he fail to see himself mounting the tortoise on the terrace of the Hall of Supreme Harmony, the recognized epitome of a student's success. Such achievement might bring wealth as well as immortality.

Occupying a walled site of about twenty-five acres, the Examination Halls included space for both examiners and candidates. It contained 8,500 cubicles, each measuring five feet by five, in which aspirants were confined for the duration of their exhausting ordeal. An average of about 6,000 candidates, those who had successfully passed the provincial tests, applied each time the examinations were held in Peking. To ensure against cheating, all applicants were required to change their own clothing for special garments provided by the board. After they entered their individual cells, they were handed the necessary materials. Then the doors were sealed like tombs and, for three days and nights, could not be opened for any reason. Under the terrific strain some candidates went insane; others died of exhaustion or committed suicide. In such cases, holes had to be cut in the door panels to remove the insane or dead. All China believed that spirits hovered over the worried competitors, either to assist them to success or to make sure they failed.

Having nothing to do with practical administration or even with any specialized knowledge, the tests took the form of an essay composed in a severely disciplined style on a text or philosophical idea selected from the Confucian canons. The calligraphy had to reach near-perfection. The examinations, idealistic and typically Chinese, nevertheless constituted the first national civil service tests in the world. All men, regardless of class or station, were eligible. Familiarity with the assignment indicated a cultivated moral rectitude, for an understanding of morality was set forth in the "good books." The facility of individual style showed poise, self-control, self-discipline, and ingenuity. The beauty of the calligraphy revealed the candidate's taste and refinement. Unrealistic as the system was, it produced hundreds of loyal, capable administrators.

In contrast to the dignified, dull receptions for scholars and officials in the Hall of Assured Harmony, those for envoys and vassals were planned to impress tributary princes with the power and riches of their overlord. The Household Department made all preparations well in advance, ordering huge quantities of tea, wine, meat, and other necessary victuals from the storerooms, the buttery, and the Pasturage Department, which managed the flocks and herds for palace use. Officials of the Wardrobe Department made ready a suitable robe and complementing jewelry for His Majesty. Meanwhile, the hall itself was hung with bright banners and adorned with great treasures of bronze, cloisonné, and porcelain on the long tables about the throne.

At the appointed time the guests were led into side courts and marshaled according to rank. The court musicians struck up one of their dirgelike hymns. As the doleful music ended, the gathering knew the emperor was about to seat himself on the throne. They dropped to the paving in a deep prostration. Rising, they were then conducted up to the terrace and into the hall. They made another obeisance in unison and finally took their places at small, low tables arranged about the room. Next, the tea bearer, an official of high rank, ceremoniously poured a cup of tea, silently ascended to the dais of the throne by the east stairway, and offered it to His Majesty. Retiring with a deep bow, the tea bearer knelt on the east side to wait for the Supreme Lord to touch his cup. The official then again ascended to the dais, removed the cup, and descended to the west. This was the signal for the imperial bodyguard, who had charge of such ceremonies, to serve the guests. For this occasion, etiquette required that all guests of the emperor perform the k'o-t'ou before and after drinking tea.

Music again filled the air, wine was offered, and the same ritual of bows repeated. Then the food officials carried in a variety of bountiful, steaming dishes, which, however, were not served until the musicians had completed another solemn dirge. The emperor, on hearing the last note, gave a signal, and at last the guests were free to attack the banquet with gusto.

The Mongols were in no way inhibited or stultified by the refinements of Chinese manners. They ripped through vast quantities of their favorite mutton like a plague of hungry locusts. Often, not satisfied with what they could actually consume during the feast, they thrust all types of victuals from the tables into the wide sleeves of their long, brocaded gowns—not so much from greed, but from a wholehearted appreciation of the honor that had been done them.

Having waited through the tiresome preliminary ceremonials that bored them to the point of yawning, these semibarbarians plunged with vigor into the spirit that characterized their own feasts on the forbidding steppes from which they came. The emperor not only permitted his guests to indulge in the raucous type of brawl they loved, but even relaxed his customary rigid formality to join in the merriment. Thus the banquets became noisy with peals of loud laughter, wild shouts, frequently refilled plates, and overflowing wine cups. As they drank more and more, they became increasingly uproarious. Each new draft of wine washed away any vestige of Confucian solemnity—for which the Mongols had little respect. Like an indulgent father, the Son of Heaven looked down with twinkling eyes on their uncouth behavior, much as he might at the pranks of a rough and obstreperous group of children.

When a food official removed the emperor's dishes from the table before the throne, the guests arose. Those who still could do so, made three prostrations to express their gratitude. Some fell flat on their faces in trying—but at least they tried. The sovereign retired on a last burst of ceremonial music, and the chamberlains led the guests from the hall and across the courtyards to the outer gates of the palace. Still noisy, still laughing, and staggering drunkenly as they departed, many could well have thought that if fate overtook them on this day, they would not be eligible for the Hell of Hungry Ghosts.

At the winter solstice of 1795, a Dutch embassy, which included the diarist van Braam, was feasted in the Hall of Assured Harmony with a gathering of the usual crude vassals. He counted over fifty courses of more than four dishes each and was considerably annoyed by the familiarity of the palace servants. They crowded around his delegation, pushed rudely in front of high officials, and gaped in wonder at the colorless foreigners. Giggling and snickering, they pointed their fingers at the European "big noses" and watery blue eyes. Van Braam found nothing to his liking at the heavy repast and saw enough mutton, he wrote, "to disgust a man with mutton for the rest of his life."

The Dutch were the last foreigners who yielded to the court's insistence on the *k'o-t'ou*. Later, when the British Lord George McCartney stiffly refused to "grovel" at the feet of a foreign sovereign, the Emperor Ch'ien Lung excused him from the traditional obeisance. But Chinese officials saved his imperial face: throughout the land they spread the rumor that when the Englishman first beheld the true majesty of the emperor, he was so overwhelmed with awe and so blinded by the brilliance of the throne that his legs gave way beneath him. They said: "The English ambassador grovelled abjectly on the ground" and "to all extents and purposes performed an involuntary *k'o-t'ou.*"

For many years the Chinese form of obeisance remained a burning and bitter topic between the Manchu Minister of Foreign Affairs and the representatives of other governments. Eventually, the court completely waived its insistence. They justified their changed attitude by announcing that the clumsy and awkward foreigners would only spoil a beautiful ceremony if they tried to perform it.

The annoyance of the "foreign devils" at the high-flown demands of the court paled into insignificance beside their irritation at the condition of Chinese roads. They had to travel them, of course, and almost no improvements had been made on them during the slow passage of the centuries. A very old Chinese proverb somewhat ruefully states: "A road is good for ten years, and bad for ten thousand." Still, from the earliest times, a fairly comprehensive system of roads had been constructed throughout the empire—initially for the swift passage of imperial couriers, and during the Mongol dynasty, their records of speed far exceeded those of the American Pony Express some six centuries later.

The standard road in China, if it could be so dignified, was a pathway of stone blocks. Each block was between three and four feet long, about eighteen inches wide, and as much as a foot thick. These were laid crosswise over a rather casually prepared roadbed. In the rugged mountain regions the routes were often incredibly steep and difficult. Small rivers and streams were spanned by arched bridges, some with marble balustrades of great beauty and grace. Larger watery barriers could be crossed by ferries. These narrow roads were adequate for mounted messengers, mule or pony caravans, single human carriers, small sedan chairs, wheelbarrows, and carts, but not heavy freight. This was transported by cargo junks slowly sailing on the great rivers and gliding in and out of the extensive network of canals. Except for the couriers, the pace of normal traffic was snail-like. This mattered little. Time and an inexhaustible labor force were the two most plentiful assets of imperial China. No wonder that Western diplomats were displeased.

Far more often than not, the roads were neglected and allowed to fall into disrepair. The stone blocks were dislodged by rains and floods, and even occasionally carted off for local building needs. Sections of the old paths remain, and some are still in use by villagers. One of the best known is the so-called Marco Polo Road. It connected Kunming in Yunnan province to Burma, its original construction having reputedly been supervised by Marco Polo when he was a Minister of State to Kublai Khan. Rebuilt under the direction of the U.S. Army during World War II, the more than four hundred miles of the Stilwell Road in south China generally followed the ancient route from Kunming to the gorge of the Salween River and on toward Wanting, where it connected with a newly constructed American highway from Assam in northeast India. The new thoroughfare was built for two-way, heavy truck transportation and designed to support the Chinese war effort.

In July, 1937, the memory of Marco Polo was revived throughout the world when the Japanese army attacked China in the vicinity of the Marco Polo Bridge, west of the town of Feng Tai near Peking. Originally completed in 1194, the bridge was rebuilt in 1698 by the Emperor K'ang Hsi and named the Reed Ditch Bridge. It was an arched roadway spanning the Hun River and consisting of twenty-four supporting arches, carved marble balustrades, and two hundred and eighty columns, each surmounted by a marble lion. Since the Italian adventurer was the first foreigner to describe the bridge in writing to the Western world, it was unofficially given his name.

PART 5
The Great Within

THE GATE OF CLOUDLESS HEAVEN

On a low, white marble terrace, its great doorways flanked by guard-rooms, the Gate of Cloudless Heaven, leading to the Inner Courts, as-sured the privacy of the imperial family and barred the outer world. Opening on a formal courtyard, an extension of the Dragon Pavement connected it with the Hall of Assured Harmony. Within its usually closed gates stood a group of three large palaces—and an intricate maze of small buildings—where the emperor could shed his semidivine role and live with his immediate family in luxurious comfort, attended by hordes of household chamberlains, guards, and servants. These were the Inner Courts, the living core of the Great Within. The private life of the emperor in this untroubled paradise was exactly that—private. This very remoteness appealed to the people and gave them a feeling of security. It was at this gate that the personal bodyguard of His Majesty took over from the outer guards of the palace.

Until the days of the Republic, when the ambitious Yuan Shih-k'ai nationalized the Three Great Throne Halls of the Outer Courts and restricted the boy-emperor P'u Yi to lesser buildings, the Inner and Outer Courts were directly connected. The importance of the great forecourt between them lay in its lateral communication with the eastern and western sections of the Forbidden City. In imperial days it was a quiet, hushed place. All comings and goings from one quarter to another within the palaces were strictly regulated. Only high officials and their secretaries crossed the stone pavement with any frequency. As they hurried to their offices in the long, low buildings to the east and west of the gate, they were soft of foot and silent. To pass through the Gate of Cloudless Heaven was a special privilege and a formal affair.

The gate's most beautiful features were the screenlike panels of rose-red walls—richly ornamented with green and yellow tile plaques deco-rated in a peony motif—and the rooflets topped with processions of fantastic tile beasts. A handsome pair of gilt bronze lions guarded the center approach and its "spirit stairway." Gilt cisterns stood in the court-yard at each side of the low terrace.

During the summer season the young Shun Chih—the first of the Manchu emperors—observed an ancient Chinese custom and held formal audiences on the shaded porch of the Gate of Cloudless Heaven. Sitting stiffly in his elaborate brocades on the high, golden throne and looking no more than a bewildered "child of heaven," his pontifical utterances were prompted by his uncle, Prince Jui.

During Shun Chih's fatal illness, according to du Halde's *History of China,*

> Mandarins of all orders assembled in the great court, passing both Nights and Days on their Knees, in order to give a Token of their Grief, and to entreat Heaven to restore his Health, not regarding either the Inclemencies of the Air, or the Rigours of the Season; for if the Emperor suffers, the whole Empire suffers in his Person, his loss being the only Misfortune which his Subjects dread.

The announcement of Shun Chih's death by smallpox was made outside the Gate of Cloudless Heaven in a document handed to kneeling officials of the Board of Rites, who accepted it with a triple *k'o-t'ou*. The senior official then carried the edict to the Gate of Heavenly Peace, where he read it from the tower to an assemblage in the courtyard below. A long, sobbing wail greeted the announcement, and the nine-fold *k'o-t'ou* was performed by those present. But instead of advancing with each obeisance, as was the custom, all moved backward.

The people of the empire received the news through the venerable *Peking Gazette,* the daily court chronicle and the official vehicle for all imperial decrees and memorials. Dating from the tenth century, it was the oldest newspaper in the world. It was printed on yellow paper until after the establishment of the Republic; then the color was changed to white. The *Gazette* went out of business about 1913.

Many refused to believe the emperor was dead. Recalling his vigorous youth and strength, they whispered that his body was not in the enormous lacquered coffin. They spoke of his wracking grief over the loss of his lovely concubine, the Lady Tung—and to follow her so quickly in death? Some pointed out how heavy the burden of statecraft had been.

Then, too, there was his deep devotion to Buddhism. The city was rife with rumors! But among all the conjectures one tale stood out: Shun Chih had told one of the regents appointed for his own small son that he hoped to kneel in a Buddhist robe and watch the child's enthronement procession. For three hundred years afterward, the story persisted that Shun Chih did *not* die as officially announced, but many years later, as the abbot of a monastery of the Western Hills. This belief was confirmed by the unusual respect the succeeding emperor, K'ang Hsi, paid to the abbot of the Temple of the Mountain of Heaven's Supremacy. The abbot had never been known to *k'o-t'ou* to his emperor! Therefore, he could only have been his father! After the abbot died, his body was mummified, clothed in Dragon Robes, and placed on the main altar of the temple. For nearly three centuries the lacquered head has worn an imperial headdress and remained slightly atilt—and this, too, had meaning! For instead of the *k'o-t'ou*, hadn't the abbot simply nodded politely, his head just tilted, to the visiting Emperor K'ang Hsi, indicating respect for his distinguished reign and recognition of his sovereignty—all the deference that the father of an emperor owed his son.

THE PALACE OF CLOUDLESS HEAVEN

Under the Ming Dynasty

A wide, raised causeway led from the Gate of Cloudless Heaven to a white marble terrace on which stood a group of three halls. Two were originally built as the state apartments of the emperor and the empress; the third and smallest, as a depository for imperial valuables. During the Ming dynasty the main hall, which was then the residence of the sovereign, was known as the Palace of Surpassing Brightness. Rebuilt by the Manchus, it was renamed the Palace of Cloudless Heaven. Though smaller than the Great Throne Halls, these three structures followed the same architectural pattern and decoration.

However, the purposes for which they were used imbued them with a personal quality that has lingered in the shadows for over five centuries. So alive with great events—as well as with greed, treachery, tragedy, and death—were these palaces that long before the dream that led to their construction the Emperor T'ai Tsung of the T'ang dynasty left an epitaph that well befitted their eventual eclipse: "By using a mirror of brass, you may see to adjust your hat. By using the mirror of antiquity . . . you may catch reflections of the rise and fall of dynasties."

The small, square building between the two larger palaces was called the Hall of the Blending of Great Creative Forces. There, guarded by a golden dragon on the richly carved and painted ceiling, were kept the marriage contracts of the empresses, all engraved on golden tablets and protected by golden seals. Also entrusted to the safety of this locked hall were the twenty-five imperial seals, in silk-covered, glass cases, standing on small tables arranged about a low throne.

The most ancient of the seals had belonged to the Emperor Ch'in Shih Huang Ti. That tyrant, in addition to completing the Great Wall, contributed a darker page to the history of China. In 213 B.C., convinced that books and writings were seditious and a danger to the moral fiber of his people, he ordered them all burned. Courageous scholars risked torture and death to save the wisdom of the past. Centuries later, to guard against any possible recurrence of the Burning of the Books, the complete text of the nine classics was engraved on three hundred flat stone monuments in the Hall of Classics, which adjoins the Temple of Confucius in the northeast section of the Tatar City.

From the earliest times in China, a seal carried far greater authority than a written signature. For this reason its safe custody was of extreme importance. Even a forged decree stamped with the imperial seal was a valid document, and a decree written by the emperor's own hand had no real authority unless it carried the impression of the dynastic device. No businessman, landowner, military or government official was ever without his personal chop, or seal. No orders and no agreements could be "signed," simply because there is no such thing as a signature when Chinese characters are used. The entrusting of family seals to another was a mark of the greatest confidence, since according to custom and ancient laws, the possessor could deed or sell any property belonging to the seal's owner.

With the incongruity so often found in the Orient, an enormous grandfather clock of European make stood beside the throne in the Hall of the Blending of Great Creative Forces, as did a huge water clock, constructed to simulate a garden pavilion and dating from the eighteenth century. (Numerous elaborate clocks were placed throughout the palaces, usually prized gifts from Western ambassadors presented in the names of their sovereigns.) In the courtyard outside were a pair of unusual Ming dynasty shrines: miniature bronze halls on vaulted marble bases. One was dedicated to the spirits of land and grain; the other to the spirits of rivers and mountains. These two miniatures were symbolic reminders of the emperor's obligation to offer sacrifices at the Altar of Earth and Grain just outside the south wall of the Forbidden City. Balancing the site of the Supreme Temple of Ancestors to the east, this important sacrificial altar was in a walled park west of the Imperial Way, between the Gate of Heavenly Peace and the Meridian Gate. Once the scene of solemn ceremonies, it was thrown open to the public after the revolution and renamed Central Park. (After the Washington Disarmament Conference of 1922, the Chinese government, in gratitude for American insistence that the Japanese army withdraw from Shantung province, which it had occupied since 1915, erected a monument to President Warren Harding near the old altar.)

Throughout the period of the Ming sovereigns, the Palace of Cloudless Heaven went up in flames frequently. After each disaster it was built anew. Fire gods were implored to protect it, and the hall was plastered with posters in their honor—all of which accomplished very little in a practical way.

In the reign of Cheng Te (1505-1521) it was destroyed during the Feast of Lanterns, which terminated the New Year holidays. For this festival the causeway, the courtyard, the terraces, and the hall itself were converted into a fairyland of colored lights at an expenditure of tons of silver from the treasury. Countless flickering candles and tiny lamps glittered like fireflies on a specially built seven-storied pagoda. Lanterns of lacquer and egg shell glowed on gaily beribboned tripods. Others of painted gauze and translucent horn hung from the eaves of halls and gates. Still others of transparent silk, painted with scenes from Chinese history or with characters for "happiness" and "longevity," and decorated with long red tassels, sparkled from high stands near the throne. And finally, to be sure the wide courtyard was engulfed in radiance, thousands of varicolored lanterns quivered like great sequins from all the connecting verandas and pavilions.

Many of the lanterns were made from the large, hollow horns of water buffaloes, the common beast of burden in the south. To prepare the rough horns, the surface was scraped, cleaned, and rubbed smooth; the base trimmed; and the tip cut off. Then, after being boiled in water for days, the softened horn was pressed and blown from the inside until it assumed a large, circular or oval shape. When allowed to dry and harden, it had a milky, translucent quality and was ready for the outer surface to be painted with characters or intricate designs.

As the emperor happily watched the festival from his golden throne and the court ladies strolled about in brilliant, brocaded gowns—each carrying a bobbing lantern at the end of a light bamboo pole—a sudden gust of wind swept in from the Gobi desert. A candle splattered hot wax. A flimsy, silken lantern flamed. Countless others flared up; and flying sparks reached the decorated rafters of the hall. Within seconds the Feast of Lanterns was a holocaust! In the panic and confusion the emperor gathered his elegant robes up to his knees and unceremoniously fled. Guests and their ladies scattered in wild, screaming terror. Encumbered by long, embroidered gowns, dozens of eunuchs rushed to the hand pumps. These implements, brightly hung with honorary red silk streamers, were able to throw only a paltry stream of water scarcely higher than a man's head—and even *their* decorations caught on fire! Other eunuchs, aware that the building was doomed, were frantic in their attempts to salvage treasures and, as usual, appropriated most for themselves. But there was a code even among this group. To give each other an equal chance to loot, all the eunuchs took turns at the futile pumps. Even the guards deserted their posts to pillage. The city firemen of Peking could not be called because they lacked sufficient rank to extinguish an imperial fire; and so, the beautiful hall was left to the mercy of its rapacious guardians and the pitiless flames.

As the blackened timbers and fallen tiles of the Palace of Cloudless Heaven slowly cooled in the night air, the chief eunuch reported the total loss of the building to the Emperor Cheng Te. He took it in regal stride, not batting an eyelash, and directed that "the hall be built again more beautiful than before. Fill it with treasures more valuable and more beautiful than those that have been lost."

The Ming emperors, with few exceptions, were worthless and extravagant rulers, and the dynasty's drift into incompetence and decadence was hastened by the presence and ambitions of the eunuchs, who, reign by reign, became more powerful in both palace and state councils. Cheng Te (1505-1521) was a typical libertine. At first energetic and interested in his responsibilities, his talents were soon misdirected by the "eight ti-gers," as his chief attendants—all eunuchs—were called throughout the city. His long-vanished pleasure palaces, known as the Leopard Rooms, were the scene of countless vicious orgies. He eventually died a horrible, nameless death in the midst of his cruelly erotic setting.

Wan Li, the Porcelain Emperor (1572-1619), like the Sung Emperor Hui Tsung, is still revered by collectors of Chinese art. He was, perhaps, the most celebrated of the later sybarites of his line. His potteries produced enormous quantities of fabulously beautiful porcelains—lanterns, flutes, scepters, pillows, footstools, images of Buddha, figures, vases, and fish bowls, as well as plates, cups, and bowls of every description and pattern. The "Wan Li five colors," as they came to be called, with their exquisite glow, elegant shapes, and fine designs, intrigued him far more than the welfare of his empire. He was constantly rebuked for the expenditure of astronomical sums of money. Nevertheless, he continued to indulge his superbly artistic taste in the lavish production of porcelains.

His grandson, T'ien Chi, a boy of fifteen at the time of his accession in 1620, was gifted but completely unresponsive to his high destiny. He spent most of his time at carpentry, casually assigning affairs of state to his chief eunuch Wei Chung-hsien, and his old wet nurse, Madame K'o. When he ascended the Dragon Throne, omens pointed to many misfor-tunes; and each of the seven years of his reign brought more than the one before. During an earthquake, when the Palace of Cloudless Heaven shook, trembled, and was almost destroyed, T'ien Chi could not be dragged from his work bench, where he was sawing and hammering away as the walls cracked and swayed around him. The quake was no misfortune to him—the necessary repairs gave him an opportunity to remodel one of the side pavilions into a small theater for the performance of the war plays he enjoyed and a chance to install an underground heating system in two other pavilions. This latter innovation was a bless-ing, for the halls and palaces were bleak and bitterly cold in Peking's winter.

T'ien Chi's design for these Warm Rooms was based on the k'ang of north China, which for centuries had been in common use in most homes, but not palaces. Usually considered the forerunner of central and radiant heating, a k'ang was a large, hollow, brick platform that projected into a room or filled the space of an alcove. The underportion had an opening in the outer brick wall of the building, into which servants or slaves stoked wood, coal, or long-burning camel dung. Similar to an oven, the fire heated the bricks of the inside platform and provided the family a warm place by day and, padded with mats and quilts, a snug bed for cold winter nights.

T'ien Chi's notorious eunuch and wet nurse recklessly squandered the wealth of the dynasty, and with it, the prestige. External affairs fell into a shocking state of disarray: Manchu armies raided as far south as the walls of Peking, and Korean pirates and Japanese ships harried the long-suffering coastal towns at will. Whether or not Madame K'o loved her foster son remains a mystery. She wept bitterly over his coffin and, as a penance, burned countless relics of his childhood that she had saved for years: locks of baby hair, the first tooth, broken toys, and many other mementos. Despite her ostentatious grief, Madame K'o was sentenced to die by the savage slicing process; and all the members of her family, including sleeping infants, were beheaded in a public square. The eunuch, however, cheated his enemies by committing suicide. But not to be done out of their vengeance, officials of the next emperor beheaded and brutally mutilated his body and exposed it in the market place. This was the epitome of revenge. A disfigured corpse meant a crippled or broken body in the next incarnation—a spirit condemned to wander for all time in the lower regions, one who could never be considered an ancestor by any of its own descendants. A permanent disgrace to all later generations, a mutilated body was the worst of all punishments. In order to have a whole body at the time of death, most eunuchs carried with them in small jars or phials their dried, shrunken testicles. Then, if a sudden end should overtake them, the devils of the spirit world might be deceived, and they could appear as men before their ancestors in the Great Beyond.

The eunuch and the wet nurse died; and the people of Peking rejoiced, especially the beautiful and appealing little empress, T'ien Chi's widow, who later became a Christian. She rejoiced because for the first time in ten years she could take an easy breath—throughout her husband's reign she had been in constant danger of her life from both the eunuch and Madame K'o.

Ch'ung Cheng, the brother of the Carpenter Emperor, succeeded to the throne. Being of the same generation, he flew in the face of all tradition and left the spirit of his predecessor unworshiped. The new sovereign was a worthy, painstaking individual, but a poor judge of men.

During the seventeen years of his reign, forty-seven prime ministers, none of whom were either loyal or competent, held office. Sensing that the empire was about to collapse, he turned in desperation to the eunuch corps for assistance. To show their appreciation, they did not hesitate to betray him at the time of his greatest need.

By the year 1641 the position of the Ming dynasty had become increasingly critical, though it could have been saved by forceful leadership. Ten years earlier a rebellion had broken out in Shensi province and, spreading to the neighboring areas, eventually found a leader in an illiterate peasant Li Tzu-ch'eng. Li's reputation for brutality soon became as frightening as his burly, savage appearance. The loss of an eye at the siege of K'aifeng had puckered one side of his face, and a scar, running down his other cheek, underscored his fierce ruthlessness.

Early in the summer of 1644 Li and his rabble army marched on Peking and stormed the city. The Palace of Cloudless Heaven became the stage for the tragic last act of the Ming dynasty. The scene was anything but a "cloudless heaven." Against a backdrop of flames, smoke, and falling timbers, of screams, howls of pain, of blood, and death, looting and rape, and the agonized trumpeting of the elephants abandoned in the imperial stables, Li pulled down and smashed into pieces the three-hundred-year-old palace-city of the Ming emperors. Galloping about on his black stallion, with one of his most notorious generals—a vicious dwarf—at his side, the city fell beneath his sword.

The following account, from the imperial archives, describes the last of the Ming dynasty:

> The Emperor's courtiers advised His Majesty to leave for the south, but the Emperor was indignant, and refused to desert his capital. He issued an edict forbidding his officials to leave Peking, or to send their families away, for he feared that if the governing classes departed, it would cause a panic in the city. Curiously, at this time, wailing was heard from the tomb of the first Emperor of the dynasty at Nanking. This was considered a bad omen. Also, at that time, in the territory to the west of Peking, the imperial troops had been constantly defeated by the rebels who, while at Ch'ang Ping Ho, had desecrated the Ming Tombs.
>
> The Emperor then sent for General Wu San-kuei, who was at that time holding off the invaders [the Manchus] at Shan-

haikuan. Though Wu pretended to rush to the relief of the
capital, in reality he made no attempt at haste. Now, the
garrison consisted of only fifty or sixty thousand troops, badly
fed, badly paid and in poor spirits. Many went over to the
well-fed rebels. The protection of the city gates was confided
not to soldiers, but to the eunuch palace guards, and several
thousand eunuchs were distributed among the troops of the
garrison. The population was greatly disturbed by flying rumors that the Emperor had already left.

Finally, one morning, a mounted soldier galloped into the
palace and announced that outside the city there was a great
cloud of dust. The rebels were approaching. Shortly after,
rebel troops armed with bows and arrows galloped up to the
P'ing Tze Men [one of the gates of Peking] and demanded
the opening of the entrance, but they were shot down. Such
as succeeded in getting into the town used guns captured
from the imperial troops still outside the city itself. Meanwhile, many imperial defenders refused to mount the walls
and shoot down the rebels, so hopeless did they judge their
own cause. The rebels shouted up to those on the walls,
"Open the gates or expect no mercy!" Receiving no reply,
they brought ladders and started to storm the Chang I Men,
Hsi Chih Men and P'ing Tze Men [three of the gates of the
capital]. They poured in first through the Chang I Men into
the Chinese City and started looting and setting fires.

When the Emperor heard this, he summoned his ministers
and asked, "Do you know that the Outer City is in the hands
of the rebels?"

They answered, "We do not know."

When he inquired if they had any plan to suggest, they
replied "Your Majesty, do not be anxious. We will fight them
even in the streets. Never will we betray our country."

Those nights the Emperor could not sleep. Then there
came a day when a eunuch reported that the rebels had pene-
trated the Inner City.

"Where are my loyal troops?" the Emperor asked.

"They have fled, and Your Majesty must also flee!" Then
the eunuch ran away.

Then, the Emperor with his faithful servitor, Wan Cheng,
went to Coal Hill and into the south pavilion, and from there
looked over the fires burning in the city. He returned to the

Palace of Surpassing Brightness and wrote a "Scarlet Edict" [one written in cinnabar ink and used only for the most important decrees], ordering Duke Chu Kun-cheng to command the troops and protect the Heir Apparent. Having done this, he called for wine, and when he had drunk several cups, sighed heavily.

"My poor people!" he said.

He then summoned his family and concubines, and his three sons, whom he ordered to flee. Turning to the Empress, he said, "Now the great event is over!"

The whole family cried bitterly, and also the eunuchs who were standing by. To them the Emperor said, "Look to yourselves!" When they had gone, the Empress said to her husband, "For eighteen years I have faithfully served Your Majesty, and never have you listened to my words. Now you see the results!"

Weeping, she then embraced her sons and bade them go. When they were gone, she committed suicide, hanging herself by her girdle.

The Emperor sent for his daughter, who was fifteen years old. When she appeared, he said, "Why have you been born of my unlucky house?"

With his left arm and sleeve he covered his eyes, and with his right hand he took a sword and slashed at his daughter, meaning to kill her rather than let her fall into the hands of the rebels. Alas! He only succeeded in cutting off her right hand! Seeing her fall to the ground in a pool of her own blood, his hand trembled so that he could not deliver a second blow. He then ordered his favorite concubine, the Lady Yuan, to commit suicide. This she did by hanging herself, but unfortunately, she recovered consciousness, so the Emperor killed her with his sword. He also killed with his own hand several other of his favorite concubines.

Once more he summoned his favorite eunuch and drank wine with him. Afterward, His Majesty changed his shoes, took a spear, and in the company of a score of eunuchs, went to the East Flowery Gate of the Forbidden City. The eunuchs on guard there, thinking that disorder had broken out within the palace, shot at the little company with arrows and stones from their crossbows. Nevertheless, the Emperor succeeded in passing through the gate and reaching the house of Duke

Chu Kun-cheng, whom he had put in command of the defenses. Duke Chu was absent at the time, examining the defenses of Ch'i Hua Men, so the Emperor made his way to An Ting Men, which was free from attack at the moment. The latter of the two gates was so strongly barricaded that it could not be opened sufficiently to let him pass, although some hours before, his three sons had escaped by it.

Dawn was now breaking. The Emperor returned to the palace. He ordered a bell to be rung to summon his ministers, at least those who had not already fled. But not one responded. He then went up Coal Hill to the Pavilion of Imperial Longevity, where he and his faithful eunuch committed suicide by hanging themselves.

The Emperor was hatless, with unknotted, flowing hair, and he wore a long blue gown. His left foot was bare; on his right foot was a red shoe; and on the front of his gown he had written a few lines on the silk: "Seventeen years have elapsed since I ascended the throne, and now rebels infest my capital. Because my virtues are insignificant and my personality wretched, I have incurred the wrath of Heaven. But nevertheless, I was deceived by my ministers. Still, after my days on earth, I am ashamed to go to meet my Ancestors in the shadowy world. Take off my diadem, hide my face in my hair, and let the rebels cut my body to pieces if they will, but let them touch not one of my people. Let all my ministers rally around the Heir Apparent."

From this last line it was evident that he hoped his Scarlet Edict was already known to his ministers and would be acted upon by them. However, by the time the eunuch delivered the edict, the ministers had already gone and no one took any notice of it.

Thus passed a dynasty begun in great hopes and great courage and ended in rebellion and death.

Once in Peking, Li's rabble seized the mistress of General Wu San-kuei. The general then was in command of the all-important fortress of Shanhaikuan, the eastern pivot of the Great Wall. In a rage at losing his famous "round-faced beauty" to a ravaging horde of soldiers, Wu San-kuei turned against his own country and made a deal with the Manchu armies then storming his position. He agreed that he and his key troops would open the gates of the Great Wall, surrender the fortress, and collaborate with the invaders. In fact, this traitorous act was a gross error in judgment made through the colossal conceit and greed for personal gain that so often characterized dealings of high policy in imperial China. The Manchus were a young, military people, hardy barbarians of the northern wilderness who only twenty years earlier had been a feuding group of jealous clans. In 1625 a chieftan named Nurhachu had made himself their acknowledged leader and had organized a central government at Mukden, modeled on that of the Chinese. Wu San-kuei presumably regarded them as mere savages who would be content to return to their own lands as soon as they were paid off with rich plunder. If this were so, the general would be in an ideal position to bring about a Ming restoration or grab the throne for himself. Later he was revolted by the first rule of the game as laid down by his new allies from the wildly bleak north, but helpless to resist. as a visible evidence of his allegiance, the Manchus forced him to undo the high knot with which the Chinese then dressed their hair, shave his forehead, and wear a humiliating queue. From that time on, the queue became the symbol of the alien domination over all Chinese men, just as bound feet became the sign of the subjugation of all Chinese women.

But not knowing what was in store for him, Wu San-kuei threw caution to the winds and joined his new masters in a battle near Shanhaikuan against Li Tzu-ch'eng and his army of nearly two hundred thousand men. Though the vast rebel horde far outnumbered the forces of Wu and the Manchus, a violent dust storm tore in from the Gobi desert. It blinded Li's undisciplined troops and obscured their opponents in dense clouds of gritty sand. When the winds calmed, Li saw to his horror and amazement that he had lost the battle. One last hope remained: China might rally to a dedicated and *enthroned* emperor. So thinking, he fled with all speed to Peking, where he made feverish preparations to assume the imperial title in the throne halls of the Great Within. On the twenty-eighth day of the fourth moon of 1644, exactly two days after his defeat, the rebel Li proclaimed himself Son of Heaven in the Hall of Martial Grace. Then he solemnly conferred upon his ancestors for several preceding generations the posthumous title of "sovereign." The proceedings were carried out in such haste that the golden seal of authority was not ready, nor had the coinage bearing his reign title been struck. Nevertheless, he had his brief hour of triumph, lording it about with all the pomp and assurance of an absolute monarch: he wore the Dragon Robe of majesty; his consort, the Lady Kao, was proclaimed empress; and his court, such as it was, made obeisance to him.

No sooner had the accession been announced than Li prepared to leave Peking. With frantic speed he proceeded to loot the city as well as the palace. Thousands of gold vessels were melted down into flat bars, each weighing about a thousand ounces, and these, with other cumbersome treasures, were loaded on transport mules. The next day the main gates and many halls of the Forbidden City were put to the torch. As the flames roared and black smoke darkened the sky, Li headed down the long road to the south, to death and oblivion, his vast accumulation of loot scattered among deserting troops or lost forever along the way.

During the Reign of K'ang Hsi

After the defeat and flight of the rebel leader Li and of his rabble army, the Manchu clans found they had suddenly achieved the impossible— they had overthrown the dynasty of the Ming emperors and had fallen heir to China's mighty empire. Their success had been ensured by the traitorous general Wu San-kuei, who had opened the gates of the Great Wall. They cared not a whit that he secretly complained he had "brought in lions to drive out rebel dogs." They were lions, the Manchus, ravenous ones, and vastly proud of it. And riding the waves of victory, they pushed southward to pursue the prey of dwindling resistance to their power.

Within a year the blackened ruins of the Palace of Surpassing Brightness were rebuilt and renamed the Palace of Cloudless Heaven. Erected on the original marble terrace, the reconstructed building glowed with new lacquer and shining golden tiles. And the charred ashes that were the heritage of the brief period of blood and terror, which ended the former dynasty, were soon forgotten.

In 1653, during Shun Chih's reign, the building was destroyed by fire and once again rebuilt. Although two Russian trade missions were considered beneath the dignity of a formal reception in the new palace, a Dutch embassy was received there in 1656. It was about this time that one of the czar's missions departed from China with a letter to the absolute monarch, expressing the emperor of China's satisfaction with his *vassal.* Fortunately, years passed before the document was ever translated. The Russians, blissfully unaware of the insult to the Romanoffs, continued to send missions to the Manchu court.

It was in the Palace of Cloudless Heaven that the first Manchu emperor died, and there that his eight-year-old son, K'ang Hsi, performed the ancestral rites before his father's coffin. The child offered food and wine three times daily, pouring the funerary libations from a golden cup onto the earth. With his head shaved in mourning, and his little figure clothed in coarse white sackcloth, he invited the spirit of his parent to partake of the vapors rising from the lavish feasts on the table before the lacquered casket. His grandmother, now the empress grand dowager, and his mother, the new empress dowager, supported by white-garbed imperial ladies, set the hall trembling with reverberations as they keened loudly from early morning until far into the night. The terrace and the courtyard outside echoed the dowagers' wails as all ranks of courtiers knelt in rows, prostrating themselves and airing their grief to Heaven.

Months later the encased remains were carried to a hall behind Coal Hill to await an auspicious day for burial. After a magnificent imperial tomb was readied in the spacious park, the funeral cortege slowly wound its way through the empty streets of the city. The weeping child-emperor, walking humbly beneath a white cloth canopy, wailed dolefully every step of the way in the most approved filial manner. The people, shut inside their houses, were much impressed with the conduct of this small son. Alien though he might be, the child—now the Emperor K'ang Hsi—was obviously entitled to their respect.

At all funerals in China—even as late as the middle of the twentieth century—dutiful sons in coarse white cloth, leaning on the arms of friends and relatives, lurched and staggered behind the processional coffin of their departed parent, loudly publicizing their grief. Actually, months might have passed between the time of death and the auspicious day named by the astrologers for the funeral, so the edge of any sorrow had probably long since been blunted. Since cemeteries were usually located outside the city walls, far from family homes, the bereaved, the hired mourners, and scores of marchers needed occasional rest as they trudged and wept through the streets. On signal, the long cortege would halt near a teahouse along the route. The eldest son—who had barely been able to stand without aid in his overwhelming show of grief—would suddenly step briskly to one of the outdoor tables and chat gaily with his friends as he sipped from his cup. A loud clacker would announce the resumption of the sad march, and the son, calling pitifully for support, would, again, with bowed head, stagger to his place in line. Trading reality for illusion with characteristic Oriental dexterity, he would then stumble forward to the solemn clamor of deep-toned horns, exploding firecrackers, wooden noisemakers, the scattering of silvery "spirit money," and the loud wails of keening women, who were paid in accordance with the uproar they created.

No matter what the family's religious beliefs might be—and most were little more than a combination of superstition and a rather sophisticated cynicism—the rich took no risks in sending the spirits of the dead to appear before their ancestors. Thus, Buddhist, Taoist, Confucian priests, and even Christian ministers, were invited to accompany the mourners to the grave.

K'ang Hsi was born in 1653 to the constant racket of saws and hammers in the palace. This was, in a way, almost prophetic, for he spent most of his life rebuilding the great structures, adhering closely to the original plans of the founder, Emperor Yung Lo. The exotic, almost feminine beauty of the Ming court was, however, edged with a firm dignity and substance, both Manchu characteristics. Dominion of the northern clans over the empire was still uncertain. Instead of lavishing treasure in wild extravagance on the palace-city, the new dynasty sent regular shipments of gold and silver ingots and works of art to their former capital of Mukden in Manchuria. Apparently this was a form of insurance against a possible reversal of their good fortune.

K'ang Hsi, an eight-year-old boy when he succeeded to the Dragon Throne in 1661, was physically robust and mentally sharp. His personality was magnetic, forceful, and commanded respect, yet tempered by patience, kindness, and understanding—even as a child. When his father lay dying, he had told the four newly appointed regents: "I have a son of eight years, and though he is not the eldest, his rare intelligence makes me hope he will govern well. Let him therefore be my successor. . . .I recommend him with confidence."

Under the guidance of his grandmother, the empress grand dowager, the promising lad matured into a brilliant, highly educated man. Even after the regency ended in 1667 and the young emperor assumed the government—with its time-consuming routine of daily audiences and decisions—he still continued his studies with Ferdinand Verbiest, his tutor in the Western sciences. Yet he managed to find time to enjoy sports with his princely brothers: riding, hunting, and particularly archery, in which he developed an astonishing skill.

Like his father Shun Chih, K'ang Hsi was thoroughly instructed in both the Chinese classics and his native Manchu literature. After he had mastered the first six books of Euclid, which Father Ricci had translated into Chinese for the Ming court, he set about translating them into Manchu for the instruction of his own sons. Verbiest introduced him to European music and, with some success, interested him in Christianity. Years later the Manchu sovereign astonished a Russian ambassador by comparing a great flood in China to Noah's deluge and quoting the appropriate biblical text. He seldom forgot even the most trivial bits and pieces of information. Twenty years after he had heard the uncommon Flemish name of a bird native to Belgium, he still remembered it though Verbiest,—who had long been absent from his homelend—had quite forgotten it. Under this close association of monarch and tutor—not unlike Yung Lo's intimacy with the mystic monk—Verbiest was permitted many freedoms. The old priest's "holy boldness," as K'ang Hsi phrased it, often proved a problem and an irritant. At the most improbable and inconvenient times there he was, under foot and all over the place, babbling his head off.

The Emperor K'ang Hsi always accepted responsibility for the errors of others and was generous in honoring those who loyally carried out his commands. He did not spend his days secluded in the Forbidden City, as most of the Ming rulers had done, but traveled about the land seeing for himself that his laws were enforced and that public funds were properly expended. His armies were never neglected. On frequent excursions beyond the Great Wall, he not only saw to it that his troops were appropriately equipped and trained, and that the camels and horses of army baggage trains were well cared for, but he also impressed his might and dignity on his numerous Mongol vassals. The weather, the crops, and the condition of prisoners received his close personal attention, too. And always, he tactfully made use of the Catholic missionaries at his court in assorted ways: they prepared maps, engravings, and detailed designs for artillery; or acted as official interpreters, mathematicians, and astronomers. Nor did he neglect the arts. One example of his patronage was the development of a brilliant color still memorialized by the name "K'ang Hsi green." All of his thoughts and actions were characterized by a sympathetic concern for the people and their lives—his children, as he called them.

As he grew older, he was considered an accomplished scholar in the polished and conceited literary circles. This was no mean feat, for the men of his race found the sword more to their liking than the pen. (Two hundred and fifty years later many members of princely Manchu houses derived a certain pride from the fact that they could scarcely read or write Chinese!)

K'ang Hsi's portraits show a face of strong character with large, brilliant eyes, described as having "double pupils"—a Chinese expression indicating their piercing, luminous quality—and strangely long, heavily lobed ears. A word portrait written by Father Ripa in his memoirs, states: "There is nothing in his appearance that is not worthy of the throne he occupies. His air is majestic, his figure excellently proportioned and above middle height, all the features of the countenance are regular . . .and the few marks left by the smallpox detract nothing from the charm which is conspicuous throughout his person."

In 1669, two years after the Emperor K'ang Hsi had reached his majority and assumed the government, the archives state that the Palace of Cloudless Heaven was again rebuilt. Though not specified, it had probably been severely damaged in the earthquake of 1666 (which had been the means of saving the life of Father Adam Schall). Less than ten years later Peking was again visited by severe earth tremors. One was so violent that it drove the entire court from the palace halls to live in tents pitched in the courtyards. Under the first of these shocks the youthful emperor took to his heels in terror and found shelter in the underground pit of the heating system installed by the Carpenter Emperor nearly fifty years earlier. Many of the halls were badly damaged, but the Palace of Cloudless Heaven survived. Though it has been extensively repaired many times since, it stands today as it did nearly three hundred years ago.

The Warm Rooms and most of the other buildings forming the sides of the courtyard before the palace of Cloudless Heaven were intimately associated with the daily life of the Manchu emperors. One was a schoolroom for imperial children. An adjoining small room contained a tablet dedicated to Confucius, before which pupils and teachers offered incense on the first and fifteenth of each month. Used by K'ang Hsi as a study, the Hall of Industrious Energy later became one of the offices for members of the intellectual Han Lin Academy who performed secretarial duties at court. Though the great halls of state could not be rearranged to suit imperial whims, small pavilions could be altered at will, and were usually adapted to the individual tastes and requirements of each ruler.

In 1673, when K'ang Hsi was but twenty years old, the strength of the young emperor was put to a test. The traitorous Chinese general Wu San-kuei, who had been given the title of "prince of the West" and the fief of the rich southern province of Yunnan, raised the standard of rebellion. He and three powerful Chinese princes (governors of the provinces of Kwangtung, Fukien, and Kwangsi) combined forces against their Supreme Lord in Peking. The uprising lasted five bloody years and eventually involved eleven of the eighteen provinces. But at the climactic moment Wu San-kuei died. The princes quarreled among themselves over the leadership, and the revolt fell apart. During this desperate struggle, the military prowess and political sagacity of the young emperor were fully rewarded, and the Manchu dynasty was saved for nearly two hundred and fifty years more of rule.

But the trials of K'ang Hsi were far from over. The notorious Koxinga and his son Cheng Ching had established a pirate kingdom of land and sea that extended from the mouth of the Yangtze river to Formosa and many miles southward. Their fleets swept the seas of all ships. They anchored off shore, poured on to land, and ravaged the coastal towns with merciless regularity—burning, raping, pillaging, and slaying all with vicious brutality. To increase their power and to enlist the semblance of a following, they supported first one princely Ming pretender to the throne and then another, deserting them when the alliances proved unprofitable. In time K'ang Hsi, with the assistance of the Chinese viceroy of Fukien (the Manchus were notoriously poor sailors), destroyed or scattered the pirate armada. Koxinga and his son died, or were killed; their heir was captured and sent to Peking.

Completely ignorant of the larger events on the mainland and the western areas of the China Sea, a small Spanish and Filipino force from Manila had set out to "conquer" Formosa and had actually won control of the principal ports and a considerable part of the island. Thus, Koxinga's pirate bases were denied to the remnants of his defeated fleet when they attempted to return to their old strongholds. The Spanish commander, fired by the success of his few hundred troops against a virtually undefended people, grew wildly ambitious. He submitted a plan through the governor-general of the Philippines and the viceroy of Mexico to the king of Spain for the conquest of the entire empire of China. But his grandiose project was either ignored or buried under layers of bureaucratic indifference. K'ang Hsi, relieved of the pirate threat to his coasts, generously agreed to receive Koxinga's heir at court and, being in an expansive mood, ennobled him with the title of "duke." But, playing it safe, he confined the new duke to the capital as a hostage for good behavior.

Peace did not endure long. In no time K'ang Hsi was leading an army into the vast heartland of continental Asia against Galdan of the Eleuths, who boasted descent from Genghis Khan. The expedition consisted of a hundred and fifty thousand men. They were organized in four groups, one of which the sovereign personally commanded. Before this force departed, the emperor reviewed its divisions in a great ceremony and, from a golden cup, drank wine to its success. In order of rank, each of his chief commanders accepted the imperial offer of wine and, by drinking it, pledged their lives and loyalty before rejoining their men on the road into the far northwest.

Complicated by the politics of Tibetan and Mongolian lamas, by the questionable suzerainty of Tibet itself, and by the unfortunate fact that certain of the imperial generals were neither courageous nor astute, his campaign was not wholly successful. A brother of K'ang Hsi survived a defeat of his army and, flouting tradition, did not commit suicide. This cowardice utterly shocked the pride of the other warring princes and shook their morale to its depths. But the Manchu-Chinese armies, partially armed with muskets, had sufficient- artillery—thanks to the ingenuity of Father Verbiest—to assure final victory. After several campaigns and intervals of ominous peace, Galdan died alone and forsaken by all his friends.

Inevitably, Manchu control extended deeper and deeper into the continent. At the end of K'ang Hsi's reign his dominion reached the town of Hami, northeast of the towering and legendary T'ien Shan. The perpetually snow-clad "spine of Asia," the T'ien Shan ("Mountains of Heaven") was a region of dark mysteries and awesome fears. Centuries before, the strange cult of the Nestorian Christians had held sway there, and terror of their extraordinary powers had not vanished from men's minds or from the land they occupied. The warlike Sungarians, who inhabited this high plateau, decided to keep the peace with their powerful Manchu neighbor. But not until they learned of the defeat of the Eleuths. Even then, they were never truly subdued.

During K'ang Hsi's reign of sixty years, the Palace of Cloudless

Heaven, its courtyard, and its marble terraces were the scene of many imposing festivities. Most appealing of all were those held in honor of the old men of the empire on the sovereign's sixtieth birthday, and again on the sixtieth jubilee of his reign.

These Feasts of Elders were considered pre-eminently appropriate. In China old age, unembarrassed as it was with the bias and misdirected enthusiasms of youth, merited the respect and honor of all men. The calm, wrinkled faces of the elderly were the accepted seals of an experience and a wisdom that made their judgment valuable. The mere fact of their longevity was regarded as an auspicious circumstance that guarded imperial China in all matters for many centuries.

When a man celebrated his sixtieth birthday, he graduated from the "college of life" and could be accounted an elder. From that day on, his opinion was worthy of deference. He had a right to the respect of others. He was entitled to a certain amount of leisure. He could use a staff and was expected to grow a beard. By the time he reached seventy, he could retire from active life entirely and spend his time enriching the younger generations with his accumulated wisdom and sage observations.

The sixtieth birthday of the Emperor K'ang Hsi was in April, 1713. Early in that month high provincial officials began to arrive in the capital, each offering presents in accordance with his wealth and station. Since gifts were mandatory, the Catholic Fathers who were attached to the court in an official capacity were not exempt. Their first offering, according to Father Ripa, consisted of: "European wine, Brazilian tobacco . . . one pound of gum storax, a piece of the finest linen, two painted quilts from Coromandel, several white pocket handkerchiefs of the finest description trimmed with lace, four embroidered purses, various kinds of scissors, knives and small padlocks, three pounds of tartar, a mathematical instrument, two pots of balsam, six bottles of confectionery, twelve jars of preserved quinces, eight stones of gaspar antonic, saffron, bark [quinine], oils and medicinal roots."

But the gifts added up to an odd number, and in China odd numbers were associated with the dead. And furthermore, no matter how valuable or how difficult to obtain, medicines did not signify auspicious wishes. His Majesty's Household Department was greatly disturbed at this near-sacrilege. It ordered the priests to take back their presents, remove the medicines, and reduce the total number to an even figure. This nonsense so annoyed the stiff-necked Father Ripa, as he recorded in his memoirs,

that he refused to have anything more to do with such "childishness."
He washed his hands of the whole matter and told his better-humored
colleagues to meet the court requirements. When the revised list was
finally offered, the elderly Jesuit rather unwillingly admitted that the
emperor was not only highly gratified, but had also sent presents to him
in return. Unfortunately, one imperial gift was a box of European paints
that had just been given to the sovereign by another courtier. This made
Father Ripa bristle. A single line in his journal states that he had little
sympathy with such a court and that K'ang Hsi never had been known
for generosity—a criticism that was not entirely justified. In 1693, when
the Jesuits Gerbillon and Bouvet cured K'ang Hsi of malaria with a
revolutionary new medicine—quinine—the emperor, in gratitude, presented their order with a sizeable tract of ground in Peking. The Old
Cathedral and other buildings were constructed on the site, and were in
almost continuous use until exchanged for land farther to the north, on
which the North Cathedral was built in 1888.

In preparation for the Feast of Elders, Peking blossomed with banners
and flowery arches, but not sufficiently so to meet with the emperor's
approval. Aware of his reluctance toward lavish expenditures, his officials
had hesitated to commit themselves to any expense for which they might
be held personally responsible. But when told that their Supreme Lord
was prepared to throw economy to the winds on this occasion, they
entered into the spirit of the celebration. Not only did they redecorate
the entire city, but the streets were cleaned and repaired as well. The
latter activities were a major undertaking. The public ways had long
shamed even the tolerant gods of the roads, who dwelled very humbly
in small, shabby shrines at each intersection. During the spring season
most of the alleys and thoroughfares of Peking were all muck and slime,
deeply rutted and traversed by ditches filled with filth and garbage, in
which starving beggars and black pigs competed for scraps. Barely wide
enough for the passage of one man, greasy "sidewalks" edging the walls
under the eaves of shops were somehow kept open most of the time.
Nonetheless, the officials achieved a miracle of beauty, cleanliness, and
repair!

Father Ripa, writing of the Feast of Elders, remarked in his memoirs:
". . . the populace was habited in gala dresses, banquets were given
without end, fireworks discharged and every kind of rejoicing carried on
as at the New Year." But the most impressive sight to his jaded eyes was

the road from the Summer Palace. It was screened by mats and "entirely covered with silks of the most beautiful workmanship, while at certain distances were erected fanciful houses, temples, altars, triumphal arches and theaters in which musical dramas were represented. So great was the abundance of silk used that we Europeans all agreed. . . . that no Kingdom in Europe possessed so much."

Emperor K'ang Hsi, having withdrawn for a rest at his favorite retreat outside the capital, returned on April 11—the appointed day for the Feast of Elders. Wearing his magnificent robes of state and riding the finest horse his stables could provide, he made an impressive progress through the city to the Great Within. To mark this special occasion, the people were allowed to gaze upon their sovereign. They poured out of their houses and shops, packed themselves solid in the streets, and kneeling on the yellow sand, watched the passage of the glittering cavalcade with silent awe and pounding hearts. As the emperor finally approached the towering grandeur of the gates to his palace-city, the elderly guests—already gathered there in excited anticipation—braced themselves to greet him.

Father Ripa wrote the following description of this scene in his memoirs:

> A vast number of aged but healthy men. . . . had come from all the provinces. They were in companies, bearing the banners of their respective regions. They also carried various other symbols and trophies, and being symmetrically drawn up along the streets. . . . presented a very beautiful and uncommon appearance. Every one of these old men brought a present of some kind for the Emperor. . . . vases or other articles in bronze. His Majesty gave to each of them twelve silver taels [about sixteen ounces], together with a gown of silk. . . . This venerable company amounted to four thousand in number. . . . His Majesty was highly gratified by the spectacle; he inquired the age of many, and treated them all with the greatest affability and condescension. He even invited them all to a banquet and made them sit in his presence.

In the Palace of Cloudless Heaven the emperor's own sons and grandsons personally served the old men with wine. Afterward, the sovereign "presented every one of them with something; to the one who was most aged in the whole assembly (being nearly one hundred and eleven years old) he gave a Mandarin's suit complete, together with a staff, an ink stand and other things."

Eight years later, on the sixtieth jubilee of K'ang Hsi's reign, the feast and reception was repeated. According to the chronicles, it greatly surpassed the first in magnificence. In 1785 the Emperor Ch'ien Lung followed his grandfather's example by celebrating the fiftieth jubilee of his reign and his own seventy-fifth birth year. On this occasion the most venerable were given special attention: those having passed the age of ninety were privileged to use a staff within the palace grounds, and each was presented a jade scepter by the Supreme Lord.

Genuine respect for the elderly continued into the twentieth century. After the Japanese surrender at the end of World War II, when the United States was attempting to unify Nationalist and Communist factions by means of American officer teams, China's traditional respect for the wisdom of old men entered the difficult Sino-American political picture. During the preceding conflict, vigor, courage, and determination had been the most desired attributes in both American officer and enlisted ranks. Younger men naturally predominated throughout the U.S. forces stationed in that area. But diplomacy and a sincere desire to honor the ancient tradition of an Oriental ally resulted in a request from the Marshall Mission, headed by General George C. Marshall, to the War Department in Washington, D. C., for the assignment of fifty senior officers with gray or white hair. It was hoped their appearance of age might win the confidence of both political rivals in China. How well this particular effort succeeded is a matter of record: a unified China, to be sure, but unified under Mao Tse-tung, not Chiang Kai-shek.

During his long reign K'ang Hsi made five state progresses to the provinces drained by the Yellow River. He was particularly interested in the network of waterways that formed the Grand Canal, the vital communication system for the immense traffic between the rich southern provinces and the governing north. In 1689 he journeyed as far south as Hangchow on the beautiful West Lake of Chekiang province. On this occasion he accepted few offerings and, as always, paid the cost of his progress from state revenues rather than making special requisitions from the districts he honored with his presence. As an additional mark of munificence, he remitted the land tax from all areas he visited. In the imperial rescript issued to commemorate the event, he stated: "Our wish is that wealth should accumulate among the people so that they can have all they need." Economy in everything but his personal life was his pride and delight, and his edicts abounded with references to his public thriftiness. Though never lavish with presents, he neither expected nor accepted expensive gifts or offerings from others.

Nor did he neglect to make pilgrimages to the sacred places of the empire. When he visited T'ai Shan, the holy mountain of Shantung province, he humbly paid homage to the tomb of Confucius, whose teachings had finally won the wholehearted respect of the conservative alien dynasty. Though the tendency during the preceding few centuries had been to deify the Great Sage, the Manchus merely ennobled him as the wisest of men—a distinction that may have been prompted by the influence of Christianity at the court. K'ang Hsi was sincerely impressed with the Western doctrine of One God and His Son on earth. It paralleled the cult of a Supreme Heaven and his own personal role as the Son of Heaven.

At the time, and for generations after, it was common talk in the teahouses of Peking that the Jesuit Fathers had almost converted the empress grand dowager to Catholicism. Had they succeeded, it is not inconceivable that the emperor, out of a sense of filial piety for his grandmother, might also have become a Christian. A number of the court nobility already had, and he had not objected. But at this crucial point, the growing jealousy and machinations of the Dominican and Franciscan orders toward their rivals in Peking so influenced the Vatican that it drastically curtailed their authority. At a later date the Jesuits were recalled entirely. Fruitless as speculation can be, what might have happened if politics in Rome had not interfered with the activities of the Jesuits? With the emperor converted, Christianity might have become the most important of the official religions of China during his reign—with, of course, certain adaptations to old and time-accepted beliefs. If this had happened, Chinese thinking, philosophy, and technology might well have been aligned with the West; and the power politics of subsequent history in the Far East could have followed a far different course.

Unhappiness tinged much of K'ang Hsi's life. His mother died when he was but ten years old. One of his empresses, to whom he was deeply attached, died giving birth to a son whom he named heir apparent, but was later forced to depose. Most of his eighteen surviving sons were greedy, overly ambitious, and unruly. On several occasions their unspeakable behavior caused their dignified father to burst into apoplectic rages. Once, he, the semidivine Son of Heaven, shocked his Jesuits by ordering twelve of his sons—including the then heir apparent—to be degraded. Their headdresses were removed, they were stripped to their skins before the assembled court, and were publicly beaten.

K'ang Hsi was sixty-nine years old when he died in 1723. He had been hunting outside Peking, in the park not far from the Summer Palace, near the hill where many years before he had watched Father Verbiest bless his cannon and christen each one with the name of a Catholic saint. After a vigorous day in the saddle, he suddenly pulled up his Mongol pony and complained that he felt faint. He was first carried to a nearby pavilion, and then to the Summer Palace, where he died. Shortly before the end he named his fourth son—known to history as Yung Cheng—as his successor. His body was then moved to the Palace of Cloudless Heaven, where it lay in an enormous lacquered coffin until the auspicious day for its burial. Mourned as one of the greatest rulers in the history of the empire, his spirit still towers above nearly all others. (Perhaps that great spirit slips silently from the ancestors in the Yellow Springs and, hovering over the Great Within, still gazes down upon the darkened courts and pavilions. In a land dedicated to spirits—for good or evil—it would be strange if he did not.)

During the Twilight of the Manchu Dynasty

The spirit of youth and hope, of strength and adventure, swelled with the noisy crescendo of giant waves over and around the palaces of the early Manchus. With scarcely a pause in its impetus after K'ang Hsi's death, the bursting ebullience and vigor of the imperial family continued throughout the reign of his son Yung Cheng. Finally, it spent itself in a dazzling tidal wave of magnificence under Ch'ien Lung—the Grand Monarch of the Eastern world, as Louis XIV of France was the Sun King in the West. But, a decade or more before this last great emperor abdicated, the surge for perfection in the arts and the creative inner spirit of grace and beauty gradually succumbed to mere technical facility. The tide had turned, and slowly ebbing over the exposed sands of history, it proved the prophetic sagacity of the ancient proverb: "As the water recedes, the rocks and pebbles begin to show themselves."

The succeeding occupants of the Palace of Cloudless Heaven, seated in duplicated splendor on the golden Dragon Throne, must have been uncomfortably aware of the jagged rocks and slippery pebbles beneath their feet. Behind them the great carved and gilded folding screen still protected the chair of state from the evil influences of the north. But the winds had veered, and chill breezes seemed to be rushing from all directions—even into the hallowed throne hall. Those who knelt respectfully in audience before the Son of Heaven, surrounded by all the elegant panoply and treasured illusions of majestic greatness, had tremulous hearts. They realized that the sovereign, for all his show of splendor in Dragon Robes and cap of state, was at best a complete synthetic. The tall mirrors on either side of the throne room reflected the perplexed and anxious faces of the Grand Council as they listened over and over to tidings of increasing ills, of misfortunes and defeats, of the white foreigners who had brazenly crossed the western horizon and were thrusting their mighty power onto China's shores. Aware of growing tension and weakness in the empire, officials traded respect for authority, and tradition gave way to avarice and sly cupidity. The palace eunuchs fed like leeches on the vast treasures that passed through their greedy hands—there being no effective control to stop them.

By 1861 the life of the empire, which usually centered about the Palace of Cloudless Heaven, had gravitated to the lesser courts and residences where the two surviving consorts of the Emperor Hsien Feng (1851-1862) —the Empress Dowagers Tz'u An and Tz'u Hsi—shared the authority of the regency. T'ung Chih, the six-year-old Son of Heaven, was left wholly in the care of eunuchs, who indulged his every whim and raised him to become an obnoxious little tyrant. His own mother, Tz'u Hsi, ignored him except for occasional sharp and unreasonable corrections. Tz'u An, childless, lonely, narrow, and pious, spoiled and petted the boy. With no stern grandmother to supervise him, the eunuchs debauched the little emperor. Had his upbringing been wiser, T'ung Chih might have grown up to become a worthy occupant of the throne. He had inherited his mother's physical strength and steady nerves, but not her mind nor iron will.

When he reached the age of seventeen and was finally married, the two empress dowagers at last complied with custom and reluctantly relinquished the supreme authority into his inept hands. Though his mother still expected to be obeyed, as was her traditional right, T'ung Chih and his young wife Aleute were indiscreet and openly flouted her will. Such unfilial conduct did not go unpunished in imperial China. After reigning but six short months, the nation was advised that the emperor had "blossomed." In less poetic language, he had contracted smallpox.

Three weeks later, to no one's astonishment, he was gathered to his ancestors. Since Aleute, his empress, was childless, though pregnant, he had not been able to appoint an heir. However, he had issued a decree —or more than likely it had been issued in his name—that beseeched the two empress dowagers to resume the regency and, in grateful recognition of their tender care during his last hours on earth, bestowed upon them honorific titles exalting their motherly virtues. In white mourning, Tz'u Hsi offered the proper funeral honors at the deathbed of her little-loved and less-regretted son. After the customary lamentations, she tied the strings of his splendid shroud and placed pearl-studded shoes on his feet. The young Empress Aleute, watching her mother-in-law perform these rites, wept and wailed, heartbroken and terrified with the knowledge that she had now fallen completely into the power of her husband's cruel and ruthless mother. Tz'u An wept tears of genuine sorrow, for she really loved the boy in her odd way. And other members of the imperial family managed a sob or two as they all crowded together in the dimly lit, airless room.

The emperor's eyes had hardly been closed before every high official, with the strong gambling instinct of most Manchus and Chinese, was wagering huge stakes on the succession. If Aleute failed to bear a son, the lawful choice of the new sovereign lay among the deceased emperor's first cousins *once removed;* but his first cousins were of his own generation and therefore ineligible to offer the ancestral sacrifices his departed spirit had every right to expect. Tz'u Hsi chose the child she wanted—her late son's first cousin—and in so doing ignored all ancestral obligations in order to suit her own plans and ambitions. The chosen one was her sister's four-year-old son by a brother of the deceased Emperor Hsien Feng. So once again, Tz'u Hsi and Tz'u An could look forward to a long regency.

Within a few months the young Empress Aleute and her unborn child joined the spirit world of the ancestors. Officially it was understood that she had committed suicide, either by starvation or by swallowing gold leaf; but it was commonly accepted that she had been "assisted on high" by the Dowager Tz'u Hsi. Had Aleute lived and given birth to a son, that son would have become emperor, and Aleute would have become the empress dowager and regent. The ruthless and conscienceless Tz'u Hsi could never have risked that!

Though a delicate, sensitive child, Kuang Hsu, who became Emperor in 1875, was, like T'ung Chih, placed largely in the hands of eunuchs. Much of his time was frittered away on the amusing toys his eunuchs found for him in the only foreign shop in Peking. When the lad clamored for more of the novel, mechanical playthings, he got them at once—including a telegraph set and, later, a telephone outfit. In time a narrow-gauge railway was laid out along the lake shores of the Sea Palaces just beyond the western walls of the Forbidden City. With mischievous delight he invited court ladies for rides on this strange and fascinating contraption and went into transports of laughter as they stared in wide-eyed fright from its windows. Next came a newfangled steam launch, chugging and puffing through the lotus blossoms of the lakes, the court ladies clinging in panic to the railings. Unintentionally the fawning eunuchs had sown the first seeds of discord between the young emperor and his imperious aunt Tz'u Hsi. They had turned the young monarch's face toward the future, toward progress, and toward the West—and all of this the dowager despised.

In 1889, the year of his marriage, the Hall of Annual Prayers (better known as the Temple of Heaven) was destroyed by fire. This disaster set the elders shaking their heads, convinced it was a bad omen for his reign. Tz'u An, the empress dowager of the east, had died with suspicious suddenness in 1881, and so the young Emperor Kuang Hsu's only remaining friend was his tutor, Weng T'ung-ho.

Weng T'ung-ho was a staunch and upright man, a brilliant official, and a classical scholar of the first order. He had passed first in the imperial examinations—and had mounted the tortoise before the Palace of Supreme Harmony—he had been president of the Board of Revenue, a grand councilor, and head of the newly established language college. Since his position as imperial tutor carried a great deal of parental authority over his student, and knowing the young emperor trusted him, Weng T'ung-ho spoke out frankly on the appalling condition of the empire. Thus, at an early age, the youthful Kuang Hsu learned of the universal abuse of public funds, of corruption and greed; he was plunged head first into the troubled waters of liberalism that were washing over the scholars of his own generation. Early in 1898, while the young sovereign still gave the appearance of ruling by his own authority, Weng brought to the palace K'ang Yu-wei, one of the leading reformers of the time. The two young men liked each other at once. There was an instant and responsive sympathy between them, and they quickly became friends—a bond that caused tragic results that neither was practical enough to envision.

With imperial formality set aside, the earnest Son of Heaven and the young liberal spent long hours closeted together in the west chamber of the Palace of Cloudless Heaven. They discussed the disarray into which the affairs of the empire had fallen. They dissected piece by piece the top-heavy bureaucracy of the government. Both shook their heads dolefully over the recent Sino-Japanese War of 1894-1895, which had been disastrous. Not only had the neglected armies of China been overwhelmingly defeated, but the navy—a large part of whose funds had been diverted to construct and embellish the magnificent Summer Palace—had been wiped out. In addition, China had been forced to cede Formosa and the Ryukyu Islands to Japan, to relinquish all rights in its tributary kingdom of Korea, and to lose all authority in Manchuria, the original home of its rulers.

As the young emperor and the young liberal plotted and planned, while the Empress Dowager Tz'u Hsi was at her fabulous Summer Palace, content with the world, enjoying the painted galleries, the marble terraces, the serene lake. If there was one thing she did not want it was *change*. Long ago she had closed her eyes to the needs of her subjects, the wild extravagances of the court, the waste and duplications in the government, the debauched dishonesty of the eunuchs—even to the pressures of the "foreign devils." She had sardonically ordered that funds allocated to build up a navy be used to construct a marble boat, which was "docked" beside a landing on the shores of the lake at the Summer Palace.

The plans for reform decided upon by the young sovereign and his liberal friend depended on secrecy and speed. The spies of the empress dowager at court kept her fully informed of every zephyr of politics and intrigue, and the two young men knew it. Supported by a cunning, relentless, and procrastinating bureaucracy, she would leave no stone unturned in order to prevent the slightest change in the existing pattern of government. This they knew too.

The Hundred Days, as the period of reforms was called, began with a flood of extraordinary edicts that poured out of the Palace of Cloudless Heaven, much to the dismay of a corrupt officialdom determined to perpetuate itself. Education was to be modernized. Many government offices were to be abolished. The wealthy were to be heavily taxed; the poor were to be exempt of all taxes. Among other innovations, all officials were to abandon their elegantly embroidered silk robes and wear simple, foreign-style clothing.

The empress dowager, in a wild tirade of fury, quickly dismissed Weng T'ung-ho, blaming all the rapid turn of events on the tutor. In alarm, the young ruler called for a hasty council with K'ang Yu-wei. The two young men decided that, in order to save their reforms, the Dowager Tz'u Hsi had to be removed from the scene as delicately as possible and placed in safe custody. Completely unfilial, this decision constituted an open revolt against the ancient social code that had bound the empire to the throne for over two thousand years.

One of the ablest of the younger officers, and the commander of a reasonably well-equipped army, General Yuan Shih-k'ai was chosen to carry out the plan. He was a blood brother of Duke Jung Lu; and the duke was not only the cousin and staunch henchman of the empress dowager, but her lover as well. Nevertheless, since General Yuan belonged to the modern school of militarists who took orders directly from the monarch, the emperor and the young liberal thought he could be counted on to obey his sovereign, rather than the orders of a patron.

On an early September morning Kuang Hsu issued orders from his golden throne to Yuan Shih-k'ai: Duke Jung Lu was to be arrested at once and executed; Tz'u Hsi was to be imprisoned. The emperor's high-pitched voice, tense with strain, was described by a contemporary as being "shrill as the hum of a mosquito." Over and over his words faltered, and the tone broke into a tremulous falsetto as his blood pressure rose. The general bowed and accepted the golden arrow, symbol of transmitted imperial authority, prostrated himself, and departed—and went straight to Duke Jung Lu in Tientsin as fast as the train could carry him. He reported the proposed seizure of Tz'u Hsi and the order for the duke's execution. Wasting no time, Jung Lu hurried by special train to Peking. That afternoon he strode without ceremony into the empress dowager's apartments in the Sea Palaces. She had just returned to Peking from the Summer Palace, and she stood, unblinking, as Jung Lu outlined the entire plot.

In blind rage and fear she ordered the Grand Council summoned immediately. Though it was late at night, the old men who represented the established order which centered about her hurried through the palace grounds and apprehensively awaited her commands. When she told of the plot, they were aghast.

Things moved rapidly after that, as they always did when Tz'u Hsi went into action. The sun had just risen when the young emperor, studying a litany he was scheduled to recite at a ritual sacrifice later in the day, was seized by Her Majesty's special attendant—the eunuch Li Lien-ying—and a group of his followers. Alone, and shocked by what had befallen, the emperor put up no resistance and was quietly escorted to the Ocean Terrace, an island in the Sea Palaces that, ironically, was a replica of the Isles of the Blessed—and there he was confined. Fortunately, before he was seized, he was able to send off a warning to K'ang Yu-wei, who managed to escape.

The empress dowager at once reassumed supreme authority. She forced the Emperor Kuang Hsu to issue an edict stating he was neither competent nor worthy to rule the empire. A second rescript of nine characters followed: "The emperor being ill, the empress dowager resumes the regency."

All orders for reforms were immediately countermanded. The emperor was permanently banished to his closely guarded island in the Sea Palaces. Many of his supporters feared for his life at the hands of the eunuchs. On orders or suggestions from Tz'u Hsi, they introduced all manner of vices and licentious living into the island prison. In his hopelessly frustrated boredom, the rightful Son of Heaven allowed himself to be led from one excess to another, drifting into a limbo. His health broke. He became a ghostly reminder of his former self. Nonetheless, he survived—a man in whom all hope had died. Only the name of the general who had betrayed him had the power to arouse him from utter indifference: *Yuan Shih-k'ai!* Later, during the flight of the court after the collapse of the Boxer movement in 1900, Kuang Hsu passed long, weary hours in various dilapidated "traveling palaces," drawing countless pictures of the despised turtle—a symbol of ignominious ancestors—and combining them with the character for *Yuan.* Often he used these drawings as targets for arrows, or with a murderous glare in his eyes, he would viciously cut them into little pieces, which he threw to the winds. His last act before his death was to draw a circle, its lines shaky from his feeble hand, betraying his desire for vengeance—for a circle is the same as the character denoting *Yuan.*

General Yuan Shih-k'ai, a ruthless opportunist, was never true to anyone or to any principle other than his own extravagant ambitions. In 1911 he again betrayed his emperor—this time P'u Yi, the boy-emperor, who had succeeded the reform-minded Kuang Hsu. It was Yuan Shih-k'ai who nationalized the Three Great Throne Halls for his own private glory. And it was he, the first president of China, who betrayed the new Republic by seeking to make himself emperor. In this effort he hopelessly miscalculated. Just as Emperor Kuang Hsu had depended on him to execute Duke Jung Lu and imprison Tz'u Hsi, General Yuan Shih-k'ai depended on Prince P'u Lun of the Manchu dynastic clan to obtain possession of the imperial seals. By this treasonous act he hoped to ascend the Dragon Throne himself. But as Kuang Hsu's plot for reforms had failed, so did Yuan Shih-k'ai's plot to make himself emperor. Having made himself ridiculous by his presumption, he never raised his head again and was said by the Chinese people to have died of shame.

For a few years longer the court, like tired puppets, danced on crazily to the powerful strings of growing Western influence. The stage began to dim, but the dance went on and the prescribed lines were spoken. The once magnificent Palace of Cloudless Heaven became a pallid hall of state. For a while, it continued as the setting for the New Year and imperial birthday ceremonies, for receptions of haughty representatives, foreign missions, and embassies. And years after the Republic had been established, the boy-emperor's wedding was held there in 1922.

But by then the life and blood and strength of the past five hundred years had drained away. A velvety cloak of darkness gradually covered the last gleaming twilight of the empire. The grandeur and beauty, the shimmering silks and flashing jewels, gave way at last to pathetic mockeries of a radiant history. (Shorn of all obeisance and display, the Palace of Cloudless Heaven was left only its calm dignity and its countless spirits. It is not difficult to imagine those ghosts slipping in and out between the lacquered pillars, yearning to revive the wonders of past glories.)

The Clan Hall and the Shaman Rites

Originally built as the state apartments of the Ming dynasty empresses and furnished accordingly, the Palace of Tranquil Earth was destroyed by fire when most of the Forbidden City was burned by Li's army in 1644. The Manchus rebuilt it in 1655. After a second fire, it was rebuilt again in 1673 as the Clan Hall dedicated to ancient Manchu family rites. Since it was the spiritual citadel of the emperor, the chief of the dynastic clan, it was in reality the inner core of the Great Within.

With relatively minor exceptions, the exterior of this hall conformed to the accepted conventions of palace architecture. But inside, it was divided into two apartments of unequal size: the imperial wedding chamber in the east section; and the much larger hall for secret clan conclaves in the west.

The ancient Manchu cult of Shamanism, a crude form of animism, still flourishes among certain tribes in northern Siberia, Alaska, and the sub-Arctic wastes. Though oddly out of place in a court observing the sophisticated tradition and the rigid formality of the Chinese—based, as they were, on the precepts of Buddhism—this black faith of their primitive forebears was retained by the Manchus who placed their altars hard by the dignified state halls of the palace-city. The Manchus reasoned that to slight their own ancestors in a land that worshiped its own would be unseemly. Also, such a tradition of worship would bind all Bannermen more closely to the throne and thus reinforce the Manchu unity of purpose in China.

The retention of ancient practices may also have been part of the mystique with which new royalty and power has so often surrounded itself. Alien and downright peculiar, which no sophisticated Chinese could ever accept, Shamanism set its devotees above and apart from the conquered peoples and created about them a separate spirit world. Yet it permitted the Manchus to follow the precepts of the long-established religions in China and, like scholars fluent in several languages, to approach Heaven and the gods from more than one path.

No outsider ever witnessed the Shaman rites. That the rites were like family skeletons hidden behind closed doors and taken out now and again to rattle their bones circulated in continual rumors. But the dignity of Confucian officialdom was never offended since no Chinese ever saw the priests or priestesses of this mysterious cult in public. Nonetheless, these wizards and witches, playing on the fears bred into the bone from a shadowy past, held their Manchu flock in thrall, the more superstitious of whom ran to them frequently for consultations. In the darkened Clan Hall, the Shaman priestesses would mount effigies of the ghost-tiger, and court ladies, listening with wide eyes to revelations obtained from oracular crows, would grow faint, tearful, or fall into fits of hysteria.

In addition to the sanctuary in the Great Within, there was only one other shrine of this kind in all Peking: the T'ang-tzu (literally a hall). Before the creation of the Legation Quarter in 1900, it stood on what later became the site of the Italian Embassy. At that time a new hall was built close to the Supreme Temple of Ancestors, where, at stated times, Heaven, Nurhachu, the founder of the Manchu imperial house, and his son T'ai Tsung were worshiped by their descendants. By custom, the emperor visited the hall at his accession and at the opening and termination of a military campaign.

From the records of the dynastic archives, the ceremonies held in the Palace of Tranquil Earth, though seldom tranquil, were almost identical to those held at the home palace of the Manchus at Mukden. In general the ritual consisted of music, dancing, offerings, prayers, and sibylline forecasts. The Shamans, frequently imperial guardsmen and their wives, were all members of the Banners.

Shaman regalia was fearsome looking. Its officiants wore the skins of wild animals, bears being preferred. Their holy hats were conical affairs of fur adorned with antelope horns. For certain ceremonies crude armor was worn, and weapons of the chase and war were carried. The most curious feature of their attire, of ancient Siberian origin, was an apron of brass tubes shaped like elongated ice cream cones that jangled loudly as they performed their sacred dances. At most ceremonies a musical instrument, similar to a tambourine and about a foot in diameter, was used —clanking with copper and iron rings and gaudy with multicolored strips of cloth. All of this barbaric paraphernalia was stored in huge cupboards built from floor to ceiling in the Palace of Tranquil Earth.

In one corner of the apartment stood a large curtained alcove, not unlike the cabinet of a spiritualistic medium, where the Shamans retired to pray and interpret the omens. At the west side of the hall a sacrificial altar was loaded down with a combination of symbols achieving a heterodox confusion of superstitions: flat-faced rag dolls dressed in silk; pictures of the primitive spirits of Heaven, the Ongots; paintings of the Chinese god of war, Kuan Yu; and depictions of the Buddhist incarnation of mercy, Kuan Yin. Near this altar a number of brocaded bags hung from the walls: "Lucky sacks" or "bags of the ancestors." They contained the "locks of happiness" that were worn in small pouches about the neck by Manchu boys and girls until they married. Each year newly cut locks of hair replaced the old ones, the old being placed in the hanging, brocaded bags in the Clan Hall.

An enormous cauldron for cooking sacrificial meats stood behind a long, altarlike table. A brick furnace for completely burning certain sacrificial offerings was built in a special alcove opposite the main doorway, and a huge cauldron, large enough to cook a whole bullock, stood on one side of the room. After the ceremonies, the cooked meat of animal sacrifices was cut up on a brick platform at the opposite end of the chamber and distributed to the participants.

When the emperor or the empress took part in the rites, a cushioned "precious seat" was prepared for them on a low platform along one wall of the hall. This was intended to recall the earlier days when a tribal chief sat cross-legged in his tent at clan councils.

A month before a sacrifice to the high spirits a fine quality of millet wine was prepared. Three days before the ceremony the animals intended to be sacrificed were carefully selected—two pigs, two sheep, or two bullocks, depending on the importance of the occasion. If the animals struggled when hot wine was poured into their ears, they were considered unfit as offerings to the gods and were sent off forthwith to the butchers in the palace kitchens. However, if they placidly accepted this test, the beasts were acknowledged suitable for the high destiny about to be visited upon them. On the day before the ceremony special cakes of yellow millet called beaten cakes were prepared by steaming a flour that had been made by pounding the grain with hammers. They were placed, along with the wine, as temporary offerings before each spirit to be worshiped. Finally, between three and four o'clock on the morning of the sacrificial day these same cakes, with wine and vegetables, were moved and placed before a tablet of the Chinese god of war on an improvised altar table hidden behind a curtain. As the emperor knelt before this drapery, the ceremony began. The master of ceremonies gave a signal. One priest cracked a long whip three times. Another priest, in the courtyard outside, struck the great drum three times, and the musicians in the hall burst into a wild cacophony of sound. A Shaman, sword flashing, leaped into a frenzied dance, shouting through his gyrations: "Offerings of cakes and wine have been respectfully made to bring blessings on the master of this house!" The participants chanted to the accompaniment of lutes and four-stringed guitars. The august Son of Heaven beat vigorously on a tambourine. A drum was tapped at a furious speed in a continuous high rolling sound—and all other instruments combined in a crescendo of savage music that filled the darkened hall like a roaring gale tearing through the trees of a primeval forest. With the incantations completed, the chief Shaman lifted his head, and with eyes closed, listened respectfully for messages from the world beyond. Behind the Shaman, on the cold tiles of the floor, the emperor prostrated himself to the spirits. His clan knelt, and a master of ceremonies commanded in a loud voice that the sacrificial animals be brought into the room. When this was done, he again poured hot wine into the ears of the placid beasts that had been chosen, and another official called out: "The gods have accepted the sacrifice!" The entire family then expressed its gratitude by performing the nine-fold *k'o-t'ou*.

A second master of ceremonies directed the cook to cut up the carcasses, reserving the best pieces for the spirits. After another invocation and more *k'o-t'ou*'s, a Shaman presented the emperor with a red silken cord for the horses in the imperial stables. After that, the sacrificial meat was divided and eaten to the last morsel, for no offerings were allowed to be taken out of the building. During the entire proceedings, even though the animals had been killed in the hall, no reference to death was permitted.

Often the ceremonies were accompanied by ritualistic dances in the forecourt. On these occasions sixteen to thirty-two Bannermen, in a phalanx of two rows, performed symbolic pantomimes that recalled the past. One of these—*mi-hu-ma-hu*—was a stylized version of the legend, showing the founder of the dynasty, still in his youth, killing child-eating tigers and bears in the forests of Manchuria. Half the performers wore black sheepskins; and half, bearskins. All wore masks of the animals they represented, and high, conical, befeathered hats. The leader, depicting Nurhachu, in an elaborate costume and helmet, pranced his horse between the rigid lines of men, discharging blunt arrows at the various "animals." The tableau ended with one of the men falling to the ground and the others running off. In another spectacle members of the Eight Banner Corps rode hobbyhorses, each rider in a different costume, a symbolic flag at the back of his neck and a number of small bells jingling on his feet and ankles. While the musicians played dirgelike martial airs, the men pranced about the courtyard, each straining to outdo the others both with motion and the racket of brass bells.

That evening a special sacrifice was made to the ancestors and to the seven goddesses who were the spirits of the Long White Mountain in Manchuria. During this service the windows of the hall were heavily curtained, creating thick darkness to symbolize the gloom of hell. Once again a sword dance, paced by the loud clamor of brass drums, accompanied further invocations.

After these ceremonies, the bones and the strips of gristly meat left over from the ritual feast were hung on a spiked wooden mast, known as the Sacred Post, which stood on the terrace of the Palace of Tranquil Earth. These scraps could be eaten only by the black crows, which swooped down from above the roofs and courts to gorge themselves.

It might be noted that this final act of the Shaman ritual could have been derived from the ancient Tibetan custom of feeding the flesh and broken bones of the dead to vultures. In the extremely high altitudes of that mountain country, the ground is frozen for more than half the year and fuel is scarce. Since either burial or cremation was virtually impossible, a practical system of disposal had to be devised. Stone platforms were constructed in the hills outside each town. The deceased were delivered there by their families and handed over to a specially trained group of priests. It was the priests' duty to cut off the flesh, break up or crush the larger bones, and toss the pieces into the air. They were snatched at once by the eager beaks of large flocks of waiting vultures. These overladen scavenger birds, flapping awkwardly skyward, were believed to carry the souls on their first journey toward heaven—not to mention providing a spiritual rationalization for a necessary but primitive form of sanitation. (A comparable custom existed in certain parts of Outer Mongolia. Centuries of experience had taught the Mongols that shallow graves in the flinty soil of the central Asian plateau were quickly scented by roving packs of wolves or wild dogs. To avoid the useless labor of digging graves, the dead were simply placed on barren hillsides not far from the felt yurts of nomadic encampments and were soon devoured by the snarling beasts. Once they had eaten their fill, off they dashed across the lonely steppes—to the Mongols this meant the souls of their dead were being transported to their heavenly rewards.)

On the morning after all the ceremonies the spirit tablets were carried to the court north of the Clan Hall, where the Shamans read more incantations to the deities and offered sliced meat mixed with rice to win their favors. This was known as a vow to heaven, and its completion meant that all the promised obligations had been fulfilled. Three days later, as cakes and varicolored silk threads were offered, a prayer asking for a blessing was recited before the tablets. Then, to indicate that the favors of the Great Beyond had been bestowed upon him, the threads were fastened on the breast of the emperor.

Among the strange shrines in that weird hall of the Palace of Tranquil Earth was that of the lovable Chinese god of the hearth. He was a homely little kitchen deity who sat quietly in the midst of his barbarous companions throughout the reigns of all Manchu emperors. Watching over the imperial family's hearth, he was expected to protect not only them but all the subjects of the empire. Before each New Year, the Son of Heaven personally feasted him and then sent him off to Heaven to render his annual report to the gods. Like the head of all households, His Majesty smeared the little god's lips with honey, so he would speak only sweet words in the hereafter. The Emperor Ch'ien Lung went even further: he poured a libation of wine for the little god, tea for his horse, and sent him on his heavenly journey with a great burst of exploding firecrackers. Five days later the kitchen god was welcomed back to his hearth in the Palace of Tranquil Earth with proper greetings. He settled down then for another year, as comfortably as he could, in the midst of his odd surroundings.

Nothing definite has ever been known by outsiders as to the worship of lesser deities in the Clan Hall: Wan Li Ma-ma, the horse; the hunting dog; and the ceremonial bath of the "jade baby." "They were the private affairs of the imperial family," according to one distinguished Sinologist —and Shamanism remained just that until the overthrow of the Manchu dynasty. For over two hundred and fifty years, on the second day of each

New Year and on the third day of each spring, the emperors honored the gods of their ancestors as had been done for ages past.

The lips of all Manchu Bannermen and their descendants—and few exist today—have remained sealed regarding the mysteries of the Shaman cult. What little has been learned has come from the tersely brief dynastic archives or has been woven by scholars into an indistinct pattern of hearsay. Information on the primitive rituals and customs has been further limited by the fact that the entire race of northern tribes has either become extinct or so mixed with Chinese blood as to be scarcely recognizable.

And just exactly how the "lucky locks" of Chinese children began is not known either, though one might conjecture they had something to do with "lucky sacks," "bags of the ancestors," or "locks of happiness," which were a part of the Shaman rites. Whenever Chinese children had their heads shaven, a "lucky lock"—tightly bound with red strips of cloth —rose in a tuft from the center of their shiny polls. In a playful mood, parents occasionally left two additional locks of black hair on each side of their young children's heads, binding them so tightly with red cloth they stuck out, straight as arrows, above the ears. The young babies of the wealthy also wore a flat gold locket, which symbolized the harnessing of the soul to the earth. And it was the habit for small boys to wear one earring in order to deceive the gods and spirits into thinking they were merely worthless girl children and therefore not of enough importance to molest.

The Imperial Wedding Chamber

Decorated in red and gold, and adorned with large characters meaning "double happiness," the wedding chamber of the Palace of Tranquil Earth was a cheerful contrast to the Clan Hall. Though seldom used, it held an important role in the drama of the state apartments. The first obligation of all emperors to their ancestors was to contract marriage and produce as many sons as possible. This meant the Son of Heaven must remain polygamous to ensure the presence of living male descendants to carry on the family rites and worship.

The emperor was not considered master of his household and the empire until he had taken an empress. Before that, he was dependent on his mother or his regent. The long delay in the marriage of T'ung Chih was a deliberate scheme of Tz'u Hsi to continue her own power and authority as long as possible. Thus, T'ung Chih's wedding did not take place until he reached his seventeenth year. This made him old. Shun Chih and K'ang Hsi—the first and second Manchu sovereigns—had been only thirteen when they entered the wedding chamber.

In the selection of an empress, family requirements eclipsed any personal preference of the future bridegroom. The Empress Dowagers Tz'u Hsi and Tz'u An chose Aleute for T'ung Chih. She was the daughter of a distinguished member of the Han Lin Academy and of noble Mongolian-Manchu descent. The dowagers' decree, as published in the *Peking Gazette*, described the maiden as "gentle, diligent, studious, and serious."

After the court astrologers pronounced that the horoscopes of the young couple were propitious for a fruitful and happy union, the countless details of the marriage and its attendant ceremonies were arranged. The first step was the issuance of an edict granting Aleute the title of "empress." Then the wedding day itself was announced, based, of course, on studies and interpretations of the heavenly bodies. It turned out to be October 16, 1872.

For this great event the marriage chamber was repainted and hung with colorful brocades and scrolls of dragons and phoenixes. The golden characters for "double happiness" were regilded. The wedding bed was draped with curtains of the finest new silk. In the midst of all this lavish splendor, T'ung Chih would come face to face for the first time with Aleute, his bride. They would share the nuptial feast and drink the nuptial wine. Then the union would be consummated and made sacred under the watchful eyes of the spirits of countless ancestors who would use their heavenly powers to make Aleute conceive a son at once. In fact, it was their ancestral duty to see that T'ung Chih's imperial seed was instantly fertile and male!

Unbending tradition prescribed that the new empress be received on her arrival at the Forbidden City by His Majesty's secondary wives or concubines who, from then on, would be her principal companions. Therefore, the court quickly announced their selection and hurriedly installed them in the palace. The possibility of future jealousies between these young ladies was not even considered. Because of her unassailable position as the first lady of the Son of Heaven, the private feelings of the empress-bride were not considered either. If her lord preferred another to his principal wife—as had happened many times in the past—she would "eat vinegar." Many hours would be spent in bitter tears and melancholy, with no recourse but to cloak her sorrow under a simulated air of dignity and resignation.

The long and complicated formalities of an emperor's marriage seemed endless. There was the sending of betrothal presents, the formalities connected with the marriage contract and the rites of the Golden Seal and the Golden Scroll. After a herald proclaimed the imperial edict naming the empress, the officials in charge of presents selected officers of state to "take the symbol of imperial authority and carry out the ceremonious sending of betrothal gifts." As prescribed by law and custom, gifts to the bride-to-be included bolts of the finest silk and cotton; saddled horses with coats of mail and a bow and arrows—as a reminder of the time when a Manchu wife was prepared to follow her husband's fortunes in war; flocks of sheep to represent the wealth of former days; gold and silver ingots to symbolize the ancient custom of buying a bride.

Gifts were also sent to the girl's family. Her father, mother, and brothers received gold, silver, horses, court robes for winter and summer, sable furs, and a gold and silver tea set. These were displayed in great style in the Hall of Supreme Harmony, and the horses were tethered in the Court of Honor. Since imperial gifts, like imperial edicts, were believed to be imbued with the actual presence of the Son of Heaven, the bride received the betrothal presents—borne in yellow-draped "dragon pavilions"—on her knees in the courtyard of her father's home.

As the colorful procession of "dragon pavilions"—elaborately decorated palanquins equipped with carrying poles—passed through the cleared streets and alleys of the capital, people massed, shoulder to shoulder, in overwhelming numbers to watch the lavish, eye-bedazzling parade, and to stare incredulously at the pavilions, balanced on poles and borne shoulder high by bearers trotting between escorts of officials in gleaming satin gowns. Necks craned this way and that as all gawked at fabulous gifts and the magnificently garbed mandarins—public officials of high rank who preceded the cortege. As each new extravagance of their sovereign passed slowly before the crowds, women of the poor districts, with babies swathed on their backs shared in the "beautiful occasion" soon to take place in the palace. With nothing in their drab lives to widen their own eyes, the gorgeous pomp brightened their dull and hungry faces, set voluble tongues clacking for weeks after, and happily immersed all in the romantic tradition of a golden sovereign in a golden palace.

Two weeks later the marriage contract and many more valuable gifts were sent to the future young empress. Finally, on the day before the wedding, the Golden Scroll, the Golden Seal, and the Phoenix Wedding Chair were placed in the Hall of Supreme Harmony for the emperor's inspection. As he strode about, formally examining these ceremonial accouterments of his wedding, the doleful strains of ancient ritual music, not too soft in the background, blended with the slight noise of specially selected officials making a deep *k'o-t'ou* in unison. That done, a command was given to carry the Scroll, the Seal, and the Chair to the home of the bride, all three to arrive at the auspicious hour prescribed by the astrologers.

Aleute, the chosen one, awaited the phoenix chair under a huge mat pavilion in the main court of her father's residence. Like the heart of a blossoming flower half-hidden by unfolding petals, she was the center of a cluster of ladies—of her family and closest friends—all glittering in gold embroidered court dresses of every glowing color in the rainbow. The pendant pearls of their elaborate headdresses trembled like drops of morning dew, their eyes shone, their cheeks were flushed with excitement. As the imperial delegate entered the outer gate, bearing the Seal, under its cover of yellow silken gauze, the Scroll, and other symbolic gifts, the bride and her attendants dropped gracefully to their knees. Then, formally accepting the seal and scroll, Aleute listened to the rising and falling cadences of the classical language in which the imperial rescript had been prepared. At the conclusion of the reading, she rose to make the womanly equivalent of the nine-fold *k'o-t'ou*—bowing six times with her arms hanging submissively; then kneeling three times and bowing thrice more. The betrothal rites, now as binding as those of marriage itself, were completed. The bride had only to enter the phoenix chair and be on her way!

What were the young Aleute's thoughts, commanded as she was to marry a man she had not even seen? She knew, of course, that by the next day she would be alone in a vast and awesome palace-city, surrounded by ungentle splendor, and despite herself, caught up in jealousies and endless court intrigues. But she would be an empress, a symbol of the empire—the pure and unsullied vessel by which the male line of her unknown husband would be perpetuated for his ancestors. Her own parents and family would be lost to her, given up for the harshness of a system that cared for nothing but its own permanence in power. Her personal feelings would be of no importance. This, of course, was the price of the highest honor that could be bestowed upon any woman in China's vast empire.

Under a glowing October sky the fading sun gently brushed the crests of the Western Hills, the leaves of nearby gingko trees glinted like freshly minted coins, and ripe persimmons hung like balls of glowing orange-red in the crisp air of that autumn evening. The auspicious moment for the departure of the Phoenix Chair had arrived at last! Its gold-embroidered trappings of yellow satin gleamed in the lights of the countless lanterns of the procession. Aleute took a tremulous step forward. The slight motion made her sumptuous silken robes of fiery red, embroidered with intertwined dragons and phoenixes, glow as with some inner fire of their own. A few more steps, and then she seated herself on tufted satin cushions in the chair, nodding with dignity as an apple—the fruit of peace and concord—was placed in her hands.

Sitting quite still, she waited, head a little to one side, listening. It was time for the traditional pink-dyed geese to be released in the courtyard of her home. If they honked and cackled loudly, there would be happiness and sons for the bridal pair. If they remained silent, the omens would be bad. There is no record of the behavior of the pink fowl on this occasion, but it can be safely assumed nothing was left to chance. At such a momentous time trusted servants would be diligently jabbing long pins into the indignant birds until their outraged cries reached the proper degree of noisy clamor.

With a heart full of misgiving, Aleute's father bade her goodbye at the gateway, his face dark with apprehension. Though the honor paid his daughter and his house was very great, he knew he might never again see his young and inexperienced offspring. He also knew the ruthless reputation of her future mother-in-law, the empress dowager of the west, Tz'u Hsi. And he had missed not a word of gossip about T'ung Chih, who had not only been corrupted by the eunuchs, but, as a young man on his own, had chosen debauchery as a way of life. As the elegant cavalcade slowly vanished from sight, its richly garbed eunuchs running beside Aleute's chair, her attendant ladies on horseback—as was proper for the wedding procession of a Manchu princess—he turned back into his house, blinking against rushing emotions.

In the gathering darkness the glittering procession wound its way through narrow alleys and along wide thoroughfares. The lights from lanterns, suspended at the ends of long poles, glowed softly. Now and then there were flashes of light from the rich, silken robes and jeweled chains of office, from the fluttering phoenix flags and embroidered canopies of dragon pavilions laden with brocades, pearls, and jade, from the gold-threaded gauze that covered the golden Seal and Scroll. Musicians beat on muffled kettle drums. Great brass cymbals clashed. Deep-toned horns of gilt and bronze were blown. Surrounding the chair itself were bearers, eunuchs, and a great many palace servants with silver incense burners, which trailed bluish veils of haunting fragrance in their wake.

The streets for the procession were closed to the public. The Ministry of Foreign Affairs had requested that not even the diplomatic corps or any of their nationals enter or cross the route to be used by the cortege of the empress. Nevertheless, Henri Cordier, a French Sinologist, managed to observe its passage from the doorway of the old home of Adam Schall.

In his *Letters from Peking* he described it in part: "Through the half open door, between eleven-thirty and midnight, we could witness amidst a most impressive silence, the procession moving on. Prince Kung, the Finance Minister, and other princes rode on horseback. We saw heralds with yellow silk batons, hundreds of servants in red gowns with white parasols, hundreds of men marching in pairs with lamps, thirty led horses with yellow trappings, and the closed yellow imperial sedan chair, carried on red poles by sixteen bearers surrounded by a crowd of yellow gowned eunuchs."

The cortege proceeded slowly along the specially opened Imperial Way. Finally it passed through the Dynastic Gate over a carpet of yellow sand that covered the stone paving, threaded itself between the marble lions and the Pillars of Victory, crossed the marble bridges, passed beneath the double-towered Gate of Heavenly Peace, the Gate of Correct Deportment, and at last, went through the gloomy vault of the Meridian Gate into the vast Court of the Golden River. Thence the elaborate chair was borne to the Gate of Supreme Harmony, and at the exact instant of midnight, was hurried through its portals.

Surrounded by his court in the Palace of Cloudless Heaven, the Emperor T'ung Chih awaited the coming of his bride. As Aleute's Phoenix Chair entered the hall, the male attendants silently dispersed, leaving only the palace ladies to receive her when she finally alighted. T'ung Chih then discharged a blunt arrow at the chair's closed curtains, in keeping with an ancient Manchu custom to dispel evil spirits, and retired through the rear door to await her in the wedding chamber. A mistress of ceremonies lifted the chair's curtain, and Aleute, in all the splendor of her pearl-fringed bridal garments, her face still completely veiled, stepped down into the hall. The apple she carried was now replaced by a symbol of the riches of the earth: a golden vial containing pearls, tiny gold and silver ingots, rubies, two little golden scepters, a handful of yellow rice, and one of white rice. Supported and guided by her ladies, Aleute was led from the Palace of Cloudless Heaven to the doorway of the Palace of Tranquil Earth. As she crossed the high threshold, she stepped over a saddle under which an apple had been placed. This symbolized not only her willingness to follow her lord into battle, but also her desire for peace.

As the young emperor at last raised her heavy veil, fragrant with the rich scent of Tibetan perfumes, he gazed upon her delicate face and downcast eyes for the first time. Her head remained bowed, partly in tradition and partly from the weight of the imperial bridal headdress— a goldsmith's masterpiece with its five filigreed phoenixes, wings and tails outspread, each beak dripping with long tassels of pearls that fell like opalescent rain about her face.

Again, guided by the mistress of ceremonies, the bridal couple was seated upon the nuptial couch, and a large, round, brass basin was set upside down between them. On this was placed a plate of "sons and grandsons cakes," which they shared. Next, the elaborate phoenix headdress was removed, and the bride's hair—still in the long plaits of girlhood—was dressed in the style of a married woman. As the couple partook of the marriage feast, drinking the wine from a single nuptial cup, behind a screen, a male and female Shaman chanted the vows symbolized by the wedding food. Finally, still a little embarrassed, no doubt, by numerous attendants and so many ceremonies, they were left alone to become man and wife—except, of course, for the ancestral spirits who had long awaited their chance to take a hand in the conception of an imperial son.

But this marriage, so carefully planned and so auspiciously begun, was destined for tragedy, as Aleute's father had feared. Aleute proved not to be the docile daughter-in-law the Empress Dowager Tz'u Hsi had expected, and T'ung Chih plunged back into orgies and erotic escapades. Their life together was stalked by one unhappiness after another, and ended in the untimely and suspicious death of the bridegroom.

The last wedding that took place in the red and gold chamber of the Palace of Tranquil Earth was that of P'u Yi, the boy-emperor, in 1922. Since the great halls in the southern part of the Forbidden City has been nationalized, his bride could not enter the Inner Courts through the great Imperial Way in the old manner. Instead, she used the Gate of Military Valor, the ill-omened north gate of the palace. The November night was clear with sparkling moonlight, and there was a crush of people in the streets. But for the few still living in the Great Within, it was a disillusionment and a sorrow—pomp and ceremony cut to the bone and many of the ancient traditions ignored.

Two days after the wedding, the boy-emperor and his empress received foreign notables and residents of Peking in the Palace of Cloudless Heaven. They greeted their guests in the Western manner, nodding to some and shaking hands with others. A mere shadow of a real Son of Heaven, the emperor mounted the dais of his throne, and speaking in English, said: "It is a great pleasure to us to see here today so many distinguished visitors from all parts of the world. We thank you for coming and we wish you all health and prosperity." Raising a glass of champagne, he bowed to the company and touched it to his lips.

The occasion was unlike any other the Manchu dynasty or the Forbidden City had ever known. Its informality flouted all tradition. *Ladies* and gentlemen were received by the emperor and the empress, who were *standing together*—an unheard of procedure! The empress was even observed to smile during some of the introductions! And one ill-mannered foreigner violated all court etiquette by wearing spectacles in the presence of the sovereign and keeping them on throughout the reception! Not only that, several male guests strutted around in white spats—and *white* was the color of mourning! The "big noses" had offended all precepts of good taste.

Though traditions had been smashed, the ancestors were not ignored. The boy-emperor, in formal ceremony, had announced his betrothal to them, and, undoubtedly to their relief and consolation, had spoken of all the rites connected with his marriage. Even if a world of the past was crumbling within and without the palaces, the emperor assured the spirits of a comfortable future in their shadowy existence, with their descendants never ceasing to honor them. But they were deceived, for within a few years their spirit tablets were forgotten in the whirlwind of the disasters to China that followed.

The tremendous cost of an imperial wedding was partly offset by the presents of high officials pouring into the palace from throughout the empire. In the Red Book—red being the color of joy and happiness— issued by the Household Department after the marriage, over a million dollars *in cash* was listed among the offerings. Also, there were vast quantities of priceless carpets, jades, and porcelains. As a measure of return, wedding honors were lavishly bestowed upon relatives and tutors; and posthumous honors on the departed members of both families. On that day of days, with the imperial line assured of continuation, the slaughter of all domestic animals was prohibited; nor could wild animals be hunted or killed. Any live fish or birds brought to the markets had to be instantly set free. Amnesties were granted to all banished officials and to prisoners not convicted of serious crimes. Thus, the happy influences of the "beautiful occasion" were assured.

THE IMPERIAL REST GARDEN

At the rear, or north of the Palace of Tranquil Earth, the Imperial Rest Garden—commonly known as the Garden of Earthly Repose—was laid out during the Ming dynasty in a manner described in the ancient architectural manuals as "The Imperial Audience Hall Style." In harmony with the rest of the palace, its formal pavilions repeated the yellow-tiled roofs, red lacquer pillars, and carved white marble of the main buildings. Standing in rows like decorously garbed officials were ornamental trees and shrubs, carefully pruned and designed. Pebbled walks wound in graceful curves beneath the branches of purposely gnarled cypresses. Peonies, blooming in a riotous profusion of white, pink, and red, were contained in terraces of green and yellow tile; the roots of perfectly tended trees within low rims of brick or cement. Only the brilliantly colored summer lizards, flashing about the fantastic rockeries like tiny comets of blue and green, violated the carefully controlled plans of man's ingenuity in this Garden of Earthly Repose.

When the welcome "grain rains" of spring fell, the curving, yellow-tiled eaves showered runlets of water on the budding blossoms, and an ethereal beauty touched the awakening garden. It became a rainbow-colored mist in the delicately fragrant air: tiny plumes of pink, white, and rose; the fragile sprouting of yellow forsythia; the pale lavender of drooping wisteria, and the inverted bells of creamy tuberoses. A new season of life had begun.

The love of the Chinese people for growing plants and flowers was epitomized in their temples, private gardens, and public parks. From the first azaleas and peonies in April and May until the last chrysanthemums of November, the walled compounds of Peking were ablaze with color. In one temple courtyard of the city, generations of priests had carefully nurtured the beloved peonies, whose roots had provided over three hundred seasons of bloom. For over six hundred years at the great Temple of the Five Hundred Buddhas outside Kunming, acolytes had specialized in growing camellias, and in 1945 the original plant, grown to the size of a spreading tree, was still blooming. Several of their younger shrubs—a mere five hundred years old—towered over twenty feet and were so weighted down with huge blooms that the branches had to be supported by props. Even the pragmatic Chinese army commanders succumbed to this floral shrine of beauty, and astonished American officers were invited to share it with them to "create a happy mood" before a series of military conferences on how to destroy the Japanese!

It was the custom for the emperor—after the last audience of the day —to come to the Garden of Earthly Repose for relaxation. Though he was never able to escape formality and was always attended by Eunuchs of the Presence, the Garden of Earthly Repose seemed carefree in comparison to the weighty pomp of the great halls. While strolling about the paths and shaded walks, he must have felt he had entered a Buddhist or a Taoist fairyland, where the purest enjoyment was to be found in philosophy, music, painting, and literature. One can visualize him, his face serene, in the refreshing atmosphere of this courtyard garden, wandering about pavilions inspired by the Five Virtues. Or, he might choose to write a poem, or gather together a few scholarly princes to recite the wisdom of the past, or indulge in a philosophical discussion of an ancient Han dynasty couplet. Most of the serious emperors—K'ang Hsi and Ch'ien Lung in particular—enjoyed these quiet hours, which were the only true liberty their positions of supremacy permitted. On the great feast days of the lunar calendar, however, the happy laughter and loud prattle of imperial children rang out in this garden. The families of the princes who lived outside the palace grounds were often invited on such occasions.

The Hall of Imperial Peace in the center of the enclosure of the Garden of Earthly Repose—a Buddhist temple that tolerantly sheltered a number of Taoist divinities—was often used as a family chapel by the emperor and his ladies. When wives and concubines needed special favors from the gods, they visited this shrine on the two monthly holidays of the moon calendar and burned sticks of incense or red candles made of mutton fat. An enormous gilt vase, sheltered by a circular canopy of wrought metal, was perched at the center of the ridgepole of this old temple, its Ming dynasty architects having adopted the design from the Mongol khans. Representing the golden urn, in which were placed the names of candidates selected for important positions in the lama hierarchy, this symbol was of the greatest importance to all Tibetans and Mongolians.

Another pavilion in the Garden of Earthly Repose—octagonal in shape and with four cleft cypresses at its entrances—was reputed to be a Taoist shrine erected in the early Ming period. Three hundred years later, Ch'ien Lung built a small library near the old shrine to house his favorite books. And beyond the east wall of the garden was the building in which the Jesuits worked to satisfy Ch'ien Lung's lively curiosity about the modern sciences of the Western world.

A high rockery against the northwest wall of the garden was crowned with the Imperial View Platform, a favorite haunt of the Empress Dowager Tz'u Hsi, who frequently watched the busy traffic of the city from this vantage point and was deeply disturbed by what looked to be Western progress—and a threat to her power. At one point during the Boxer Rebellion in 1900, standing on the Imperial View Platform, she indulged in one of her terrifying tempers as she saw the Han Lin Academy going up in flames.

The Pavilion of the Ten Thousand Springs and the Porch of the Red Snow stood above the garden on a marble terrace reached by four flights of steps. In the latter building the more literary emperors had entertained special guests with verse-making competitions. And just beyond was an open pavilion built over a pool, its deep, still waters stocked with fat, tame carp. Fishing parties had long been approved as a proper pastime for leisurely scholars—as was constant flattery to the Son of Heaven. In the

T'ang dynasty the poet Li Chia-ming consoled his emperor's bad luck on such an occasion with the lines:

" 'Tis rapture on the warm spring days to drop the tempting fly
In the green pool where deep and still the darkling waters lie.
And if the fishes dare not touch the bait Your Highness flings,
They know that only Dragons are a fitting sport for kings."

Tz'u Hsi had a high platform built in the garden for the pleasure of the Dalai Lama when he came to Peking on one of his rare visits of fealty. And in another corner, a large, two-storied, L-shaped pavilion was assigned as a study for the boy-emperor's British tutor, Sir Reginald Johnston.

The essential quality of formal elegance in the Imperial Rest Garden was reflected in the palace-gardens of the princes and wealthy nobles. Unlike European palaces, great establishments of the Chinese nobility often consisted of numerous pavilions set in the midst of gardens, many containing streams large enough to float small fishing craft and pleasure boats. Frequently they were "more garden than palace," with courts and buildings for various wives and concubines separated by parklike spaces of trees, shrubbery, flowers, and small lakes.

As an added pleasure, many of the nobles and wealthy Chinese maintained large flocks of homing pigeons. Attached to the base of the pigeon's tail was a tiny gourd, or bamboo, whistle; and when the birds were released to circle in great swooping arcs of red, steely blue and soft gray, their motion in flight created a wondrous symphony of sounds. To ensure the return of the flocks to their rightful owner, a coaxer, who led all the other birds, was guided from the ground by servants waving long bamboo poles, to which were attached brightly colored strips of cloth. With a busy flutter of wings, the pigeons would eventually light on their own roofs and were returned to the dovecots. Some of these flocks numbered in the hundreds. Whether rich or poor, the neighbors tried by every conceivable means to lure away coaxers and followers, and often did—with dire results to the peace and quiet of the district.

A somewhat less cultural activity involving pigeons was practiced by the thieves of Bamboo Wattle Lane in the Chinese City. Great flocks of birds trained to steal grain—euphemistically called food distributors— would wing their way to the imperial granaries each morning and feed on rice until their expanded craws were full to bursting. Once back in their cages, the owners would give them water mixed with alum, and they would instantly vomit up the contents of their gullets. The rice, washed and dried, was either sold or used by the families of the prospering thieves. This was actually a profitable means of livelihood, for a flock of one hundred pigeons could collect about fifty pounds of rice each day.

But the emperors, though their imperial granaries were being robbed, were so enslaved to magnificence that nothing so mundane as the Bamboo Wattle Lane racket ever touched their ears. Even the simple pleasures of their own garden were often denied them by the cold and formal monotony of daily routine. Each morning, long before the first pale glow illumined the eastern sky, a Eunuch of the Presence awakened His Majesty with a cup of tea or almond gruel. By the light of lanterns, the dutiful sovereign was then dressed in his stiff, official robes. Before the sun pierced the still-darkened sky, he entered the Hall of Audience and was greeted by bowing ranks of officials who had come to conduct the business of the day. With only the respite of the New Year, there were reports each day from every corner of the empire. All awaited his perusal and decision.

State audiences were regularly held on the fifth, fifteenth, and twenty-fifth of each month, and whenever officials came to offer thanks for new posts or promotions. Since the emperor received the Grand Council, the senior councilors, and his household officials every day, it was eleven o'clock before he could enjoy his early rice, a substantial meal which he ate in lonely state. Then, for a brief hour or so at noon, the emperor usually slipped away for a stroll in the Garden of Earthly Repose, a favored lady or honored guest at his side. In the afternoon his schedule often called for more interviews with officials; there were more state papers requiring his attention, and preparations for rituals or sacrifices, which usually included fasts, purifications, and a host of details, none of which could be slighted. Except at the Summer Palaces outside Peking, where life was more informal and less demanding, his time was seldom his own until the end of the long day.

When darkness fell, the gates of the Forbidden City, like the gates of the city, were closed and barred. Until the break of day the emperor was theoretically the only man—one of his many titles—inside the palace-city. The other members of the imperial family who slept in the Inner Courts were his empress, his concubines, and his young children. As soon as his sons reached early manhood—thirteen or fourteen in imperial China—they would be moved outside the high walls and towers into spacious palaces of their own, either in the Imperial or the Tatar City.

The early Manchu emperors varied their dull routine with state progresses and imperial hunts. Usually they spent the summers at Jehol in Inner Mongolia or at the nearby Summer Palaces. The great emperors accepted their responsibilities and managed distractions with a reasonable amount of dignity. Everyone knew that Ch'ien Lung visited the teahouses and bookshops outside the great Front Gate of the Tatar City. But he never neglected the empire, so his private amusements were his privilege. But when the Emperor Hsien Feng or his scapegrace son T'ung Chih made nocturnal pleasure excursions, the people were deeply offended. T'ung Chih's escapades in the more licentious houses of pleasure were a scandal and a disgrace. Each evening a blue, cotton hooded Peking cart—a solid, springless vehicle balanced on a single pair of heavy, iron-tired, wooden wheels and drawn by a strong mule—awaited T'ung Chih by a small gate that had been cut in the west wall of the Forbidden City. Disguised in the traditional long, dark gown and black cap of a respected citizen—which deceived no one—the emperor was in and out of the lowest haunts of the Outer City.

The day finally came when T'ung Chih failed to appear for morning audience. His Peking cart did not return to the palace until almost noon, when he staggered out of it, still drunk. Polite excuses were made for his absence. But when the same thing occurred on several later occasions, all officials were horrified at this flagrant neglect of duty. One courageous dignitary even risked banishment from court by removing several eunuchs who were suspected of encouraging their imperial master in his depraved behavior. Even the empress dowager, his mother, went into action and brought down her wrath and punishment on his drunken head.

There was an old saying in China that compared the emperor and his people to a cup filled with water. "If the cup is square, the water will appear square. If the cup is round, the water will conform to that shape." But even if T'ung Chih had taken his pleasures in scholarly meditation in the Garden of Earthly Repose, it was then too late to right the wrongs that crowded like hungry locusts around the Manchu throne. The vigor and imagination of the dynasty had begun to run thin before his birth.

He was also under the iron grip of an ambitious and unscrupulous mother who had no love for him—nor for anyone else.

Tz'u Hsi was motivated by one thing: a driving urge for supremacy over all others—to rule China!

Time had been a friend to the trees and rockeries of the Imperial Rest Garden. But time was the enemy of the warrior Manchu clans. As the end of the dynasty neared, Tz'u Hsi realized that the bold dreams of lasting grandeur were growing more elusive with each passing decade. But she hung on by her back teeth—a spark of the Manchu conquerors still glittering behind her steely black gaze and ruthless pursuit of power.

PART 6
The Eastern Sections of the Palaces

HALLS OF THE OUTER COURTS

In contrast to the orderly procession of gates and halls that made up the central core of the Forbidden City, the general plan of the eastern section of the palaces appears at first glance to have followed no pattern. Actually, its many courts and buildings were arranged with complete attention to precedence and decorum. Some of the civil functions of the emperor were conducted in the numerous government offices adjoining the parklike expanse of trees and shrubs. Behind them lay more offices a vast L-shaped court, the Hall of Abstinence, the Imperial Schoolroom, the Chapel of the Ancestors, and an enormous retirement palace.

The official entrance from the Imperial City to the Forbidden City was the East Flowery Gate, its two-storied tower rising high above the parapets of the palace wall. The daily procession of scores of officials with business to conduct inside the Great Within had to pass through its tunneled sally port. A few paces inside the gate, the canal of the Golden River turned south and flowed under the southern outer wall into the lotus-clogged waters of the palace moat. The imposing Halls of Literature and Learning as well as the two-storied library with its green and black tiled roof stood west of the gate.

The majority of those who entered the Forbidden City by the East Flowery Gate were clerks and lesser secretaries, whose records and accounts of the empire were kept in small, unpretentious office buildings. Those of higher station, having business with the secretaries of state, or even an audience with His Majesty, were always accompanied by palace flunkies. They crossed the marble bridge over the Golden River, passed through a wide gate and several of the important courts, proceeded past the palaces of the young princes and finally crossed the wide paved area to the Palace of Cloudless Heaven. There they were confronted by a huge sign that bore the single character: DOWN. At that silent command the most pompous officials and arrogant princes, riding ponies or being carried in chairs, descended and proceeded humbly on foot. Having already submitted to several inspections—and payments of bribe—their credentials were again examined by the guards of the Inner Courts. Again money slyly passed hands, and the great personages were permitted to enter the main section of the palace.

The buildings in the northeast quarter, with the exception of the Great Theater, were usually closed and deserted. Only during the last decade of Ch'ien Lung's reign, and from 1888 until the death of the Empress Dowager Tz'u Hsi, were the main halls opened for formal audience.

THE EAST FLOWERY GATE

The high, double-roofed tower of the East Flowery Gate overlooked the Imperial and Tatar Cities as well as many of the great palaces of princes and dignitaries who resided in the east section of the capital—a quarter that later became known as Mayfair, owing to its wealthy homes and spacious gardens. All the officials—even the emperor on occasion—used this entrance to the palace. The outer guards always angled to be posted at this gate, and with good reason. It was the most lucrative of all the openings into the Great Within.

In accordance with the custom that required all visitors to pay for entrance into the palace, the tariff exacted by the guards was known as the gate squeeze. The amount levied depended on rank and income and was solicited at every barrier by the outstretched palms of hundreds of servants, guards, and eunuchs. Though these "tips," or graft, seldom amounted to more than a few hundred ounces of silver, a wealthy seeker of imperial favor would disgorge as much as five thousand ounces before he could pass through all the gates and courts leading to his goal.

The gate squeeze was not only a palace prerogative, but prevailed in the homes of important officials, nobles, and, in varying degree, of all Chinese and foreigners who maintained servants. For at least thirty years after the fall of the last dynasty, a squeeze of ten per cent of the value of all goods, food, and necessities delivered at the outer gates of all houses was generally accepted as being an "honest" share for the servants.

Because of the extremely low wages, this form of kickback was the only means by which household staffs found it possible to raise families of their own. In great houses the percentage was usually considerably more.

On days of formal audience and lunar festival days the East Flowery Gate and its adjacent park swarmed with life and activity. Hours before the first light paled the eastern sky, the area was jammed with carts and sedan chairs carrying both civil and military officials in full court dress, and young nobles astride ponies, the heavy embroidery and silver of their long saddle skirts glittering under the glow of swaying lanterns.

As the official world assembled, each individual, flanked by his own servants, outriders, and lantern bearers, took a sort of swaggering pride in the protocol that pervaded the air. Palace eunuchs singled out the visitors according to rank and wealth, and so designated them. As each was beckoned forth, he moved with a feeling of superiority over those left behind him, and was conducted straight off to the waiting room nearest the prescribed hall for his audience. After the topmost rank came less important officials, unimportant assistants, and finally the lowly heads of minor bailiwicks, each having mustered as imposing a retinue as he could. The last to be summoned, having no one to look back at or down on, somehow held his chin high. After all, weren't there some two hundred million subjects who could never get *this* far? He was therefore a person of consequence, and it was expected that all persons of consequence would make their way to court at one time or another.

Those who preceded all others bore either great inherited titles or the ranks and honors they had won in the service of their lord. Some had been granted special privileges—the right to wear the Yellow Jacket, the sable robe or the triple-eyed peacock feather, which hung down their backs from their hats. Many had barely sufficient rank to warrant an appearance at all.

The most important daily visitors to the Forbidden City typified the entire government of imperial China. They were the heads of the six boards through which the sovereign ruled his empire. These powerful officials, usually Manchu princes, were automatically members of the Grand Council, which corresponded to a cabinet in Western governments. In the present-day world some of their titles and functions sound archaic; but their influence and authority provided them the means to amass enormous personal fortunes and achieve great power—which they did as an accepted concomitant of their high position.

The six boards were:

Rites, which dictated court etiquette and supervised all imperial sacrifices.

Civil Office, which controlled official promotions and awarded posthumous honors.

Revenue, which "kept the lists of population in order to aid the emperor in nourishing all the people," directed the provincial government of the empire, and collected taxes.

War, which recruited, trained, and equipped the Banners that made up the army. In times of war or rebellion its senior officials—princely generals—conducted the campaigns.

Punishment, which meted out justice through courts and local magistrates.

Public Works, which conducted the internal affairs "for the purpose of aiding the emperor to keep all the people in a state of happy repose."

The lesser boards and officials were:

Colonial Office, which collected annual tribute from vassals and tributaries and distributed suitable gifts in return. It also kept in submission the semi-independent border peoples and the mountain tribes.

Imperial Tutors, who educated the emperor's sons.

Secretaries, from the Han Lin Academy, who had secretarial duties at the court.

Heads of the Imperial Household Department, which ran the finances and conducted the operation of everything in the Forbidden City.

Presidents of the Boards of Music and Astronomy.

Board of Censors, commonly called "eye and ear officials," but officially known as the "court for examining everything," which remonstrated with the emperor to correct wrongs. They were supposedly prepared to commit suicide to emphasize their protests—and often did. Though some were men of the highest principles and all were theoretically exempt from punishment or censure of any kind, most were paid government spies with high sounding titles who pried into the public and private lives of the official classes. Many censors whose advice was not palatable to the emperors they served were either executed or banished.

On the long city street called the Eastern Thoroughfare, leading toward the East Flowery Gate, a number of undistinguished-looking buildings were hidden by high, mud-brick walls. They housed the Eunuch Clinic and were of the greatest importance to the Great Within and the dynasty in power. Though the system of emasculating men dated from antiquity, it was not adopted by the Manchus until after their reign was well established in the Forbidden City. During the early periods of history the source of supply was prisoners of war; later, condemned criminals as well, whose sons, born prior to their emasculation, were already deprived of an ancestral line because of the father's crimes. In theory each imperial prince was required to furnish the palace with eight eunuchs every five years. At their own residences princes and princesses of the blood had the right to maintain thirty eunuchs to care for their households; nephews and younger children of the emperor could have twenty; imperial cousins and descendants of the eight Iron capped Princes, who had aided in the Manchu conquest, were allowed ten. Since the supply was limited, and the demands of the Forbidden City endless, a register of all those desiring to enter this profession was kept by the Eunuch Clinic.

Though still in their twenties, many volunteers were married and fathers. By having themselves eunuchized, they hoped to advance in rank among the palace attendants and amass sizeable fortunes through squeeze or outright theft. By sacrificing their manhood, they earned a degree of merit in the eyes of their impoverished families, despite the relinquishment of their right to be worshiped as an ancestor. The sons and nephews of rich eunuchs, instead of becoming mendicants or laborers in the fields, were educated, accumulated capital to launch profitable businesses, and, in turn, raised their own sons in comfort. When their emasculated benefactor departed this world, he was given every possible earthly honor by his grateful relatives and the descendants of his early virility. For many years after the collapse of the imperial dynasty and the dispersal of the palace servants, a special Eunuch's Cemetery was maintained by a small clique of gray-clad monks outside Peking. Under the dappled shadows of age-old cypresses, the large walled area contained the elaborate tombs of the powerful—for example, the last grand eunuch Li Lien-ying under the Dowager Tz'u Hsi—as well as those of the most humble. Li Lien-ying's wealthy relatives in Tientsin—beneficiaries of his generosity—hired guardian monks to burn sticks of incense and to maintain offerings of fresh flowers and fruit before his spirit tablet—until the Japanese army invaded north China in 1937. His official ancestor portrait was kept in a huge chest before a stone altar in his private shrine until the eunuch-monks were driven out by the Japanese.

Most of the eunuchs were recruited from a few large villages near Peking. The required operation was performed by a "surgeon"; his position, a hereditary one. He was considered highly trustworthy by the Household Department; he received no stipend from the government, but was paid by his clients. Since he and his family dared not risk their livelihood, teahouse gossip that false eunuchs often entered the palace service was bound to be patently untrue.

Considering the crudity of surgery in China and the ignorance of postoperative shock, it is surprising that any young men ever volunteered for the operation—regardless of later rewards. The records indicate that about half of the candidates died within a few days of the operation. Under the usual procedure the candidate was first given a large dose of opium to partially dull his senses. Then, with his lower clothing removed, he sat over a six-inch hole in the seat of a chair. The "surgeon," reaching from under the rear of the chair, would grasp the testicles and, with one deft stroke of a sharp knife, cut them off. In most cases the patient fainted from either pain or shock. The bleeding wound was quickly packed with mud—believed to have healing powers—and bandaged to hold the pack in place. The survivors were given daily dosages of opium and permitted to rest until the wound healed. When fully recovered, they joined the palace staff as apprentices or were sent to a prince's household to be trained.

The East Flowery Gate had more than its share of history. Ch'ung Cheng, the last Ming emperor, in a final attempt to communicate with his ministers as his capital and palace were about to fall into the hands of Li's army, made his desperate way to the East Flowery Gate, but had to turn back. It was also through its portals that the first Manchu regent, Prince Jui, entered on June 5, 1644, with the traitorous Chinese General Wu San-kuei at his side. On that day the sturdy Manchu conquerors were greeted in silence by those of the humiliated Peking populace who were brave enough to venture out into the streets. The more craven of the defeated Ming officials, accompanied by the always craven eunuchs, opportunistically awaited the Manchus at this gate, bringing with them the imperial sedan chair. When Prince Jui was invited to enter it, he demurred with the remark: "I wish to follow the precedent of the duke of Chao in acting as regent for the emperor. Therefore, I should not ride in the chair."

But under pressure he finally yielded. He was carried forth in imitation pomp to the Hall of Martial Grace beyond the charred and blackened ruins of the main gates and throne halls. There he received the handful of Ming officials who had not fled the city and those of the household staff who had nervously quit their hiding places in the labyrinth of palace buildings and had come trembling into view.

THE HALLS OF LITERATURE AND LEARNING

The twin Halls of Literary Glory, elevated on white marble terraces and secluded by high, red walls, were designed to proclaim the close bond between the emperor and the sages of the land. During the second moon of each year they were the setting for the most distinguished savants and Han Lin academicians to join with their sovereign in observing the Feast of Classics. As a part of the ceremonies, the Son of Heaven offered incense before the spirit tablets of long-dead scholars and imperial tutors in the adjacent Hall of Proclaimed Intellect. In Chinese eyes this act was especially appropriate, since tutors traditionally wielded almost as much authority as parents. Alive, they took precedence at court over all but a few imperial princes; dead, their impartial opinions and influence on all matters were thus gratefully acknowledged.

Enjoying many privileges denied most courtiers, an emperor's tutor was permitted to ride a horse or pony within the palace precincts. At lesson time he merely bowed, rather than making the k'o-t'ou, and usually sat beside the emperor, instead of standing opposite him. When it was necessary to wait for his imperial pupil, he was fed from the palace kitchens. To stimulate scholarly interest by competition, he was authorized to recommend a student companion of noble birth for his imperial pupil. There was one restriction: the lad so chosen must never outshine a faltering or slow-witted young sovereign.

The Emperor Ch'ien Lung once pontificated: "The ruler of an empire must know the classics. For otherwise, being ignorant, how can he govern properly? Now, the only road to learning is through books. Therefore, the collection and study of books is the first principle of government."

In this pompous, approved style, his words emphasized the ancient origin and remarkable continuity of Chinese learning. Its direction had changed little since the bronze age prior to the Shang dynasty (1766-1122 B.C.), and it has always differed from the more analytical studies of the Western world. Only now and then throughout Chinese history did a radical mind challenge the accepted records and teachings. But the strength of conviction was never sufficient to divert the stream of culture into new channels. During the later Ming and Manchu eras, intellectual criticism was often a wasted effort—as in the case of a scholarly author who painstakingly collected one hundred and sixty ancient pronunciations of a certain word. The work of the Jesuits in mathematics and geography was stimulating; but since official qualifications for scholarship remained unchanged, there was little incentive to explore liberal, radical, or new ideas in these fields. "Learning in China was literary; and literature was learned."

Since Confucius looked upon the early Chou dynasty (1122-255 B.C.) as the golden age of life and intellect, his precepts and analects were generally fixed on the thinking of that time. Though his teachings were often considered a religion, they were basically concerned with principles of conduct. In Confucius's ideal world, each man had his own preordained place in an existence whose five principal relationships were those of ruler and subject, father and son, elder and younger brother, husband and wife, friend and friend. When amplified and expounded, much of the so-called philosophy of Confucius contains little more profundity or inspiration than Benjamin Franklin's *Poor Richard's Almanac.*

This narrow concept of conduct, which in time pervaded all Chinese thought, remained stubbornly in force with little change until the Western powers rudely nudged it aside in the nineteenth and twentieth centuries. Its basic conceit and its failure to adjust to modern influences during all the intervening centuries created rulers and people who could neither accept nor understand the changing world around them. Though sanctified by conservative sages, Chinese poetry, on the other hand, has always sung as freely in the hearts of the people as the spirit of the land itself. Through all its many forms, its subtle essence was distilled for an instant or for an eternity—according to its theme and nature.

Though other emperors in their line had no "ink in their stomachs," K'ang Hsi and Ch'ien Lung were both proud of the "twelve-dragon guests who dwelt in their ink," just as they themselves "dwelt in the ink" of every scholar with literary talents. Both men were flattered when intellectuals came to court to lend it a grace and sparkle that imperial princes, Mongolian vassals, and Tibetan lamas could never achieve. At one time it was not uncommon for a victorious prince to imprison a learned man as a prize of war. In the fourth century an Indian sage, Kumarajiva, became the trophy of first one warring kinglet and then another. One of Kumarajiva's Chinese captors, hoping to ensure himself of a host of little scholars, provided the Indian intellectual with the finest of quarters and presented him with ten beautiful young wives. Before the closing down of the Bamboo Curtain in 1949, descendants of Kumarajiva were still living in Sianfu and still proudly using the Chinese equivalent of their learned ancestor's name.

Many of the intellectuals were possessed of the highest principles, for which they were ready to sacrifice their lives and fortunes. Several emperors, snubbed by men of this caliber, accepted such rebukes in accord with their individual temperaments. Yung Lo, the founder of the Forbidden City, barbarously executed the savant Fang Hsiao, who, busy at work on a history of the preceding Mongol period, refused to leave Nanking and attach himself to Yung Lo's court at Peking. Shun Chih and K'ang Hsi, when unable to tempt distinguished Ming scholars to their courts, gave in and bowed before the prejudices that considered any honors from the Manchus a degrading indignity. Notable among such refusals was that of Ku Yen-wu, a philologist, who, rather than submit to the conquerors whom he looked upon as barbarians, became a common farmer.

The prodigious literary production during both the Ming and Manchu dynasties was most noteworthy for encyclopedias, dictionaries, and commentaries. The Emperor Hung Wu (1368-1398) set the pace in the early days of his reign in Nanking. He commissioned many great scholars under the renowned Sung Lien and set them hard at work producing a history of the Mongol period.

In 1578 Li Shih-chen completed his monumental *materia medica*, many of whose ingredients have proved valuable to modern medical science.

Hsu Kuang-ch'i, a minister of state who had been converted to Christianity by Matteo Ricci, compounded an elaborate agricultural encyclopedia, various mathematical treatises, and a lengthy document on the system of astronomy the Jesuits had brought from the West. The Emperor K'ang Hsi bitterly complained that his reign had failed to produce any pure literary works of lasting value; but he was wrong, for two of the finest Chinese novels—among the earliest novels in history—emerged under his patronage. Pu Sung-ling, who had failed in the examinations but later was celebrated as the "last of the immortals" because of his incomparable style, produced the classic *Strange Stories.* And in the seventeenth century an unknown author turned out the famous *Dream of the Red Chamber.*

If K'ang Hsi was disappointed in the intellectual achievements of his reign, the Emperor Ch'ien Lung had reason to be proud of the literary output of his, which became a golden age of literature. His prefect of Canton, Lan Ting-yuan, even dared to write a book of "good advice for women," which achieved only a partial success, since most Chinese women were illiterate, or nearly so, and in any case were not inclined to take advice from any but their husbands. But one of the more noted writers, Ch'en Hung-mou, the viceroy of Kwangtung and Kwangsi, so immersed himself in literature to the exclusion of all else—including his official responsibilities—that he was dismissed from his high post "for alleged incapacity in dealing with a plague of locusts." However, the poets, their works radiating delicacy and charm, led happy and fairly prosperous lives as the result of their efforts. One of the more outstanding, Yuan Mei, abandoning poetry for the moment, wrote what today would be called a cookbook. With a verbal bow to the ancient principle of the yin and the yang, he stated; "Cooking is like marriage. Two things going together should match." Another, who signed his work "The Flower Hermit," produced a lyrical appreciation of nature. The famous Chao I, in the midst of his prolific writings, compiled a complete history of the Manchu wars. But the topmost scholar in the best classical taste, Yuan Mei, did not reach prominence until 1798 at the end of Ch'ien Lung's reign. Succeeding emperors rewarded him with many high offices. He became Viceroy of Kwangtung and Kwangsi provinces, and eventually presented his library to the Emperor Chia Ch'ing.

The greatest production during the enlightened era of Ch'ien Lung was a monumental compilation of all the works of antiquity. Revised, rewritten, and edited by hundreds of scholars, it was divided into four categories—classics, history, philosophy, and belles-lettres—and called the Four Libraries. When completed, copies were distributed to all the centers of learning throughout the empire.

While this great literary task was still in progress, a special envoy was sent to Ningpo to study the building and the stack system of the famous Fang family library. This structure was the model for the library of the palace—known as the Pavilion of Literary Profundity—which was completed in 1776. Its air of quiet austerity—the result of Ch'ien Lung's careful planning—represented the affinity between the "superior man" and the harmony of nature. Sheltering pines shaded the garden and sighed as gentle winds slipped through their swaying branches. The arch of a white marble bridge was reflected on the glassy surfaces of a dark pool—a circle symbolizing the oneness and completion of life. Singing birds, blooming flowers, the leafy greenness, all combined to create a spirit of peace, meditation, and untroubled throught in the mind of a scholar. In the words of the poet Yuan Mei:

> ". . . the wind custodian sings,
> 'I guard the fragrance of a thousand springs.
> Draw near! Draw near!
> Ten thousand yesterdays are gathered here.'"

Unlike the golden roofs of the other great halls in the palace-city, that of the library was tiled in black and green. Its beams, rafters, and balustrades were blue and green, as were its decorative motifs and frescoes, while the mythical beasts and dragon heads on its curving eaves and ridgepole were of green tiles. Within the two-storied building a throne faced the south door, opening on to the serenity of the garden. Placed before the state chair, a table held all the writing paraphernalia of a scholar: a porcelain brush stand, a carved ink stone, a jade bowl for water, black sticks of dried ink, sable brushes, and silklike sheets of the finest paper.

In a land so steeped in custom and tradition as China, the caliber of learning mattered little to the average man in the street, provided the illusion of great scholarship and erudition was obviously present. Poets were more or less expected to follow in the footsteps of the famous Li Po (700-762) who, according to legend, was such a hard drinker that he reeled home one night, after a carousal with his cronies, staggered into a canal and drowned trying to embrace the reflection of the moon. In order to advertise his scholarly character, the mouth of a great calligrapher or painter was expected to be stained with ink from pointing the ends of his brush between his lips. Those who professed to any degree of learning wore the long robe of a gentleman and grew their fingernails inordinately long to prove to the world their hands had never been soiled by the slightest form of manual labor. Some permitted their little fingernails to grow to such excessive lengths that they had to be encased in protective bamboo tubes. An interesting sidelight of affectation was the true scholar's constant companion, the "ink monkey"—a creature that either never actually existed or has long been extinct. These tiny, jet-black animals were supposedly carried about in their master's loose sleeves. Their function was to rub his ink sticks on the wet ink stones so the flow of his profound thoughts would not be interrupted by even this minor chore.

The huge single room of the upper floor of the library was lined with books and scrolls and, for the emperor's relaxation, contained the only really comfortable, well-cushioned chair in the entire palace. When the aging Ch'ien Lung retired to this quiet room, surrounded by his most cherished possessions—his books—he could rest and meditate in the midst of the mellowed essence of the collected wisdom and thoughts of a thousand years. He could gaze with pride and pleasure on volumes bound in carved jade and ivory, scrolls of the most delicate silk and paper, page after page of exquisite calligraphy, and countless books printed from hand-carved wooden blocks.

In each successive reign the vast collection grew, until the very floors under the stately hall began to sag with the weight of accumulated learning. Ch'ien Lung's Four Libraries alone included thousands of volumes. Original editions, printed nine hundred years before, during the Sung dynasty, filled the shelves and crowded against the lacquered pillars. Hundreds more from the Mongol and Ming periods struggled for space against the colossal encyclopedia of five thousand volumes, which had been printed in 1723 from moveable blocks on the best paper. In addition, the library was the repository for innumerable historical records, the Manchu imperial family's private papers, instructions from the emperors, daily accounts of the imperial household, official reports of the privy council, a vast number of unpublished edicts and memorials, and nearly a thousand priceless old maps and portraits.

What has become of this enormous treasure-trove of learning and history? Much of it is known to have been placed in the National Library in Peking, where, before 1949, it was properly cared for. But much was stolen or lost. What remained on the slowly rotting shelves was probably nibbled by industrious rats and mice, or, perhaps, thrown away by its present masters.

THE INNER COURTS OF THE EAST

The Archery Ground

Behind the library the Archery Ground's wide expanse of gray paving stones lay like the bed of an empty lake and was enclosed by the rose-colored walls that guarded the great halls and palaces beyond. The solitary Archery Pavilion stood at its center to emphasize the manly nature of its purpose. Conveniently situated, the huge, open courtyard provided easy access to the state apartments and the retirement palace, the imperial schoolroom, the building for ritual fasts, and the Chapel of the Ancestors.

Both in hunting and battle, archery in imperial China was one of the arts in which every gentleman was expected to be proficient. Its practice was a cult with an elaborate ritual that could be compared to the knightly tournaments of medieval Europe. Twenty-five-hundred-year-old bronze inscriptions from the Chou dynasty record the fact that royal princes and young nobles attended schools of archery, and kings of various Chinese states took part in the ceremonial contests. Even in those ancient times every detail of the competitions was minutely prescribed, including the accouterments of the archer and his exaggerated postures.

The Manchus, a martial people, knew the value of training all their men in archery. They admired physical strength above any cultural attainment. Given a pen or a bow, the pen would have been thrown onto a trash heap. Archery practice revived the wild exhilaration their forefathers had known as they had galloped across the plains of the northern wilderness. The feel of the bows in their hands made them see themselves in pell-mell pursuit of tigers, bears, deer, antelope, elk, and wolves —and the defeated troops of enemy clans. The proficient use of the bow and arrow was a must for all young princes of the blood. They practiced almost daily in the Archery Ground and were awarded prizes for excellent performances by the emperor. When imperial sons and grandsons became old enough, they were taken first to the Hunting Park outside Peking. Later they went on lengthy expeditions to Jehol province in Inner Mongolia, where the great hunts might last for weeks and include thousands of men in semimilitary exercises. On these sport and troop training maneuvers, the robust Emperor K'ang Hsi started out on the chase hours before dawn and seldom returned to camp until well after darkness. On one occasion, while hunting with his sons and grandsons, Ch'ien Lung was so impressed with the prowess of one small prince of nine years that he gave him as an award the Yellow Jacket. The child grew up to become the Emperor Tao Kuang, the last of the Manchus with any greatness.

The Tatar bow was a formidable weapon with an average pull of one hundred and sixty pounds. As a protection against the cutting power of a released bow string, the archers always wore heavy thumb rings of jade or other stone. Despite the increasing use of firearms during the later Manchu period, bows and arrows remained the principal weapon of the Bannermen. Up to the very end of the dynasty, cavalry troops, training under the massive walls of Peking, stood in their stirrups on their shaggy, hard-mouthed ponies and galloped like the wind toward targets against which three arrows had to be discharged in one mad rush.

However, not all Chinese were good archers. A centuries-old tale was often told of a pre-Manchu general, a poor archer, facing an important battle on the morrow, who prayed to the gods for success. In his sleep that night a strange spirit came to him and promised victory. "Who are you," the general asked, "for I must offer incense before your shrine." "I am the spirit of the target," the apparition said, "and I award you success because you have never hit me!"

Aware that only a strong man, able to command respect from his armies and civil officials, could hope to rule successfully, the early Manchu emperors chose their heirs with the utmost care. But in the case of Chia Ch'ing, who succeeded the great Ch'ien Lung in 1796, the new sovereign lacked the inner fortitude to face the multitude of troubles that beset the Dragon Throne during his reign. Confronted at the outset with a comparatively threadbare treasury, and being of a parsimonious nature, he became renowned for his tight fist and avariciousness.

Dissatisfaction throughout the empire gave fresh impetus to numerous secret groups, notably the White Lily Society, already in existence for over four centuries. In 1811 astrologers interpreted the appearance of a comet as an omen from Heaven and predicted that the Manchus would leave China on October 13, 1813. Since this fateful date would occur during an intercalary month of the lunar calendar, Chia Ch'ing simply commanded the court astronomers to remove it from the official method of reckoning time. Unwilling to accept this arbitrary change, a band of conspirators scoffed at the godlike proclamation and planned to seize the Forbidden City on October 13, as prescribed in the old calendar. On that day the emperor and most of the palace guards were at the imperial tombs performing the prescribed annual rites. But before departing, Chia Ch'ing placed his second son, Tao Kuang, in charge of the palace.

Lin Ch'ing, the leader of the conspirators, had haphazardly organized his rebel task force of about two hundred men. His plan was to enter the palace in two disguised groups and, with the aid of disloyal eunuchs, to seize it from within. But on the day of the planned predawn coup, this ignorant, burly giant of a man completely forgot his mission. He was blind drunk at an inn six miles outside the city, boasting loudly about what he would do on the *next* day.

Leaderless, the two armed bands decided to go on with the plan—even though they faced an ill-omened wind from the Gobi desert. After only a part of the first element succeeded in passing through the East Flowery Gate, one of their number bumped a coal carrier and dropped his concealed sword, which clattered loudly against the paving stones. When the guards heard and then saw the forbidden weapon, they at once slammed shut the great brass-studded doors of the gate. Those rebels who were still outside fled in panic. Those who had managed to get inside frantically rushed toward the throne halls.

Meanwhile, the second group, guided by a treacherous eunuch, entered the Forbidden City through the West Flowery Gate. A few men of this band immediately climbed the outer wall of the palace and hoisted a great white banner to proclaim the restoration of the long-defunct Ming dynasty.

With the first gray light of dawn the remnants of the east group of rebels fought their way to the Gate of Cloudless Heaven, defended at the time by a mere handful of inner guards. As great bronze bells and drums clamored in a general alarm, Tao Kuang ordered all gates closed and barred. When he saw the white banner flying above the west wall, he rushed to a second-story porch near the treasury, took careful aim with his fowling piece, and brought down two of the rebels. Then he plunged into the thick of a skirmish at the gate of Cloudless Heaven, where he fought with great courage. By this time the imperial princes, with their armed retainers, and Duke I Hou, with a large body of troops, reached the scene.

The rebels scattered, some to hiding places in the kitchen areas of the palace, some to occupy the northwest Corner Tower, whose guards they overwhelmed. By nightfall most of intruders had been killed; and with the first light of the next morning, the others were hunted down like animals and slain. Those who had seized the Corner Tower threw themselves into the outer moat—and the leaderless little band vanished into history.

Meanwhile, rumors of further uprisings swept like dry leaves through the silent, deserted alleys of the capital. The emperor had been attacked! He had been killed! He was safe and returning from the tombs! Finally, after two days, Chia Ch'ing approached the gates of the city and, following custom, at once issued an edict accepting sole responsibility for the disorders. Then he rode slowly through the streets to reassure the people that he and his dynasty still occupied the Dragon Throne. In recognition of his energetic action, the emperor bestowed the title of "Wise" on his son Tao Kuang and doubled his emoluments.

Born in 1782, this "young prince," as Chia Ch'ing called him, was then thirty-one years old, and had several children of his own. A short time later he was named heir apparent, and eventually succeeded to the throne as the Emperor Tao Kuang.

But personal courage and skill with weapons served Tao Kuang little purpose in the following years. His far from peaceful reign met the pressing onslaught of modern times with a truculence that sometimes bordered on stupidity. He suffered his first serious humiliation in the Opium War of 1840. This was brought about by the British in their attempts to force the sale of opium in China, though its use was prohibited in their own colony of India, where it was grown. Tao Kuang issued an edict prohibiting sale, purchase, or use of opium in the empire, except for medicinal purposes. The viceroy of Kwangtung energetically enforced this wise decree and flatly refused to permit the sale of the large quantities of opium the British had unloaded at Canton. When he ordered part of the cargo burned, English warships opened attack on the flimsy junks of the Chinese fleet at the mouth of the Pearl River and proceeded upstream to Canton, the viceregal capital. It was a one-sided war and resulted in the island of Hong Kong being ceded to the British Crown; several Chinese ports being forcibly opened for trade with Great Britain and, under additional later pressure, with France.

Thus the practice of smoking opium was forced on the Chinese people by an enlightened Western power seeking a sales outlet for a vicious drug. Regardless of the severity of the punishments for its use, successive governments in China failed to wipe out the practice of opium smoking. Clandestine operations eluded government suppression for decades.

When Tao Kuang died after a reign of twenty-five years, the T'ai P'ing Rebellion, led by the self-appointed "emperor" of an agrarian reform movement, was ravaging the Yangtze valley. This catastrophic uprising actually continued until after the death of his son and successor, Hsien Feng. Before it was finally suppressed in 1864, with the aid of a Britisher known as "Chinese" Gordon (later, Gordon of Khartoum), the fourteen-year struggle was estimated to have caused the deaths of over fifty million people.

The Chapel of the Ancestors

Austere, silent, and aloof, the Chapel of the Ancestors was the most venerated and hallowed shrine in all the Forbidden City. Its location was ideal: near the great Retirement Palace, the Imperial Schoolroom, and the Archery Ground, it was situated so that the spirits of the past could dwell within earshot of the cultured tones of the elders who were soon to join them, the eager voices of the young at their studies, and the twang of quivering bow strings that bespoke the healthy vigor of their descendants.

Throughout Chinese history the spirits of the dead were expected to guide and influence the living. This belief—the cult of the family—had its rites but no mysteries and no priestly orders, and it had a far deeper hold on all Chinese than did any formal religion or philosophy. But ancestor worship was never in any real sense an actual form of worship in Confucian society. Essentially characterized by deep respect, honor, and affection, it is comparable to the biblical commandment: "Honor thy Father and thy Mother."

The essence and practical expression of the cult was the safeguarding of family continuity and the passing of the fire of life from one generation to the next. Each male in the line was a member of the group or unit, the needs and desires of which far eclipsed his own. Of little importance as an individual, his sole function—as in nature—was to father sons. His greatest sin was childlessness, for the spirits of ancestors lingered in their descendants as well as in their former homes—and for all time. Like all loving parents, these spirits advised and shielded the rising generations. A woman belonged to her father's family until she married. Then she and her spirit ceased to be members of that clan and joined her husband's clan forever. This changeover required that she be formally introduced to the tablets of his ancestors, who then had the right to expect her to become the mother of a son.

The departed ancestors were enshrined in a simple wooden tablet called the house of the spirit, and they heard and observed all that happened in the home. Of plain wood and about twelve inches long and three wide, the tablet was inscribed with the appropriate names and placed upright on a small block of wood. This represented a connection to the World Beyond, through which ancestors could share family joys and sorrows, and happily accept the remembrance and the affection of the living. The memory of generations acted as a spiritual guardianship for filial descendants, who, in turn, were able to share the past with remote but still-loving ancestors.

The personal relationship between departed spirits and their living, earthly relatives, and even friends, was best exemplified by the Chinese manner of expressing that a member of the family was dead: "My father is not here." In other words, the deceased was simply away in the spirit world and could return at any time to his honorary tablet.

The spirits demanded little in material ways. For nourishment, the mere vapor of food was sufficient; for comfort and contentment, the periodic salutations by their descendants were all they expected. But they were exacting in the fulfillment of these simple duties, and the danger from ignoring them was recognized in the code of laws for the empire. If neglected or forgotten, spirits could become vengeful and inflict harm, instead of good. Another of their expectations was that a dutiful son would not fail to sweep the graves of his ancestors at least once each year, during which ritual he could not be disturbed nor interrupted by any business, no matter how important.

In humble homes the number of spirit tablets kept in the house seldom exceeded five or six—parents, grandparents, and the recently dead. The names of more remote forebears were inscribed on a scroll, which also received proper attention. In the mud-brick hovels of the peasants, the "dwellings" of the spirits might be preserved in a cupboard or on a shelf. But rich families habitually set apart a special room or a separate building for them and called it the hall of ancestors.

As the natural protectors of the dynasty and the empire, the imperial ancestors required an official place of worship—the magnificent Supreme Temple, or T'ai Miao, in a cypress-studded park just east of that section of the Imperial Way between the Gate of Heavenly Peace and the Meridian Gate. On great occasions, such as the winter solstice, the New Year, and the Spring Feast of the Dead, the sovereign went there in person to greet the spirits and perform the sacrifices. If he was too young or too ill, an imperial prince was delegated to carry out this sacred obligation on his behalf.

Preparations in the Supreme Temple began days before the time prescribed for the ceremony by the Board of Rites. The grand councilors always composed the special prayers. They were written on a square wooden tablet, encased in white paper, and placed facing south on a table in the throne room. The emperor prepared himself both mentally and physically by fasting and purification. A red tablet of abstinence was published and set up in all government offices. Every official wore a silver medal to indicate his participation. Like their imperial master, they, too, were required to observe the seventeen ritual rules of fasting. The condemnation to death of convicted criminals was forbidden, as were visits to the sick, attendance at funerals, the sweeping of tombs, and the playing of music.

Three days before the ceremonies the household officials presented to the emperor a small bronze statue of abstinence, portraying the figure of a man holding a wooden tablet on which were pasted the rules for the fast. During that time the statue stood in front of the Hall of Abstinence, inside which the sovereign spent the entire three days. Meanwhile, the court abstained from eating certain so-called gross foods—principally onions, garlic, meat, and fish.

Two days before the sacrifices were to be offered, an official selected the cattle, which were draped with satin trappings and then solemnly led to the palace butchers for slaughter. After inspection, if they proved to be satisfactory, the blood and hides were burned and the carcasses cleaned. When a careful rehearsal of the ceremony was completed, the spirit tablets were reverently borne from the inner shrine to the hall of offerings in special lacquer cylinders between carrying poles—a contraption comparable to a sedan chair—which were shaded by yellow satin umbrellas.

The feast for the spirits was as elaborate as one prepared for a banquet in a state throne hall. Dishes of sweet cakes and vegetables were set before each tablet. The larger animal sacrifices, however, were placed on a separate long table; the carcass of a red bullock in the place of honor at the center, a white sheep at the east end, and a black pig at the west. After the actual rites, the emperor presented all the offerings of food as well as bolts of satin and silk to those who had assisted in the ceremony.

Following the reading of the prayer to the ancestors, the spirits were notified of important events that had taken place since the last rites, both in the empire and the imperial family. Thus they were kept minutely informed of the next state progress or campaign, of betrothals, marriages, and of the birth of children.

The smaller Chapel of the Ancestors, within the walls of the palace-city, was entered only by members of the imperial family and their retainers. Under Manchu rule no Chinese officials or servants were ever allowed to take part in these intimate family ceremonies. The unusual ceiling of this building's outer hall was lacquered in different shades of bronze, with clouds as the principal motif, rather than dragons. A long row of intricately carved and thick-cushioned throne chairs were placed for the use of the spirits, each departed emperor and each empress being assigned to the thrones in order of precedence. Nurhachu, the founder of the dynasty, and his consort occupied the central position, as befitted the dignity of the chief ancestor. The chairs of his descendants were ranked by generations, alternating to the left and right of the founder in the same manner as guests were seated at a dinner. The yellow cushions of the throne were brocade, embroidered with dragons for the emperors and with phoenixes for the empresses. After the spirit tablets were brought from the inner shrine, they were balanced upright by small wooden stands on the seat of each chair. Though the older ancestors were honored first, their least distinguished descendants shared equally in the offerings. No Ming emperors were honored, for at the downfall of their dynasty all their tablets in the Temple of Ancestors were burned, and the Manchus installed their own.

Shafts of rainbow-colored light, like sunshine filtering through stained-glass windows, spread a soft mosaic of bluish tones on the floor of the gallery that connected the inner and outer halls. Darkness pervaded the resting place of the ancestors and accented the invisible presence of spirit eyes peering from the deep gloom, of spirit ears straining to listen, and of ghostly souls noting all thoughts and deeds.

The inner hall was divided into a series of stalls by screens painted with dull gold tracings of dragons. Before each partition stood a pair of horn lanterns on high stands, a low table draped with cloud-patterned brocade, which held candle sticks and an incense burner, and a similarly covered throne table. Each of the narrow throne chairs—wide enough for spirits, but not for mortals—was adorned with scarves embroidered in imperial dragon and phoenix patterns. Behind them, hanging from ceiling to floor, were silk curtains that could be parted to reveal the inner shrines where the spirits rested. These were miniature throne halls. Each was magnificently carved and gilded, and contained a tiny bed with a yellow satin mattress, on which the souls of the sovereigns and their consorts could relax in privacy.

Since the tablets were impregnated with the spirits of those invited to enter and dwell therein, they were treated with all the honors due to the reigning monarch. And because a spirit might choose to inhabit more than one tablet, those in the neighboring Supreme Temple were regarded with equal veneration. When the small wooden slab bearing the inscription of an older generation was brought into the hall, those of its juniors were temporarily removed until the senior had been properly received.

Tablets for all past emperors were also placed in the Temple of Successive Generations of Emperors, in the northwest section of the Tatar City. An imperial hall of fame, all sovereigns were included except tyrants, usurpers, enemies of literature, those who had been assassinated, and those who had lost their thrones. Since all were somewhat tyrannical, the omission of tyrants makes one wonder how any got in. Kublai Khan was at first admitted; then removed. Later, he was restored to his honored place by the Emperor K'ang Hsi who also added the first Ming emperor and all the monarchs of the Liao and Ch'in dynasties. Still later Ch'ien Lung confirmed every Ming ruler except two—because of their "love for debased eunuchs"—Wan Li, the Porcelain Emperor, being one.

Among the Chinese and Manchus, a sovereign was remembered in history by his temple name. Each, of course, was given a personal name at birth and assumed a reign title at the beginning of the year following the death of the preceding monarch. During his lifetime the personal name of an emperor was taboo. He was referred to only by his imperial title *Huang Shang*, which can be somewhat freely translated as the "Highest Yellow One." In the Western world they are always called by their reign titles (with the single exception of P'u Yi, whose reign title was Hsuan T'ung).

The empresses, who were also given temple names, were installed in the Chapel of Ancestors in accordance with rank and seniority. She who had shared the nuptial wine and feast with her husband, and was therefore senior consort for all time, was known as the Central Palace. The second consort raised by decree to the rank of empress was referred to as the Eastern Palace, and the third as the Western Palace. But regardless of whatever august position she may have attained in life, if she had been designated the third consort of her lord, she retained that position—and that only—in the ancestral hall.

The same strict set of precedence applied to the succession. This fixed dynastic rule was designed to prevent any possible break in the continuity of the line. The empress dowager Tz'u Hsi sinned grievously against her own son, T'ung Chih, by ruthlessly settling the succession on Kuang Hsu, who was of the same generation. Numerous upright officials were so disturbed that they risked calling her attention to the injustice done her son. One imperial censor even committed suicide to emphasize his protest. When Kuang Hsu died, she attempted to make amends. To comfort her own conscience, in a most unusual decree she arranged for *both* the deceased sovereigns (T'ung Chih and Kuang Hsu) to adopt as their *joint son* the two-year-old P'u Yi.

In 1911, after the outbreak of the revolution, the spirits in the Chapel of the Ancestors heard a momentous announcement. On behalf of P'u Yi, his regent solemnly swore to observe the new constitution of nineteen articles, in which the National Assembly declared that the empire was no longer the private estate of the Son of Heaven, but a constitutional monarchy. A few months later the child-sovereign and the ancestors were deprived of even the shadowy rights laid out in that document. On February 11, 1912, a strange edict of abdication was promulgated by the Empress Dowager Yung Lu, the widow of Kuang Hsu. This most curious of all rescripts ever produced read:

> Some time ago the Republican soldiers started an uprising and the provinces responded eagerly; the whole country seethed with revolt; and ruin was brought upon the people. Yuan Shih-k'ai was specially commanded to depute a delegate to discuss the general situation with the Republican representative and to arrange for the holding of a national convention to decide on the form of the government.
>
> Two months have elapsed, and no practical or certain mode of operations has been evolved. The North and the South, separated as if by a barrier, are struggling against each other. Merchants tarry by the roadside, and soldiers are exposed in the field. So long as the form of government remains undecided, so long will the minds of the people remain unsettled.
>
> The majority of the people in the whole country are in favor of a republic. The southern provinces first propounded the idea; and it was afterward supported by the northern generals. Such being the overall inclination, Heaven's ordinance may be divined.
>
> How could I dare to disregard the wishes of the millions for the sake of the glory of one family? Judging, therefore, by the general aspect without, and public opinion within, I specially direct the Emperor to bestow the administrative power upon the whole country, in order that a Constitutional Republican Government may be adopted.
>
> Thus will the hearts of the people, wearied with trouble and yearning for orderly government, be appeased. I also accord with the principles of the ancient sages that the country should be owned by the public.
>
> At this transitional period from the old order of things, there should be a union of the North and South. Yuan Shih-k'ai was formally elected Premier by the Senate, and he shall have full power to organize a Provisional Republican Government. He will therefore confer with the Republicans on a united plan of action, with a view to secure peace to the people and the country.

The territories of the Manchus, Chinese, Mongolians, Mo-hammedans and Tibetans shall be consolidated into a great Republic of China. The Emperor and I will retire into leisure to pass easily through the months and years and see the con-summation of a wise government. This will indeed be excel-lent!

The last "emperor" and the spirits of his ancestors parted from their once great estate—but not by any means as willingly or as gracefully as the Empress Dowager Yung Lu pretended in her decree. She had no choice, for the Manchus were bankrupt—in spirit, in strength, and in their squandered treasury.

The tablets in the Chapel of the Ancestors still enjoyed the care and reverence of the boy-emperor and his court, though sadly enough, he had nothing but misery to report. He had been born under an unlucky star. On the death of the empress dowager and the puppet Emperor Kuang Hsu in 1908, P'u Yi, then two years old, ascended the Dragon Throne under the dark clouds of the coming revolution. After Sun Yat-sen estab-lished the Republic in 1912, this powerless boy-emperor and his court were allowed to remain in the Forbidden City for the next twelve years. The new government provided him an allowance of four million dollars a year—scarcely more than a pittance—to cover the enormous expenses of palace upkeep, greedy relatives, servants, and eunuchs. Meanwhile, China was torn between the struggles of various warlords, one of whom, Feng Yu-hsiang, called the Christian General, seized Peking. This burly, almost illiterate ruffian is best remembered for two deeds: first, he ousted P'u Yi and the remnants of his court from the Forbidden City and forced them to flee to Tientsin, where the former emperor took refuge in the Japanese legation; and second, he marched his ragamuffin troops under spraying water hoses in one great wholesale ceremony to baptize them all as Christians.

When the Japanese army invaded Manchuria in 1931, P'u Yi was se-lected "emperor" of their new puppet nation of Manchukuo. Seated on this flimsy, synthetic throne, he led a miserable, degraded existence for the next fourteen years. With the surrender of Japan in 1945, he was dragged off his throne and made a prisoner of the Soviet army. After the seizure of all mainland China by Mao Tse-tung he was once again impris-oned, and confined until 1959 in a "labor reform camp," his "rehabilitation" including the most menial of tasks. One of his ignominious jobs was that of a guide. Herding scores of tourists through the palace-city, his duty was to point out this and that marvel in what had once been the home of his ancestors. Finally, the Soviet government appointed him to the impotent National People's Congress. He was serving in that post when he died at the age of sixty. He left no son or grandson to revere his tablet in the Chapel of the Ancestors—or anywhere else—and no family or courtiers to bear his remains to the once magnificent tombs of the Manchu dynasty.

The Palace of Peaceful Old Age

The Palace of Peaceful Old Age, a costly fancy of the Emperor Ch'ien Lung, occupied the site of some of the most fantastically lavish buildings and gardens of the elegant Ming sovereigns. Though both his grandfather, K'ang Hsi, and his father, Yung Cheng, had disapproved of the luxurious royal hobby of depleting the treasury to construct and maintain unnecessarily expensive palaces, Ch'ien Lung was no pinch-penny. He was congenitally unable to deny himself any pleasure his active mind might devise, regardless of cost.

Using the excuse of his doting love for an aging mother, he converted a rather simple rustic retreat near the Western Hills into a fabulous Summer Palace for her occupancy. There were lakes and gardens, temples and shrines, and scores of palaces, audience halls, ceremonial and view pavilions, and even a miniature fortress where he enjoyed playing at war. He basked in the delight of having his mother think him a wonderfully generous and dutiful son as she gradually and happily declined toward senility. He knew she would never question expense or realize his motives were strongly underscored with a desire to please himself. In the simplest terms, this Son of Heaven had a passion for building.

Throughout his sixty-year reign Ch'ien Lung's excited eyes fastened on the numerous temples, pagodas, shrines, and sacred places that dotted the Western Hills and the plain about Peking. His grandfather, the great K'ang Hsi, had repaired many. This was the only excuse he needed to plunge into expansive and expensive construction—and he set to with an open-handed vengeance. One of the most beautiful of his projects was the Temple of the Azure Clouds. Originally built in 1366, it had a sweeping view of the plain, with the towers and walls of Peking in the misty distance. Its largest hall contained row after row of altars from which the so-called five hundred aspects of Buddha—as well as a figure of Marco Polo and the female Goddess of Silk Culture—gazed serenely through drifting smoke of incense.

Another of Ch'ien Lung's projects was the Temple of the Sleeping Buddha. It was originally built in 635 and rebuilt several times. The greatest treasure it housed was a fifty-foot-long bronze figure of a sleeping Buddha that was cast in 1465.

When the construction of the official retirement palace was commissioned in 1769, Ch'ien Lung seemed to suffer a twinge of conscience over the enormous cost of rebuilding most of the northeast quarter of the Great Within. He announced that this new plaything, which was to cover nearly twenty-five acres of ground, was to be no more than suitably dignified, comfortable, charming, and as refined as good taste could make it. After its completion in 1773, and with the inclusion of numerous additions in the ensuing years, the Palace of Peaceful Old Age emerged. From the beginning he had intended that it was to be one of the most costly and varied groups of buildings within the walls of the Forbidden City. Yet loath to relinquish his imperial powers, he delayed taking up residence there until after the three-year mourning period following the death of his mother in 1780. This coincided with the celebrations for his own seventieth birthday.

But for all his vast wealth, energy, and imagination, Emperor Ch'ien Lung's building programs would have availed him nothing had it not been for the simple and kindly Lu Pan, the god of carpenters, masons, bricklayers, paper hangers, and house painters. All honest contractors knew that when they experienced difficulty with plans or materials, Lu Pan—often disguised as a bearded old man—would suddenly appear. The complicated roof construction at the Hall of High Heaven on Coal Hill could not have been completed had not Lu Pan offered his help at exactly the right moment. He appeared and gave one of the workmen —who passed it to the foreman—a wicker cricket cage of an extremely ingenious design, which, of course, proved to be the correct pattern required for the roof. The great White Dagoba (temple) on an island in the Sea Palaces would have collapsed but for his unseen and rapid skill in repairing the cracks that threatened the entire structure. The Mongol Temple, which contains a ferocious idol of the lama sect—the Black Protector of Buddha's Laws—had a double set of eaves because Lu Pan corrected an error in calculations and design. The little god had achieved this by appearing in the guise of a cook whose repeated explanation of the overly salty food he had prepared for the workman was a play on words to advise the frantic contractor to "add another set of eaves." When this was done, the roofs were completed in perfect proportion—thanks to one of the busiest and most helpful of all the gods in the entire pantheon.

As a gentleman of taste and refinement, the Emperor Ch'ien Lung fully enjoyed his declining years in the Inner Courts of the Palace of Peaceful Old Age. Its halls and pavilions were beautiful, the gardens charming, the libraries and studies comfortable. Though he had lavished a thousand fortunes on the lakes and parks of the Old Summer Palace, he once again plunged into wild extravagance for his own pleasure. Under the Ming emperors this quarter of the Forbidden City had been a succession of garden palaces with "trees and towers and high roofs horned or curved like the moon"—a domain of such loveliness that during the Emperor Wan Li's reign of nearly fifty years, life seemed one long extravaganza of taste and beauty. Ch'ien Lung emulated this epitome of Ming elegance, his eyes and thoughts fixed firmly on surpassing the Ming reputation for luxurious perfection.

The garden came to reflect his personality, his philosophy, and his concept of the worthwhile things of life. Its dimensions were those of his imagination; its horizon limited only by his own. Trees and curious stones, winding walks and "tiger walls" of varicolored mosaics, miniature pools, clumps of bamboo, quaint bridges, rockeries, and resting places were merely symbols to him, as they were to all gentlemen-gardeners of old China, who happily devoted more thought to making a scholar's garden than to a perfect poem or painting. Art expressed a mood; a garden was an interpretation of nature and life itself.

Such a haven might follow many forms in its design—meandering quietly along contemplative walks or standing in almost rigid geometric formality. But each contained certain essentials: a moon gate—beloved by young women as a frame within which they could pose their willowy beauty; the trickle of running water; a pool of glassy stillness; a rockery of porous "volcanic" stones; a marble figure—perhaps of Kuan Yin or of the Great Sage; pines or conifers, a willow tree, a clump of bamboo, water plants, and pink lotus in the summer, a blossoming peach in the spring, wisteria and peonies in season. Always, there was a shaded pavilion and a seat for undisturbed thought—around which could be planted vines, shrubs, and flowers to enhance this quiet retreat. When a tree was planted, the young sapling was at once visualized as a stately giant standing proudly for the enjoyment of a grandson or a great grandson. The eye of the true scholar ignored the present and looked only toward the distant future of his beloved garden. A long-ago Chinese poet summed up his thoughts when he wrote: "For twenty years I started to build a garden. I sat a sit, I thought a thought, I rested a rest. It was still not very good. Only when I gave my whole heart to my garden did it become perfect."

A garden offered the intellectual and spiritual refuge found only in nature, where "the heart might be open" and at peace with the world. It was to such a place that the tired old emperor, relieved at last from the pressing realities of statecraft, retreated with the scholars of his day to compose a verse or to sit in quiet reverie looking back on his crowded and colorful life. He particularly liked the sunset hours. In the last moments of the day the aging Ch'ien Lung relived the great campaigns of his reign, the annual hunting excursions to the wastes of Jehol, the mad chase in pursuit of swift wild creatures across the plains of Mongolia, and the glory that came with unlimited wealth and power. His daydreams were often peopled with rebellious Mongol princes and mysterious lamas, with his own imperial clan and bold-riding Bannermen, his mother and his wives, his sons and grandsons. But so crystal clear in his thoughts that she seemed more than a memory was the so-called Fragrant Beauty—the one real love of his life. With no effort at all he could see her again as she had been—perfect, mysterious, glorious, and untouchable.

When Ch'ien Lung reached his eighty-fifth year, he celebrated the sixtieth jubilee of his reign by abdicating in favor of his eleventh son, Chia Ch'ing. Refusing to admit any deterioration in his mental powers or his declining interest in state affairs, he announced an official reason for his decision: it would be presumptuous and disrespectful to reign longer than his grandfather, K'ang Hsi. Never one to overburden himself with consistency—when it suited him not to—he continued to enjoy all the glory of being an emperor who had divested himself of the drudgery of office, while reserving the right to interfere at will in the actions of his reigning son.

After slowly declining during his last three happy years in the Palace of Peaceful Old Age, the Emperor Ch'ien Lung finally "mounted the dragon and ascended on high to the abode of the yellow springs" on February 7, 1799. Mingling with the shades of his ancestors, his spirit could smile contentedly with the knowledge that during his eighty-nine years on earth he had learned the art of living far better than most men.

On his death the gates of his garden were closed. Time, as pitiless as an old and envious eunuch, slowly despoiled the bright faces of the buildings and blurred the outlines of their design. The winds of spring and autumn tore the paper from the latticed windows and settled dust on forgotten gods within. Winter frosts and summer rains stained and scarred the lacquered pillars, weathered the jades and bronzes, and discolored their marble pedestals. Flagstones buckled, and pebbled walks were so washed away the lantern stands fell or leaned like drunken soldiers, afraid to stay but too tired to go. A rustic garden throne of gnarled roots fell apart. Unkempt trees and hoary cypresses, whiskered pines and the famous phoenix tree, drooped over weed-grown paths. And faded poetry pavilions, gently falling into ruin, seemed to mourn the master who had left them so long ago.

The Gate of Imperial Supremacy

The main approach to the Emperor Ch'ien Lung's Palace of Peaceful Old Age, through the twin gates of the Bestowal of Awards, opened on a narrow court shaded by ancient acacias and cypresses. Directly across this grassy space, the magnificent Nine Dragon Screen protected the Gate of Imperial Supremacy, the ceremonial entrance to the complex of buildings. Designed for privacy as well as to frustrate the influence of evil spirits who traveled only in straight lines, screens—known as curtain walls of respect—stood just inside most outer gates throughout China. But Ch'ien Lung's screen of encaustic tiles on its white marble base surpassed all others in the perfection of its large panel of yellow, white, plum, black, green, and blue. For its design, the kings of all the dragons had been chosen to guard the imperial hearth. Against a background of flying spray, flaming rocks, and moving clouds, these beasts of the deep seemed to writhe and struggle in their efforts to protect the treasured pearl of mythology that fulfilled all wishes. Sealed in this wondrous tile panel, the loyal and obedient dragon vassals had deserted the breaking waves of the oceans, the mists of the highest waterfalls, the rolling clouds, and the life-giving rains, and had come to court to protect the Son of Heaven from all harm.

The ancient technique of creating encaustic tiles—fixing with extreme heat the color and glaze on baked clay—was introduced into China in the fifth century during the Wei dynasty from the Indo-Persian area. Tiles for use in the Forbidden City were made in imperial kilns a few miles west of Peking. They were carefully packed in straw to prevent breakage and transported by canal to the Liu Li Ch'ang district of the capital. There they were inspected and sent on to their final delivery at the palace. In modern times the difficult craft of fine glazing so deteriorated that many newly constructed government buildings in the 1920's and 1930's (including the National Library in Peking) were roofed with green tiles imported from Spain.

About one hundred and fifty years after the creation of the Nine Dragon Screen, a number of old storehouses at the tile factory were dismantled. In them was found a complete duplicate set of tiles stored as a reserve in the event of possible damage. Duplicating fine works of art was a common practice in China for well over a thousand years. Paintings by great artists on either silk or paper were usually copied by apprentices at the time of their execution, including even the seals, to ensure preservation of the work against loss of the original by theft, fire, or deterioration. In modern times this procedure has caused much confusion as to whether or not a surviving painting was actually from the hand of the great master who had first created it.

Differing from all other official entrances within the Forbidden City, the Gate of Imperial Supremacy consisted of three arched doorways, framed in carved white marble, which were set into the rose-colored stucco of the adjacent walls. From there another court led to the Gate of Peaceful Old Age and the broad terrace of the Hall of Imperial Supremacy. A white marble causeway connected with another large building to the rear. This hall was dedicated to the special rites and cult of the imperial clan. The closed, secretive aspect of its exterior reflected the basic character of the Manchus, who accepted no strangers at their hearths and altars.

This introversion characterized the entire social organization of the Manchus, and the great importance of the clan lists. These lists, on which the names of all members and of the spirits who governed their activities were inscribed, were the responsibility of the heads of each clan. Since the lists identified rank, past generations, and spirits, they were essential to individuals, families, and the Shaman priests. There were nearly fifty Manchu clans—some large, some small. Those who had acquired family names during the Mongol dynasty were classed as "ancient." Others, able to boast of but a few generations of lineage, were "new." In the formation of new groupings, bitter family quarrels often ensued. The imperial family was the senior subdivision of a large clan of four groups, the Gjoro, meaning "gold." When the Shaman hall in the Tatar City was burned during the Boxer Uprising, most of the lists of the lesser clans were destroyed. Their loss almost broke the Manchu spirit and regime, for their organization was left in shreds.

The Hall of Imperial Supremacy

The Hall of Imperial Supremacy was furnished with all the magnificence becoming the dignity of his Majesty. The Emperor Ch'ien Lung's high, golden throne was surrounded with gilded screens, dramatic with immense peacock feather fans that fitted into blackwood and cloisonné supports. Though filled with the finest of porcelain vases and handsome braziers, the large room was best known for its collection of nearly a hundred clocks. They were all gifts of foreign embassies to the Son of Heaven in his capacity as Master of the Year, which carried with it his responsibility for the calendar. Time pieces of every description crowded the throne hall. There were several huge, ornately carved grandfather clocks, one of which was over ten feet in height. Other clocks were set with jewels. Some were of gold or richly gilded. Many had fantastic mechanical devices that announced the hours with singing birds, dancing European shepherds, ringing bells, and beating gongs. Since the instruments were all the products of "Western barbarians," no clock was relied on to keep accurate time, and no attempt was made to correct any divergences. This resulted, of course, in a continuous bedlam of bells, gongs, and chirping birds.

When the aged Ch'ien Lung gave audience in this hall, he occupied the high throne chair since he was of the senior generation. His son, though the reigning emperor, sat on a stool at his father's left. The old man had delegated his powers, but not the privileges that went with his position. Similarly a hundred years later, in 1899, following the marriage of the Emperor Kuang Hsu, the Empress Dowager Tz'u Hsi took up residence in the Palace of Peaceful Old Age and occupied the central place of honor. The lawful sovereign was seated by her invitation only on a stool at the left of the throne. Even in the presence of a secondary stepmother the emperor had to sit in the lower position.

After the coup in 1898, which ended the liberal Hundred Days, Tz'u Hsi held audiences with all the ceremony and formality due a reigning sovereign. On these predawn, candle-lit occasions, each official was designated an exact spot on the floor where he was to make his humble obeisance, a kneeling eunuch having first announced the official's name and the exact time of his arrival for the audience.

In the time of Ch'ien Lung the announcing eunuch, having directed the official to his appointed place, promptly left the hall, shutting the door behind him with a great, but silent, show. If he failed to close the door—or, indeed, even lingered—he knew full well the law prescribed that he be decapitated. This was designed to prevent eavesdropping and to protect state secrets from such minions. The same law also enjoined officials not to start their business or begin any report until the retreating footsteps of the eunuch had died away. But when the regent empress dowagers, Tz'u Hsi and Tz'u An, gave audience, etiquette *required* their eunuch guardians to attend them—which indicates the power and prestige enjoyed by these emasculated creatures during the last decades of the Manchu dynasty. Private audiences were the only way to reach a sovereign's ear, and the information overheard by a eunuch could be worth a fortune in bribes.

Members of the Grand Council knelt on one of five cushions placed at a prescribed distance before the throne. Lesser officials were relegated to the bare stones of the floor beyond. To avoid discomfort, the latter often strapped heavy pads to their knees, well hidden under the long court robes. The more affluent among them sometimes succeeded in bribing the announcing eunuch to move a cushion from the row before the throne and make it available to them. But this could create problems. If the bribe was considered insufficient or the eunuch harbored a grudge, the floor pads were placed so far back that the unfortunate official could neither hear nor be properly heard. Since he could not move until the emperor (or the empress dowager) had finished speaking, and since etiquette forbade him to raise his own voice, his bribe money was wasted and he was helpless to do anything but *k'o-t'ou* and make as graceful an exit as possible.

On one occasion the powerful Prince Kung, a brother of the Emperor Hsien Feng, was publicly humiliated for failing to observe the prescribed courtesy to the throne. In the tradition of Chinese rulers, his imperial sisters-in-laws always screened themselves behind a suspended curtain of yellow silk when holding an audience. This not only prevented them from being seen by officials, but also rendered courtiers almost invisible to them. Never missing an opportunity to humble a real man, one of the eunuchs guarding the imperial ladies whispered to Tz'u Hsi that Prince Kung had carelessly risen to his feet before she had ceased to speak.

"Stop the audience!" Tz'u Hsi shouted. "Call out the guard!"

Her orders were instantly obeyed. And a prince of the blood was ignominiously hustled from the hall as if he were no more than an ill-mannered secretary. This delighted Tz'u Hsi and made her grateful to her waspish eunuch. It had given her an excuse to publicly degrade a man whose power and wealth she had good reason to fear.

But Tz'u Hsi never succeeded in exciting either fear or awe in Prince Tuan of the imperial clan. A tall, red-faced man with an honest, blunt manner and a caustic tongue, he was a heavy drinker and notorious for his insatiable appetite for dog meat. Being the grandson of an emperor, he haughtily looked down his nose at the dowager. She was an outsider, and he never lost an opportunity to reveal his contempt for her. He disapproved of her fondness for off-color stories and once shamed her before the entire court by forcing her to forbid the eunuchs to tell them in public. And again, at an obscene play presented in the palace theater, he insulted her before all her guests by his loud, raucous applause and insinuating remarks regarding her predilection for obscenity. After the Boxer Uprising, the victorious foreign powers demanded he be beheaded for having played a prominent part in the disturbances; but they later allowed him to go into exile in distant Kansu province, where he eventually died.

During those breathlessly hot summer days of 1900, with the besieged legations almost out of food, ammunition, and medicine—and praying hourly for the arrival of the Allied Relief Expedition—the Hall of Imperial Supremacy was the scene of innumerable audiences. Tz'u Hsi was in a controlled rage during most of them. Nothing had gone according to plan. Under the bull-dog determination of the British minister, Sir Claude Macdonald, to remain in Peking and not to surrender, the representatives of the other foreign powers in the Legation Quarter had fallen into line behind him and were—with only a handful of "foreign devil" guards—holding out against hordes of Boxers. It looked as if they would never surrender or flee, even though all the reports stated the imperial army had defeated the Allied Relief Force near Tientsin and had forced them to turn back from their march to Peking.

As Tz'u Hsi and her councilors met to discuss these strange events, she knew that all the foreigners were huddled together in conference at the British legation, which had become the main bastion of the hated "big noses." And how strange, too, that the legation was still standing. On June 23, Tung Fu-hsiang's Mohammedan soldiers had put the torch to the library of the Han Lin Academy, hoping the fire would spread to the adjoining British legation. But the wind had shifted, and the Han Lin Academy was burned to the ground along with most of the Emperor Yung Lo's great encyclopedia. The legation had not suffered even a broken window! And how impertinent Sir Claude Macdonald had been —sending a despatch through the lines to the Chinese Foreign Office stating that his barbarian soldiers had attempted to save Yung Lo's library from the devouring flames and please to send for the volumes that had been salvaged! (Tz'u Hsi refused indignantly, and so a few of the priceless books are now in the Oriental Libraries of Cambridge University and the British Museum.) Nothing had gone according to plan. After Tung Fu-hsiang's Mohammedans and some of the troops belonging to the Boxer princes, armed with swords and spears, had fought savagely with heavy losses for the first three days, they quit the battle and turned to the less dangerous pursuit of looting and murdering their own countrymen on the pretext of hunting down Christian converts. All was chaos! And as for the artillery turned on the Legation Quarter—three hundred shots a day from the ramps of the city wall, and all aimed too high! They had skimmed over the quarter like winged birds, striking right into the Tatar City. And what about Prince Tuan who had always despised her? Was he actually loyal to the throne despite his hatred? Or, under all of his "patriotic" Boxer activity, was he fomenting a palace revolution to destroy her power in favor of that misguided reformer, the Emperor Kuang Hsu, whom the foreigners wished to see on the throne, since they felt they could deal with him? In any event, her control was slipping. Defending the Forbidden City were Boxers who were only a little less a rabble than Li's rebel army of the earliest Manchu days! No. Prince Tuan could not be trusted. And instead of fleeing or surrendering, the stupid barbarians had dug in their heels and refused to budge. Despite their casualties, it looked as if they were all prepared to die to the last man if need be.

The climax of these councils of Tz'u Hsi came on August 14, a day on which interminable and frantic discussions piled one on top of the other until far into the night. While the last audience was taking place, Duke Lan, the governor of the nine gates of Peking, ignored all formalities and rushed in to announce in a loud shout that turbaned soldiers had entered the park of the Temple of Heaven.

"Ah!" Tz'u Hsi cried out with delight. "The Mohammedan troops from Kansu!"

"No, Your Majesty," Lan corrected. "They are foreign devils—the Indian troops of the Relief Force."

Tz'u Hsi had two choices: to flee or to surrender. Earlier in the day she had assured her cousin, Duke Jung Lu, that, rather than leave Peking, she would commit suicide and force the Emperor Kuang Hsu to follow her example. But her steely pride gave way to cunning, and her feminine intuition hit on what might be a vital key to the situation. At midnight, with only three ministers present, Tz'u Hsi decided to flee and to compel the powerless Kuang Hsu, wasting away in his enforced imprisonment, to accompany her dressed as a peasant. Again her reasoning was sound: with Kuang Hsu at her side, she would be able to bargain with the Allies and thus prevent them from restoring him to real power as the rightful sovereign, a contingency which would have ended her authority and probably compelled her banishment from court.

The empress dowager left much of her capital in ruins—as was described by the Reverend Arthur Smith a few days after the relief of the legations:

> It is impossible to say exactly how great an area has been destroyed by fire, but the places are numerous and some of the tracts are large. From the Russian and American Legations west to Ch'ien Men [the Front Gate] for a width of many hundred yards and over a quarter of a mile in length there is now a stretch without a single building intact. A similar devastation is seen to the north of the northern gate of the Imperial City, and on a smaller scale in multitudes of other places as well. When it was possible for foreigners again to traverse the streets of Peking, the desolation which met the eye was appalling. Dead bodies of soldiers lay in heaps, or singly, in some instances covered with a torn old mat, but always a prey to the now well-fed dogs. Dead dogs and horses poisoned the air of every region. Huge pools of stagnant

water were reeking with rotting corpses of man and beast; lean cats stared wildly at passers-by; gutted shops boasting such signs as "Perpetual Abundance," "Spring of Plenty," and so forth. Over the door of a place thrice looted and lying in utter ruin one might see the cheerful motto "Peace and Tranquility." For miles upon miles of the busiest streets of the Northern [Tatar] and Southern [Chinese] Cities not a single shop was open for business, and scarcely a dozen persons were anywhere to be seen.

There had never been a woman in China's history like Tz'u Hsi; nor is history ever apt to forget her. Her father, an obscure and penniless Manchu official, died when she was three years old, leaving his widow and children dependent on the charity of rich connections. She could never forget this impoverished beginning. It limited her vision and bound her horizon to the material aspects of the present.

Devoid of high ideals and aspirations, her heart never echoed any responsive chord to the deeply spiritual meaning of the Dragon Throne. Concerned only with the mundane aspects of the empire, she relished, and even fostered, the intrigues, bribery, and cynicism in the palace-city. Being a woman, she could have no part in the Great Rites, nor could she even enter the solemn precincts of the Hall of Supreme Harmony. The stately rituals at the Temple of Heaven and at the Supreme Temple of the Ancestors were also forbidden to her; as were the great hunts in far-off Mongolia and in the hunting park, about fifteen miles outside Peking.

Earthy, a gambler at heart, and extremely superstitious, the Empress Dowager Tz'u Hsi pinned her tenuous faith on the all-embracing understanding of Kuan Yin, the goddess of mercy, whom she often impersonated at court festivals. A practicing but cynical Buddhist, she accepted for her own convenience the Great Teacher's belief that by simulating goodness, the heart itself would eventually become good. But the selfless areas of Buddha's philosophy were completely beyond her grasp. Egoism and self-interest devoured her thoughts and motivated her actions, though as a matriarch, her family and clan were integral parts of her very being.

Blessed with a steely heart and a good digestion, her amazing vitality set her apart from nearly all her contemporaries. Her eyes were large and brilliant, her head shapely and well poised, and though she was almost diminutive in height, the high Manchu shoes lent her stature. When she entered the palace, she was a sturdy girl brimming with a health and energy that matched her crafty intelligence. Looking about, she determined at once to make the most of her opportunities. As time went on, she developed a flair for clothes. She had great style and the knack of keeping the elaborate winged coiffure of her hair in utter perfection—a feat many palace ladies failed to achieve. In addition to great quantities of priceless jewels, Tz'u Hsi favored a gold pin-on watch studded with small pearls, a teenage gift from her cousin, Jung Lu, to whom she had been betrothed. The watch created frequent gossip. Court circles whispered that during formal audiences when Tz'u Hsi touched this ornament with the tip of one finger it was a signal to Duke Jung Lu that she desired his company that night.

In 1853, at the end of the court mourning period for the late Emperor Tao Kuang, Tz'u Hsi and a number of other Manchu maidens were summoned to the Great Within. Twenty-eight, including Tz'u Hsi, were chosen as concubines for the already-dissolute young Emperor Hsien Feng. Although she was scarcely sixteen years old at the time, Tz'u Hsi was nevertheless keenly aware of the fate of palace ladies who failed to exert themselves. Though only a concubine of the third rank (and nicknamed the Yi Concubine), she was possessed of certain great advantages. Muyanga, her father's most important kinsman, had given his own two daughters to the emperor. The elder daughter, who had died a month before Hsien Feng's accession, had been posthumously created "empress." Her younger sister, Niuhulu—later to become the Empress Dowager Tz'u An—was the sovereign's senior concubine and the most important lady in the palace-city, after the emperor's mother. Though Tz'u An looked down with some disdain on Tz'u Hsi and considered her to be a pushing young relative, she could not ignore their bond of kinship. And in the Outer Courts Tz'u Hsi could always count on her most loyal friend and cousin, Duke Jung Lu, then an officer in the imperial bodyguard.

Much has been said and written about Tz'u Hsi and Jung Lu. Betrothed from infancy, the two were constant childhood companions. They rode together on galloping Manchu ponies, explored the city side by side, and frequently ignored all rules of propriety. On one occasion they were said to have surreptitiously entered the palace-city, risking their lives to do so. There was seldom a day when the young Jung Lu was not hanging around Muyanga's great compound in Pewter Lane, where Tz'u Hsi lived with her wealthy kinsman—either showing himself outright or slipping about the garden shadows to whisk his betrothed off on some new escapade.

Jung Lu grew up to be a tall, extraordinarily handsome man, with flashing black eyes and a magnetic personality. Though Tz'u Hsi was not a beauty in the classic sense, Jung Lu found her perfectly formed little body, high patrician Manchu nose, compelling eyes, and commanding personality an irresistible combination.

Gossip has long been rife regarding Tz'u Hsi and Jung Lu. It began in their youth, persisted through the years, and still makes lively romance for historical chroniclers. There were few who did not firmly believe they were young lovers and that their alliance continued right up to the time she was summoned to the palace. But gossip it had to remain, even though based on strong conviction, for Tz'u Hsi would have been ineligible as a consort for the emperor were she *known* not to be a virgin.

When ordered to the palace, each young girl was carefully examined by trained midwives under the alert supervision of the eunuchs. On the day of her examination Tz'u Hsi wore a pair of valuable jade bracelets. Wise beyond her years, she knew that when she lay on the couch in the examination room, the practiced hand of a midwife would discover in a second whether or not she was a virgin. When her turn came at last, she went into a theatrical tantrum and indignantly refused to be pawed over. As she did so, the story goes, she deftly slipped off the costly bracelets and, unseen by the eunuchs, dropped them into the eagerly waiting hand of the midwife. For an instant the two women's eyes met and locked in a glitter of mutual understanding. Finally, the elder nodded her head; and Tz'u Hsi was able to stand in line with the other selected maidens, holding her breath as she waited for the empress mother to drop the colored silken handkerchief at her feet. If *that* happened, she would be a chosen one.

It did, and she was designated a concubine of the third rank.

Unlike her counterpart in the Western world, a concubine in China occupied a position of dignity and respect. She was completely accepted by all of her consort's family, who usually called her "little sister." If she produced a son before the first wife did, she exercised considerable authority and power in the household.

The custom of multiple wives, supplemented by official concubines, was considered necessary in order to ensure the birth of a large number of sons to perpetuate the family line and accord proper respect to the spirit tablets of the ancestors. A high rate of infant and childhood mortality had long ago taught the heads of Chinese households that they could not depend on the few sons of one wife to live long enough to become fathers themselves.

They had also learned that harmony in the home was best achieved if each of the women had separate quarters—a home without peace was not a home at all. So general and so ancient was this wise practice that from the most remote times the character for the word meaning "discord" was represented by the stylized basic pictographs portraying two women under one roof.

Tz'u Hsi's first success on the path of her ambitions was with her mother-in-law. The older woman was so pleased with her "daughterly" attentions that she quickly brought her to the attention of the capricious young sovereign. When the dowager died in 1855, Tz'u Hsi was not only promoted one grade in rank, but was also with child. Until now, apart from one delicate daughter, Hsien Feng had had no children.

Tz'u Hsi's son was born in April of that year, and suddenly enough to make her head spin, she found herself a person of considerable importance. Not only had she produced an heir, but the emperor was stricken with partial paralysis, and her influence over him was so strong the impact was felt throughout the court.

At the time the T'ai P'ing Rebellion had been raging in central China for years. Imperial troops had had almost no success in suppressing it. Tz'u Hsi strongly urged the emperor to recall to active duty General Tseng Kou-fan, a capable and loyal old soldier who was in retirement and temporarily taboo because of the recent death of his mother. Mourning in imperial China was a filial obligation recognized and enforced by the state; it could not be lightly dispensed with. Nonetheless, the emperor heeded Tz'u Hsi's advice, excused the general from mourning requirements, and placed him in command of the Yangtze valley army—all of which steps resulted in an immediate improvement of the military situation. In this, her first move into state affairs, the girl had shown a bold readiness to break with tradition if it suited her purpose. Heartened by results, she set out to acquire a grasp of all the internal affairs of the empire. She learned to judge officials cynically but well and, in so doing, made herself a useful consultant for her lord and a real power in the palace.

But her advice on foreign policy—the weakness of her whole life—was not followed in 1860. An expeditionary force of foreign powers had assembled in Tientsin with the avowed purpose of marching on Peking to avenge the deaths of their envoys and the betrayal of a flag of truce. Tz'u Hsi advised the emperor to remain at the Old Summer Palace, which Ch'ien Lung had so fondly built for his mother, and to defend the capital. The emperor weighed her words against the advice of a clique of former companions (Prince Yi, better known as Tsai Yuan, Prince Ching, and an imperial clansman named Su Shun) and took their advice. He fled the area of the capital and took refuge in the safety of the palace at Jehol. Tz'u Hsi was not only humiliated by this personal loss of influence, but embittered. For the rest of her life she despised the Western world and could not think of the barbarian "foreign devils" without visualizing their wanton destruction of the beautiful old palace from which the court had fled.

Once established in Jehol, it soon became evident that Emperor Hsien Feng was dying. Having gained his ear, the Tsai Yuan conspirators also gained control of his person and excluded Tz'u Hsi and his other consorts from the death chamber. They then persuaded the rapidly weakening sovereign to appoint the three of them regents for his five-year-old heir by Tz'u Hsi. But in their haste they overlooked the one item that was vital to the legality of their plans: the Great Seal of Lawfully Transmitted Authority. Somehow the seal had mysteriously disappeared, seemingly just before their lord ascended on high to join his ancestors. They dared not make an open search for it. Their popularity with the powerful boards in the capital was not sufficient to weather the scandal such a loss would create. They knew, of course, that Tz'u Hsi, having foreseen the situation, had somehow managed to get hold of it. Her possession of the seal cemented her alliance with Tz'u An, the Empress Dowager of the East, who was furious at the three because they had excluded her from their proposed regency. Though the lives of both the women were in peril, the plotters were also in an extremely dangerous position. Without the seal, the empress could not even be bargained with by offering her the title of official "dowager." That could only be bestowed by an imperial decree, which required the imprint of the Great Seal.

Fortunately for Tz'u Hsi, the commander of the imperial bodyguard was her beloved Duke Jung Lu, and partly because of him, she had always been popular with the Banner troops. She had the allegiance, too, of clever An Teh-hai (known as Little An), a eunuch of the Presence, who was her devoted attendant.

The three conspirators would have liked nothing better than to wrest the Great Seal from Tz'u Hsi's custody; but they were frustrated in setting about it. With the court in deep mourning for the Son of Heaven, their hands were tied; any overt action was impossible. In Peking, where the late emperor's able brother, Prince Kung, had reached an accord with the allies, angry protests against the regency began to be heard from all quarters. By the time the court reached the capital, the edict of regency had to bear the imprint of the Great Seal, or it would have no validity. To further complicate matters, Prince Kung and his supporters had their own ambitions and were determined to thwart the conspirators.

This was the state of events as the mourning rites for the deceased emperor were punctiliously observed in the palace at Jehol, with the notable deviation that owing to the deathbed machinations of the three princes, the consorts had not been raised in rank as was customary when a sovereign died. When the court and the huge imperial coffin began the slow and laborious procession toward Peking, the conspirators, being members of the Grand Council, were obliged to accompany the long cortege. Also, since it was obligatory that the heir and the imperial widows receive the remains of their lord at the capital when it arrived, Tz'u Hsi and Tz'u An started off ahead of the enormous retinue and its bodyguard of Duke Jung Lu's Banner troops.

Jung Lu was apprehensive. Only minutes before the imperial cortage began to move, Tz'u Hsi's devoted eunuch, Little An, arrived to inform him not only of her possession of the Great Seal but of the dangerous position of the two ladies. Jung Lu listened to the eunuch's words and decided that without an escort of troops, a convenient "accident" could overtake Tz'u Hsi and Tz'u An on the road. His fears were correct, for before taking their positions in the late emperor's long and gloomy cortege, the three conspirators had ordered the assassination of both the imperial consorts at the mountain pass of Ku Pei K'ou. So when night fell on the first day's dragging progress from Jehol, Duke Jung Lu and the Yehonala Bannermen, who composed the guard of honor, deserted the main column and rode off rapidly to the aid of the dowagers. Amply protected, both ladies proceeded toward Peking, observing all the courtesies that custom demanded on their unhurried progress.

When they were both safe within the walls of the Forbidden City, new edicts were drawn up and stamped with the Seal of Lawfully Transmitted Authority. One created Muyanga's daughter, Niuhulu, "empress dowager of the east," and Tz'u Hsi, "empress dowager of the west." They were also designated as joint regents for Tz'u Hsi's son, the five-year-old T'ung Chih, and for the first time were officially known as Tz'u An and Tz'u Hsi respectively—names by which history knows them best.

When the three conspirators arrived at the east gate of the capital, they were at once relieved of their self-assumed responsibilities as regents and had the new edict rudely shoved under their noses. Outraged, Tsai Yuan still boldly claimed himself to be chief regent and dared anyone to divest him of his authority. In reply, the new Empress Dowager Tz'u Hsi ordered the bodyguards to arrest all three princes.

Politics temporarily out of the way, the young dowagers settled into deep mourning in the seclusion of the Forbidden City—though both secretly rejoiced at their complete success. Shortly thereafter, Tsai Yuan and Ching were presented with silken cords. Of the third, the vindictive Tz'u Hsi wrote: "Su Shun fully deserves the punishment of the slicing process." But since this was too much for even her cruel nature, he was beheaded. His enormous fortune, most of which had been squeezed from the people of Peking, was confiscated at once, to become the nucleus of Tz'u Hsi's great personal wealth.

With this tidy ending to the Tsai Yuan conspiracy, the first of Tz'u Hsi's three long regencies began. Only twenty-two years old at the time, nearly fifty years of power lay ahead for her.

The Hall of the Culture of Character: The Daily Life of an Empress

For nearly twenty years the Empress Dowager Tz'u Hsi made her official residence in the Inner Courts of the eastern section of the palace-city. Guarded by the Gate of the Culture of Character, its high, rose-colored walls were inset with windows of unusual designs—shaped like vases, diamonds, and circles. Her private apartments and courtyards reflected her love of beauty with an emphasis on comfort. Each season the courts were filled with a riot of flaming pomegranates, sweet-scented acacia, the spicy perfume of the October moon flower, the pink and white of blossoming peach, plum and cherry trees, a kaleidoscope of brilliant late-blooming chrysanthemums, and the scarlet berries and glossy leaves of "heavenly bamboo." Her favorite of all was a delicate, yellow-green orchid, which she liked to consider her personal "name" flower. With the indulgence of a smiling grandmother, she watched over the growth of chrysanthemum seeds that her ladies in waiting nurtured through the spring and summer to assure a variegated burst of color in the late fall.

Though seldom able to relax from the stiff demands of duties and etiquette, she somehow managed to find time to supervise the breeding of her Tibetan sleeve dogs and Pekingese—miniature, lively replicas of the lion-dogs that supported the throne of Manjusri, the Buddhist god of wisdom. For generations these little creatures were reserved for the imperial household only. However, as a mark of special favor, a male might be given to a prince or an important noble. But to preserve the purity of the strain, a female was never given away. Though this tradition was considerably relaxed toward the end of the dynasty, neither breed became common until many years later. Contrary to their appearance, they are excellent, if cautious, watchdogs. Their instinct is to hide in a safe place on the approach of an intruder and by shrill, incessant barking arouse master and servants.

In view of the centuries of care lavished on these pet dogs, the indifference to the breeding of horses and ponies—except in imperial or princely stables—was typical of the many anomalies encountered in certain Oriental countries. To the Mongol and Manchu warriors, strong, swift steeds were as essential as the very air they breathed. But as time passed, their principal means of fast travel and successful combat was allowed to degenerate into a runty, pot-bellied, short-coupled, coarse-haired, hard-mouthed, club-footed, stiff-gaited jug-head—usually strong and hardy, but stubborn and ill-tempered. The original stock of wild ponies from the plains of central Asia was once bred with Arabian horses taken as spoils of war by conquering Tatar armies when they ravaged Persia and its adjacent lands. But with haphazard supervision, the Mongol herds did not benefit for long. Today an occasional throwback trait may be observed: the large, wide-spaced eyes; the slightly "dished" face; or the proudly arched neck of a remote Arabian ancestor. But the overwhelming majority of horses now found in China—some no larger than a

Shetland pony—are a sad example of careless breeding and casual feeding. The breed, if it can be so called, has survived despite its human masters. The animals are still useful for the simple reason that there are no better available.

Sparsely furnished by Western standards, the Hall of the Culture of Character contained only a low throne chair. Its sitting and waiting rooms, however, provided cushioned benches, low tables, and a few stiff blackwood chairs. All the windows were curtained with long draperies of the finest blue silk. A variety of clocks, ticking away the minutes and striking the hours with utter disregard for correct time, took the place of bric-a-brac and personal souvenirs. However, the Empress Dowager Tz'u Hsi greatly admired the queen-empress of England, and on the walls were two large engravings of Victoria in robes of state. Not only Victoria, but Prince Albert and the children too—all staring down rather incongruously on scenes of a very different royal household.

On the north side of the room an alcoved bed was framed and surmounted by elaborate, carved wooden panels inset with blue and gold cloisonné bats—the symbol of family unity. Similar to all the *k'angs* of north China, this large platform-bed was equipped with a thick mattress of yellow satin, silk sheets, a quilt of embroidered yellow satin, rock-hard pillows of the same material, and bed curtains of yellow brocade.

A hidden stairway led to a richly furnished private Buddhist chapel directly above her bed, and Tz'u Hsi often climbed there to pray in solitude or listen to masses sung by the eunuch lamas of the palace. Light filtered softly through mussel-shell window panes and shone on a frieze of saints that decorated the walls and on the yellow silk rug covering the floor. Encircled by jeweled candlesticks and enamel vases holding flowers of coral, amethyst, and jade, a golden Buddha looked down from his throne on the high altar.

The joy and peace of being alone was denied the empress dowager. Her daily life was crowded with attendants: two maidservants on constant watch in her room; two eunuchs on guard in the antechamber, four more by its red lacquer doors, and a dozen others hovering within call; and at least six ladies, waiting until needed, in the rooms on each side of the flower-filled courtyard.

Nevertheless, she contrived many a rendezvous with Duke Jung Lu that were completely private. The ground beneath the Great Within was honeycombed with tunnels leading to the Theater, the gate to the Sea

Palaces, the moat, and various halls. Constructed over a period of many years for quick and easy passage from place to place, they were also used for the temporary disposal of unfortunates who had been poisoned or otherwise done away with by the eunuchs. Duke Jung Lu used one of these secret underground routes, too—one that terminated under Tz'u Hsi's antechamber, which could be reached by a stairway built to replace an earlier, crude ladder. A bolted trap door, hidden by a rug, opened into Tz'u Hsi's room.

On at least one occasion an attempt was made to assassinate the duke in the tunnel. But the sturdy Jung Lu drove his dagger into the heart of his assailant and fought off others who pounced on him from the inky darkness. (Hearing the sounds of the violent struggle under the floor, the empress dowager shuddered with fear. Who might appear at her trap door—her lover or his murderers? When the door finally opened, Jung Lu's flashing eyes gazed up at her. And since she admired strong, forceful men, it can be supposed that that night in her lover's arms was one she long remembered.)

At one period of their close association Tz'u Hsi gave birth to a child, a girl. Having been a widow for a number of years at the time, the difficulties of concealing the pregnancy and avoiding a ruinous scandal would have been insurmountable to anyone but Tz'u Hsi. Wide ceremonial robes of state helped, but that was not enough. She established at her side a guest in her own apartments, a younger sister who feigned pregnancy. When Tz'u Hsi's daughter was born in deepest secrecy, the infant was passed off as her sister's child—a well-kept secret betrayed only years later when it was safe to do so. Shortly after, the infant was taken by Jung Lu to his own palace in the city, where she was raised with his other children as his own—which she undoubtedly was.

The Hall of Pleasure and Longevity: The Daily Life of an Empress

Tz'u Hsi occupied a second and larger suite of apartments in the Hall of Pleasure and Longevity. The center hall of this rather somber group of rooms was distinguished principally because it contained an enormous block of carved jade, known as Shou Shan, or Jade Mountain. About five feet in height and weighing close to three tons, this lapidarist's masterpiece was carved to represent in minutest detail a cypress-studded mountain, with tiny bridges spanning its gorges and ravines, and the figures of hundreds of immortals strolling about its paths. When the original, uncarved piece of jade reached Peking in the eighteenth century, tribute from some Asian country, it was considerably larger; but much of the rough block had to be wasted in the carving. Probably because of its weight and size, the Jade Mountain was not moved to Nanking when the Nationalist government transferred most of the palace treasures in 1933.

The north salon of the hall contained painted flower panels and finely carved woodwork, and opened onto a small paradise of winding paths, pavilions, and flowers, which had been one of the favorite retreats of the Emperor Ch'ien Lung. Though otherwise rather delicately planned, this room also housed another huge block of finely carved jade called The Mountain Pagoda of the Diligent Yu the Great, Governing the Waters. It depicted the story of the legendary sovereign Yu, who built the original dikes to control the waters of the Yellow River and thus saved the land from famine and flood. Though the Diligent Yu had solved the problem of containing China's River of Sorrow in his own time, his engineering genius failed to carry over into later centuries. In modern times, the increased height of the dikes could hold the normal flow of the Yellow River, but the annual deposits of silt during flood stages constantly raised the level of the muddy bottom until, along its lower course, the river was often as much as twenty to thirty feet higher than the surrounding farm lands! When a violent flood crested, washing out a section of the dikes, the resulting disaster was far worse than any the Diligent Yu had been able to foresee. In order to impede the advance of Japanese troops in 1938, the Chinese army deliberately blew up a wide section of the centuries-old levees east of K'aifeng and flooded the countryside. As a military expedient, the action failed, and great areas of farms and villages disappeared under water. The main flow of the river eventually found a new natural outlet, in the channel of the Yangtze River not far from Chinkiang. Thus, the geography and the location of the mouth of the Yellow River was once again changed.

After the marriage of her nephew, the Emperor Kuang Hsu, Tz'u Hsi spent most of her days in the Hall of Pleasure and Longevity. Like all Manchus, she rose with the first graying light of dawn, drank a bowl of lotus root gruel or hot milk. Then she had herself dressed in state robes. If a formal audience was scheduled, this process was long and tedious. When she donned the imperial yellow vestments, she usually snapped a pearl collar around her throat and threw a webbed pearl cape, as part of her official regalia, over her slight shoulders. By the time her hair had been arranged in the elaborate Manchu coiffure, she was ready to receive the greetings of her ladies. It was a colorful moment. Led by the young empress, the secondary wives and imperial princesses followed in order of rank—each gowned in satin brocade, thin tapestry or embroidered silk —as they fluttered in their mincing steps across the courtyard like a congress of brightly colored birds. As each, in turn, made her formal courtesies to the Great Ancestress, she took her assigned place beside the throne, the younger girls stealing looks of longing at the porcelain bowls heaped with fragrant fruits—apples to signify peace, peaches for longevity, and the lemon-scented "hand of Buddha," an inedible fruit from the south.

With the morning reception of her ladies at an end, Tz'u Hsi proceeded at once to audience or to the hard business of the day. That completed, she retired to her own apartments, exchanged her ceremonial robes for a comfortable loose gown, and sat down to her early rice —a meal she always ate alone. She was gifted with a natural ability to eat, sleep, and feel at home wherever she happened to be. Though usually content with the simplest of food, she was not averse to the richer and more complicated dishes for which Chinese chefs have long been famous. One of her favorites was "Chicken Velvet"—steamed and gently pounded chicken breasts that were simmered in milk for hours, flavored with a few bland vegetables and a little wine, and served in a slightly thickened sauce.

Though Tz'u Hsi's tastes at the table were delicate—almost picky— those of her deceased husband, the Emperor Hsien Feng, and her son, T'ung Chih, were not. Their satiated palates demanded the most exotic dishes the restaurants of the Chinese city could provide: small green snakes from the rice fields of Kwangtung in a highly seasoned sauce (the main ingredient could be replaced by a similar but deadly poisonous reptile able to "create a sickness in the stomach" of an unsuspecting enemy); the soft, cushioned pads of bears' paws, which to Westerners tasted like axle grease; deers' tendons, whose only recommendation was their cost; duck à la Fukien province, which combined physical and gustatory sensations. But the supreme thrill was live monkey brains, a delicacy from Canton. For this dish, a saucer-sized hole was cut in the center of a round table, under which a live monkey was chained immobile and so that the dome of its head projected from the hole. The diner, provided with a small silver hammer, beat in the skull. Then, using his chopsticks, he picked out bits of the still-warm, living brain and fastidiously transferred them to his mouth. (Most Chinese deny that this has ever been a custom in any part of the country at any time. But the fact remains that as late as the 1930's, the Nationalist government considered it necessary to promulgate a decree forbidding the practice.)

On the other hand, Tz'u Hsi was revolted at the tales of the eating habits and table manners of Westerners. They used knives; and they even allowed *women* at the same table with men. As reported by Chinese so unfortunate as to be invited to their homes, what could be more barbarous than the way the British served the flesh of a bullock: "huge chunks of half raw, bloody meat of cows from which they cut slabs of dripping flesh with great swords [carving knives] right at the table!"

As fastidious in her table appointments as in everything else, Tz'u Hsi's fine china was imperial yellow, her chopsticks and spoons of silver, and the serving dishes all had elaborate silver covers. As she had a horror of soiling her gowns—always difficult to prevent when eating in the Chinese style—she fastened a large blue silk napkin to her dress, using a gold pin. Although she followed the custom of eating only twice a day, she was a nibbler. Between meals she was constantly sipping milk, fruit juices, and tea, or munching on cakes and melon seeds.

When she finished her early rice, she went to her sitting room and stretched out on the bed for a brief rest. Then she changed her gown and inspected the fruits, flowers, silks, satins, and brocades that arrived as daily offerings of good will. Some items she selected as gifts to be sent off in her name; others went to the palace kitchens. But the silks, satins, and brocades she often reserved for her own personal use. Although fifty-four years old when she took up residence in the eastern palaces, her vanity was colossal. She looked far younger than she was, knew it, and acted accordingly. The "Old Buddha"—as she liked to fancy she was affectionately called—chose her clothes with the greatest care. She had over three hundred gowns in constant use, each kept in its own shallow box and covered with yellow silk. For winter wear she preferred brocaded satin; for summer, a delicate type of needle point called *k'o-ssu*, embroidered gauzes or thin silks. Always on hand were a great variety of detachable sleeve bands and collars as well as numerous magnificent fur linings, which, in the ill-heated palace, were worn both indoors and out during cold weather. Her priceless collection of jade and pearls was stored in some six hundred padded boxes, which were kept in a special room. Among the jewels was a perfect pear-shaped pearl to be worn on her forehead for special occasions, ropes of pearls for her hair, tassels made up of eight strings of pearls for the wings of her headdress, an enormous baroque pearl that had been hollowed out to make a snuff bottle, many fringes and tassels of pearls to be worn with various robes, the fabulous cape of hundreds of large pearls, and innumerable jade ornaments of every type and color.

After Tz'u Hsi's death, most of this incredible accumulation fell into thieving hands—great quantities into those of the eunuchs and thence to merchants, who disposed of them for a fraction of their real worth. Some of the most valuable, placed in her coffin, were seized by the bandits who rifled her tomb. Eventually this loot ended up in the shops of Shanghai and Hong Kong. The share claimed by the imperial treasury was later stolen by warlords and government officials; and many fine pieces went into the jewel boxes of the wives and mistresses of the richest and most powerful men in Nationalist China.

Behind the sleeping apartment in the Hall of Pleasure and Longevity, a secret passage led through a series of grottoes to a hidden room in which the empress dowager placed her jewels in August, 1900, just before she fled from the Allied armies. Though parts of the palace were ransacked and much of the city looted, the jewels were intact when she finally returned from Sianfu.

During those bitter days many treasures that disappeared from palaces and temples were either lost forever or came to light in strange places. The Temple of the Five Hundred Crystal Buddhas was completely cleaned out by Russian troops. Though not large, this shrine contained a figure of Buddha on its main altar, which had been carved from one huge single block of rock crystal. Five hundred smaller crystal replicas of the altar figure sat on crystal lotus leaves in wall niches in the inner shrine. After the Allied troops departed, the decaying edifice stood for many years, its altar vacant and its wall niches dark and empty.

A string of forty-nine large pearls, which had undoubtedly come from the Forbidden City, turned up in Shanghai. They had been secreted inside a palace bed-pillow that had been covered over with coarse material. The soiled pillow was bought for one Chinese dollar by an impoverished coolie, who, on examining his purchase, found a package wrapped in white silk waste—and the forty-nine pearls!

Tz'u Hsi had a touch of the poet in her, too. She often visited the Sea Palaces, where she picnicked on the dragon barges as they glided slowly through avenues of open water between great patches of blooming lotus. Drifting idly, she would dreamily watch the water birds and white herons along the shore line, and the arching flashes of gold and silver created by leaping carp. On winter afternoons that were free, she passed the time in painting and calligraphy, and later sent the results of her facile brush as presents to deserving officials. Like all imperial gifts, the simple mountain-water scenes or bold black characters on squares of red paper flecked with gold were sent off to the flattered one's dwelling in palanquins festooned with yellow silk. Thus all the world knew to whom Her Majesty was doing honor.

Though mah-jongg and other games of chance were common throughout China, betting among rich women and court ladies of the capital often reached astronomical proportions. The gambling debts of many Manchu women of high position could have fed whole villages of peasants for more than a year. If Tz'u Hsi lost when she gambled with her ladies, she paid her debts cheerfully; if she won, she always forgave the losers. With all her faults, Tz'u Hsi was generous to the point of extravagance and gave lavishly to all those who claimed her interest or sympathy. She showered gifts and money on her mother, brothers and sisters —even on her long-deceased father, whom she posthumously created "duke" and reinterred with almost regal splendor. She so flagrantly favored her cousin Jung Lu and all other members of her own Yehonala clan that jealousy of their great good fortune aroused many sleeping tribal enmities.

The Grand Eunuchs

High and austere as were the noble ideals of sovereignty enshrined in the Forbidden City, they were more than counterbalanced by the evils that thrived in the enforced seclusion of palace life. Though the Son of Heaven might rise above the clouds to the highest spirituality, the double evils of iniquity and deceit often spread throughout the Inner Courts like a turgid, miasmic fog—and that murkiness was caused largely by the emperor's first ladies! Most of the thousands of palace personnel came from the strata of society where grim necessity choked out all higher ideals and standards. No amount of carefully devised etiquette or dynastic law could alter their basic personalities.

During the Empress Dowager Tz'u Hsi's regime in the Forbidden City, scurrilous gossip and intrigue flourished like sinister jungle creepers tightly binding the vitality of the court and its attendants. The dowager's preference for informality made her a perfect victim. Yet the palace inmates schemed endlessly for the favor of this powerful woman their vicious tongues often sought to destroy.

In her position, Tz'u Hsi was forced to rely on the eunuchs for much of the information she needed, since an empress could not make friends of her ministers. Members of the six boards usually referred to the palace eunuchs as "rats and foxes," and most agreed that the influence of these slyly evil creatures eventually would be one of the chief factors in contributing to the downfall of the Manchu dynasty. All the eunuchs were Chinese, and few, if any, loved their northern conquerors. It is remotely possible, therefore, that some distorted form of patriotic hatred may have motivated their twisted souls. But however unlikely such a feeling might have been, the fact remains that their power during the last decades of the regime was formidable. Though many were harmless creatures—fat, lazy, and dull—others developed the dangerous cunning of the sexless and frustrated. As confidantes, they had the interests of their ladies at heart, for on their service to a mistress depended either prosperity or ignominy. Many were devout worshipers at the shrines and temples of the Great Within. Finally, when age or ailments precluded any further real usefulness, eunuchs usually retired to one of the religious homes for them outside the city.

I. AN TEH-HAI

Little An, as his brethren called An Teh-hai, was the first of Tz'u Hsi's notorious grand eunuchs. He was cheerful and witty, good looking in a rather plump way; he had an engaging, bouncy manner, a talent for acting, and a tongue as sharp as a rapier. A loyal servant during her first years in the palace, he was promoted to eunuch of the Presence when Tz'u Hsi's influence with the Emperor Hsien Feng first made itself strongly felt.

Spiteful tongues whispered that An Teh-hai had fallen in love with his mistress. But whatever the nature of his attachment, his daring enabled the young widow to thwart the Tsai Yuan conspiracy and seize the regency for herself. Though private messages between imperial ladies and any male other than the emperor were forbidden, An Teh-hai repeatedly risked his life to arrange the necessary communications between Tz'u Hsi and Duke Jung Lu. Tz'u Hsi did not forget her debt of gratitude to the little eunuch, and she appointed him her grand eunuch with unusual rights and authority.

After the prescribed three years of mourning for the emperor, the young Tz'u Hsi and An Teh-hai became bored with the stiff proprieties of the Forbidden City. To relieve the tedium, they devised elaborate festivities and indulged in many wild extravagances. Tz'u An and the Board of Censors sternly remonstrated with Tz'u Hsi and lodged complaints against her eunuch. And to make matters worse, Tz'u An, to the horror of her conservative soul, had heard that Tz'u Hsi was again corresponding with Duke Jung Lu. She protested about this, loudly and vociferously, and Little An, overhearing her complaints, came haughtily to the defense of his mistress. He was impertinent and rude to Tz'u An. In no uncertain terms he reminded "the pale, scrawny woman" that she owed her life to him, and had he not carried messages to Duke Jung Lu for Tz'u Hsi, she—Tz'u An—might now be rotting in the ground. Tz'u An was silenced; but this insult raged and rankled within her. Gratitude was not one of her strong points, and she grimly put a lid on her bubbling fury as she sat back to wait for the day when she could wreak her vengeance on An Teh-hai. It was not long in coming.

An Teh-hai, certain that the protection of his powerful mistress would give him immunity from punishment under the dynastic house laws, decided not only to test but to curb the power of Prince Kung, a brother of the deceased Hsien Feng. The support of this senior imperial prince had been essential to both imperial ladies during the Tsai Yuan conspiracy, but Prince Kung's growing preference for the conservative, stodgy Tz'u An had become more and more obvious. Knowing that his mistress looked upon Prince Kung with mistrust and fear, the impertinent grand eunuch had the temerity to harbor an open grudge against the great man and to make an issue of it. For a long time An Teh-hai had coveted a green jade thumb ring that was owned by the prince. He brazenly asked for it, and Prince Kung angrily refused. Aware that even an imperial prince could not refuse a request from Tz'u Hsi, An Teh-hai asked her to obtain it for him. She reminded the little eunuch that Prince Kung was not of a generous nature, and it would be wise not to offend him. "The prince is fond of his ring," she said. "We have many others just as good in the storehouses. Select any you wish and be at peace."

An Teh-hai bowed, but stubbornly repeated the request.

"It would be wiser to ask some other favor," Tz'u Hsi cautioned.

Later, since her favorite continued to sulk, she asked Prince Kung the price of the ring. He bowed, instantly removed it from his thumb, and presented it to her. After his departure, she sent for the eunuch.

"Here is your ring," she said, "but do not allow the prince to see you with it."

An Teh-hai bowed with profuse thanks, his eyes glittering with delight. The next time Prince Kung came to the palace, the eunuch was all over the place, openly displaying his ringed thumb and boastfully showing it to others, to be sure the prince's humiliation would be complete. This was an insult no prince of the blood could ever forgive. Long before this he had despised An Teh-hai. Now he swore the impudent eunuch would be punished. When Tz'u Hsi heard of the prince's threat, she became alarmed, remembering with a chill that only a short time before a fortuneteller had predicted a violent death for her eunuch. Again, she warned him not to trifle with members of the imperial family. But An Teh-hai ignored her concern. He continued adding to his fortune at the expense of all those he could gouge. Thoroughly alarmed at last, Tz'u Hsi decided to send him on a trumped-up mission to central China. She knew it was against the dynastic house law for a court eunuch to leave the capital, but she packed him off anyway, bearing her written order to circumvent the law. Once on the canals, An Teh-hai traveled in luxurious fashion on a magnificent barge, making certain the imperial flag flew at the bow and stern. Flaunting these symbols of the throne, he knew that provincial officials would hasten to fulfill his demands, which were always exorbitant.

Among his unwilling hosts was the civil governor of Shantung province. This was unfortunate. Some years earlier, when the governor had gone to court to thank the Dowagers for his appointment, he had inadvertently dropped his hat on the steps of the throne hall. An Teh-hai had quickly retrieved it, but had refused to return it to its owner. As grand eunuch in charge of the audience, he gloated: "So great an official as you to lose your hat! What a disgrace! But for ten thousand taels it can be returned."

"Ten thousand taels!" cried the outraged governor. "You must be joking! Keep the hat."

"Very well, I will," said the eunuch. "And I'll hang it on the great

Meridian Gate with the notice: 'This is the hat of Ting Pao-chen, the newly appointed governor of Shantung!' "

Such an indignity would have constituted an unbearable loss of face. So, through the medium of a peacemaker, the governor bought back his hat for three thousand taels (several thousand dollars in purchasing power at the time).

It was no pleasure then for the governor of Shantung to be forced to entertain An Teh-hai. He bore up, however, suffering indignities and gritting his teeth at the imperious demands of his upstart guest. It was while the eunuch was lording it over him and his staff that the governor suddenly recalled the dynastic house law forbidding under pain of death any palace eunuch from leaving the capital. At once he sent off a private report to Prince Kung, telling of An Teh-hai's arrival and giving a complete account of his misdeeds on the journey. Prince Kung hastened to Tz'u An, whose black eyes lighted up at this chance to get even with Little An. With her delighted connivance, the prince despatched a decree ordering the governor of Shantung to execute the eunuch without delay for defying the laws of the imperial household. Then Tz'u An sat back to see what Tz'u Hsi would do when she heard. Palace gossip being what it was, she had not long to wait. That same afternoon, Tz'u Hsi, outwardly calm but boiling with rage, sought her out. To Tz'u An's satisfaction she even admitted her error and begged that her favorite be brought back alive to Peking.

To forestall his execution, Tz'u Hsi sent off a special edict of her own, which could have saved the eunuch; but her courier made such slow progress that before he had covered half the distance to the provincial capital, the original death warrant had been received. An Teh-hai was arrested immediately. His possessions were seized, the neck yoke of an ordinary criminal was slapped on him, and he was rushed pell-mell to the courtyard of the governor's yamen, or headquarters. Screaming in protest and fighting for his life, he was forced to his knees and summarily beheaded before a group of smiling officials. Then his body was tossed into an unmarked beggar's grave.

This event marked not only the beginning of open enmity between Tz'u Hsi and Tz'u An but also of Tz'u Hsi's bitter distrust of the Manchu imperial princes. Nonetheless, she had to wait until the throne became vacant, to exact her revenge. Then, on the death of her son T'ung Chih, one of her first acts was to exclude all the descendants of Prince Kung from the succession.

2. LI LIEN-YING

Li Lien-ying, who succeeded An Teh-hai as Tz'u Hsi's grand eunuch, wasted no time in acquainting all those who had business in the Forbidden City that, compared to him, his predecessor had been a bumbling amateur. Where An Teh-hai had been shallow, boastful, and peppery, Li Lien-ying was deep, crafty, suave, and patiently vindictive. The minions in the palace-city soon began to call him the Lord of Nine Thousand Years—an expression conceived by a notorious Ming dynasty eunuch in mockery of the imperial title Lord of Ten Thousand Years. But the officials of the government nicknamed him the King of Squeeze and the Kangaroo of China. He was tall and gaunt, with a strong jaw, a prominent nose, cruel eyes, and a heavy, protruding underlip. Before he died, the telltale years etched on his lean face the story of a lifetime of greed and avarice, of treachery and brutality, of cynicism, and, strangely enough, a certain quality of cold dignity.

Coming from the lowest, most poverty-stricken level of Chinese life, Li Lien-ying had as a youth but two possible careers: beggar or eunuch. Though families similar to his own had no compunctions about submitting their sons to mutilation, he was left an orphan at an early age and thus had no parents to enter his name on the list of applicants. While still quite young, his nimble wits led him into a brief career of smuggling saltpeter—and a term in prison. After his release, he made his way to Peking, where he apprenticed himself to a street cobbler and earned the life-long nickname of "Cobbler Wax Li."

When nearly twenty-two years old, Li was hard at his job of mending shoes one morning at a sunny street corner. A passing court eunuch named Shen paused, frowned, and recognized him as a lad from his own home village. Since the claim of a fellow villager in a strange city was only slightly less strong than one from a member of his own family, Shen could not refuse the youth's instant plea for help. "I beg of you," Li cried, "find me some work by which I may rise from my poverty." The eunuch understood exactly what type of work the young man had in mind. So he told Li to think hard on it during the night, and if by morning he felt the same way, then meet him at the palace Gate of Spiritual Valor.

Gossip in the city claimed that Li was never castrated, that he became a lover of the Empress Dowager Tz'u Hsi, and even that the pair had been seen embracing, she on his lap and he with his arms wound tightly around her. These gems of scurrilous palace tongues can be dismissed as emanating from out-of-favor princes and disappointed officeseekers. The picture of a Manchu empress on the lap of a Chinese peasant-eunuch is too preposterous to warrant any credence. Besides, the records of the Eunuch Clinic clearly state the day and the hour on which Li Lien-ying had submitted himself for the operation and that he actually had been eunuchized.

As an apprentice to his benefactor, Li learned to serve, to speak politely, and to follow the rudiments of palace etiquette. Because of his height and strength, he was appointed a runner for the sedan chair of the Dowager Tz'u Hsi. His next promotion made him her hairdresser, reportedly because he introduced a new style of arranging a lady's hair. The old Manchu headdress, with its flower trimmed, jewel decorated, great wings of hair, had long been the despair of the empress, though it had never bested her. Stately and picturesque as this style might have been when first arranged, it was easily ruined by wind, rain, or fading flowers, and by midday it could look untidy, ridiculous, or slightly drunken. To assuage the sorely taxed patience of the court ladies, who could not cope with the problem as well as Tz'u Hsi did, Li devised the black satin wings, which the empress dowager immediately ordered for general adoption.

Step by step Li made his way cautiously through the maze of palace jealousy and intrigue until he managed his first big squeeze from an official for whom he had wheedled the post of minister of cummunications. From then on his innate astuteness and judgment of character achieved offices for many of his recommendations, each of which increased his personal fortune. He was always careful, too, to be sure his successes were well known; his failures forgotten or ignored.

Tz'u Hsi had never permitted the degree of familiarity to Little An that she later allowed Li Lien-ying. They gradually grew closer, and understandably so, since an old servant in a Chinese house was always considered almost a member of the family. Li was given a place next to her at the Great Theater, and he was permitted to sit in her presence in private. Eventually, he was allowed to speak to Tz'u Hsi without being asked to do so; and he reportedly shared Her Majesty's meals. Once firmly entrenched, he hung a carved tablet outside the door of his quarters inscribed in gold characters: "The Principal Palace of the Li House."

All this infuriated the co-regent Tz'u An, who disliked Li and his growing power quite as much as she had Little An. One afternoon, turning into Tz'u Hsi's apartments unexpectedly, the empress of the east left in a state of shock. She found, she reported, her imperial colleague resting a foot on Li Lien-ying's knee—an item of spiteful gossip that spread like wildfire through the Inner Courts. The hostility between the two ladies was now so obvious that even the thin outer shell of official friendliness was hopelessly shattered. Tz'u Hsi faced facts and decided she could do without her co-regent. The latter's sudden death in April, 1881, solved the situation in a most opportune manner.

With her colleague dead, Tz'u Hsi no longer recognized any restraining authority. When Prince Shun, the father of the young Emperor Kuang Hsu, made an inspection tour in 1886, she again ignored the house law forbidding a court eunuch to leave Peking and sent Li Lien-ying with the official entourage. Like An Teh-hai, Li Lien-ying was impeached, but, this time, only by the censors; nor did Tz'u Hsi find any difficulty in overruling their criticism. She stated flatly: "His mission was to look after the health of Prince Shun, who found him to be as faithful as any eunuch he could have brought from his own household."

On Li's fortieth birthday Tz'u Hsi showered him with gifts of gold bullion, jade, and even a dragon robe. Later she adopted him as an imperial prince, which entitled him to wear the ruby button on his hat, the phoenix pattern embroidered on his robe, and the yellow under robe —as he is depicted in his official ancestor portrait. Imitating her birthday largesse, the court and members of the government loaded Li down with lavish gifts. Some of the offerings were disguised or hidden. One undisclosed individual sent a simple, potted dwarf tree with a quantity of gold concealed in the earth in which it was growing. In all, some ten thousand gifts were listed on this occasion.

During a severe illness, Tz'u Hsi realized her devotion to her servant had been justified! Li cut flesh from his own thigh, ordered it cooked, and had it served to her. When all other remedies failed, human flesh was regarded as a cure if offered by a near relative, a faithful friend, or a servant. This prescription was specifically recommended in the "Twenty-Four Rules of Filial Piety," but the emperor should have been the first to make the sacrifice. He had failed to do so. After her recovery, Tz'u Hsi eyed him with a certain bitterness and harbored a grudge against him because he had not offered his imperial flesh. This implied a lack of affection and devotion to her. If Kuang Hsu's conduct had not been entirely filial, it certainly could not be called hypocritical—for he had good reason to hate her.

As Li Lien-ying grew older, his patience and temper grew noticeably shorter. When obsessed with rage at some infraction, he took sadistic pleasure in watching the younger eunuchs writhing and screaming with pain under the strokes of lashing whips. At times he administered the punishment himself, viciously thrashing them with his own most cruel of all whips—a long, heavy, leather thong wrapped tightly with coils of fine wire that was able to rip off skin and flesh. Gradually, the close confinement of palace life and the demands for his constant attendance on Her Majesty frayed his nerves. He seemed to forget it was he who had made himself indispensible to her. And, dependent on him for company and advice, she ignored the possibility that he might desire an occasional few moments to himself—if for no other reason than to count up his growing hoard of wealth. Still, for all his irritability, they were nearly inseparable, sharing not only many memories but even a common purse during the wanderings of the court in 1900. Tz'u Hsi had few resources at the start of those long travels, but Li never failed to take all that could be squeezed from their unfortunate hosts in the provinces. Together they made common cause against the rising tide of change and were closer than ever when they returned to Peking and Tz'u Hsi once more sat on her golden throne.

Those who saw the old eunuch after the death of the Empress Dowager spoke of him as a pitiful creature without hope or interest in life. As Li Lien-ying walked behind the magnificent catafalque in her funeral procession, his tears never ceased. Later he seemed to deflate like a pricked balloon; and he spent day after day weeping bitterly. Whether his behavior was motivated by fear for his own bleak future or by genuine sorrow can only be answered by his spirit, which did not linger long on earth after the departure of his imperial mistress.

Of Li's vast estate most was seized by palace officials, and little saved for the family he had adopted—and that only because of the intervention of the new Empress Dowager Yung Lu. No estimate could ever be made of the actual size of his enormous fortune. However, three million taels in gold bullion (about three million dollars) was found hidden under the bed in his palace. This was seized by the Household Department, ostensibly to buy foreign furniture for various halls of the Great Within.

The Pavilion of Pleasant Sounds
(The Great Theater)

The Great Theater of the Forbidden City was built in the late eighteenth century by the Emperor Ch'ien Lung as a part of his Palace of Peaceful Old Age. A large three-storied structure containing a stage on each floor, its balconylike platforms were open on all but the south side so the Son of Heaven could always sit facing the direction from which came all good influences. Three entirely separate plays were often in progress at the same time, one on each floor. These multiple dramas did not disturb the imperial audiences. They were well conditioned to confusion and conflicting voices. Though the joys of quiet contemplation were constantly proclaimed, they were seldom achieved in the grating cacophony of everyday Chinese life. And similarly, though forever talking peace, they were far more often at war.

A large adjoining building behind the stages contained the complicated mechanism for changing scenery, storage space for props, dressing rooms for the actors, and a complete set of musical instruments. The imperial box, known as the Loge for Inspecting Truth, was in a separate building facing the stages, directly across an open court. It was a fifty-foot-long room with adjacent antechambers, whose open sides were protected from winter weather by panes of glass that reached from floor to ceiling.

Low structures on either side of the court were divided into stall-like booths for the accommodation of the princes and officials who might be honored by an invitation in the form of a decree. To make certain that their presence should in no way impinge on the privacy of the emperor and his ladies, twelve-foot-high screens of painted silk, hung so that they did not interfere with the guests' view, extended diagonally from the imperial loge to the lowest stage. Except for this contrivance and the sumptuous decorations throughout, the entire plan was patterned after the traditional outdoor theaters of China.

In later times theater buildings in Peking and in the larger northern cities were similar in construction to those of the Western world. But the behavior of the audiences was entirely different. Whole families, including young children, habitually brought along light snacks, which they enjoyed lustily throughout the performance. Mothers silenced their howling babies by nursing them in the midst of the crowded house;

friends called out greetings, gathered together for chats, and strolled about the auditorium; tea and melon seeds were sold by noisy attendants —the entire hubbub completely ignoring the right of any spectator who preferred to listen to the play or opera. Steaming hot towels, used to wipe sticky hands and sweating faces, were wildly thrown in all directions to the agile attendants—*hsiao-kuei,* or "little devils," in the hope that the young servants would miss the catch. But like professional ball players, the attendants lunged, darted, and at times almost took off in flight to snatch the small white towels out of the air. During this pandemonium the opera ground through its course—magnificently costumed actors strutting and mincing through tragic or comic roles, their voices high-pitched and straining. Stage hands and tea servers moved casually across the platform as though their soiled workclothes rendered them invisible. When not too wrapped up in their own personal affairs, the audience shouted their disapproval of any actor who might make the slightest divergence from the well-remembered classical scripts.

The Chinese theater was a happy blend of the dramatic arts; of history, legend, and fiction; of opera, straight drama, ballet, and oratory. Virtue was always shining white; evil, inky black. The mingling of comedy and tragedy occurred with little regard for either logic or rationalization. The theater flourished for the enjoyment of the people of all classes, and each passing dynasty added its own style to the favorite classical plays.

As a people, the Chinese were hedonists. Their attitude was a combination of extreme egoism, a determination to enjoy life to the fullest, and a form of permissiveness that accepted the right of others to enjoy their lives as they saw fit. The result was described by one astute observer as a "nation of peace in the midst of cacophony," whose three greatest pleasures centered about food in any form, sex, and the drama. As a people, they were all natural actors and posturers. They were either trying to "make face" in order to put themselves in a good light, or privately relishing their performances before an audience. The often repeated Western expression, "the inscrutable East," had little to do with true inscrutability. It was no more nor less than an ability to perform in a poker face manner. All the philosophical dissertations on peace, quiet, the cadence of an ordered life, and contemplation are automatically refuted by the bedlam of China's history, rife with war, rebellion, aggrandizement, enslavement, and cruelty that matches that of any other people on earth.

The elegant residents of the Forbidden City enjoyed the drama as much as did the humble tradesmen of the cities and the cotton-clad peasants of the villages. Dramatic entertainments in the palace-city, to ensure an air of make-believe, had to outshine the color and magnificence of the court itself. The costumes were a riot of blazing shades and required the use of vast quantities of gorgeous fabrics and extravagant designs. The Prince Charmings and the generals of the imperial stage wore velvet suits of armor, stiff with gold embroidery and studded with beautifully wrought glass medallions. Their helmets were adorned with trailing plumes and the long tail feathers of pheasants, which rippled and waved as the actors battled each other in exaggerated ballet manner. Buddhist priests wore patchwork robes glistening with gold. The ordinary garb of lamas was glitteringly transformed. Even the meanest beggar was dressed in finest silk. Warriors and judges were fearsomely bearded below their vividly painted faces. And the "ladies"—whose roles were always played by men—were given cheeks of peach-blossom freshness and wigs of graceful braids or coils, bedecked with flowers and jewels.

The performance of a play might last all through one day and well into the next, or a series of short plays might follow one another from early morning to late afternoon. At great festivals some theatricals lasted for several days. The regular troupe of palace actors was made up of eunuchs; but occasionally performers from the city were commanded to appear at the Great Theater.

When Tz'u Hsi attended the theater with the emperor, she sat in a large yellow chair and he on a stool at her left. The empress, secondary consorts, princesses and ladies in waiting were grouped around them in a bright splash of color. Once the dowager and the sovereign had seated themselves, the principal actors moved to the front of the stage. They all made a deep obeisance and opened the play with an introductory poem in praise of their Majesties, after which they started the first act. If Tz'u Hsi and her nephew were pleased with the performance, they "applauded" by repeating the expression for "good" twice. This signal commanded all members of the Court to join in the acclamation— whether they liked the performance or not. Neither the old lady nor the powerless emperor ever stayed for an entire play; nor did they bother to give their undivided attention to the stage, but often held informal audiences in the royal loge. And while the drama was in full swing, they usually settled down to the midday meal that was served.

Miss Katherine Carl, an American who painted a portrait of the old dowager, which was exhibited at the St. Louis Exposition of 1904, wrote the following account of her experience as a guest at a theater party in honor of the emperor's birthday:

> The eunuchs brought tables of sweetmeats to the veranda of the imperial loge, setting them before the young Empress, the princesses and ladies. There were pyramids of crystallized fruits, macedoines, nut pastes, almond creams and fresh fruit, all served with delicious Chinese wines. After this repast was finished, we were served a regular meal in the court of the theater.
>
> When the elders had finished eating, the children of the princes and nobles who had been invited to the festivities seated themselves at the tables. No one under sixteen years of age was allowed to sit with the adults at ceremonious palace dinners.
>
> When we had finished our luncheon, the ladies retired to their loge next to that of Their Majesties. The screen which hid the guests from the imperial party was removed by attending eunuchs, revealing the great princes and nobles in their splendid Court robes. The servants then passed refreshments consisting of slightly sweetened hot milk flavored with almonds.
>
> Following the removal of the bowls and dishes, an army of eunuchs entered the court in pairs, each of whom carried trays of imperial yellow decorated with the character for longevity in red. These contained the presents from the Emperor for every guest, for His Majesty gives as well as receives on his birthday. Each tray held a pair of porcelain vases from the imperial potteries, a bronze incense burner, a scroll with a quotation from the Classics, a jade scepter and an archer's ring. After the presentation of the gifts, the dividing screen was again placed between Their Majesties and their guests, and the theatrical performance resumed.
>
> At four o'clock, with the three superimposed stages all occupied by actors, the grand finale began with another hymn in praise of the Emperor. A pageant of floats representing mythical animals, Buddhas, fairies, personifications of the

higher attributes and gigantic fruits that opened to disclose figures symbolizing eternal beauty, perfect happiness and serene old age crowded on to the stages. The spectacular procession ended with an imperial dragon of huge proportions, attended by gorgeously costumed warriors and servants bearing banners and escutcheons, who finally stopped in the middle of the lowest platform to make obeisance to His Majesty.

At the end of the pageant, the screen was again removed and the glass doors of the imperial loge thrown open so that Her Majesty and the Emperor could be seen by all. The princes and nobles came forward in a body and, kneeling three times, bowed their heads to the ground nine times to express thanks for the entertainment they had been accorded. After the guests retired, the actors came to the front of the stage and performed the *k'o-t'ou* to Their Majesties.

The last gala performance at the Pavilion of Pleasant Sounds took place to celebrate the wedding of the boy-emperor in 1922—thirty-three plays presented on December 3, 4, and 5. This was the first time in many years that the Great Theater had been the scene of such a brilliant gathering. It was the last time, too, that all the guests arrived in full court dress—resplendent in satins, brocades, furs, jeweled chains of office, and peacock feathers—as if the days of the Manchu empire had not ended a decade before.

The enchantment of the Pavilion of Pleasant Sounds has long since vanished. Its decor and scenery have faded. Its orchestra is the whining sound of cold drafts sweeping across the dusty, deserted stages.

The Well of the Pearl Concubine

Throughout its more than five hundred years, the high walls and wide courts of the Forbidden City have hidden many tales of love, cruelty, triumph, and disaster beneath their stones and tiles—but none are more pathetic than the broken spirit of Chen Fei, called the Pearl Concubine, the beloved of the unhappy Emperor Kuang Hsu.

With her thirteen-year-old sister (the Lustrous Concubine), Chen Fei entered the palace as a secondary consort at the time of the young Emperor Kuang Hsu's wedding. His empress-bride was a niece of the Dowager Tz'u Hsi named Yung Lu—a cold young woman completely lacking in charm or vivacity, who harbored such an inordinate admiration for Tz'u Hsi that the whole pattern of her life was one of copying the older woman. Her cheerless disposition soon drove the sensitive bridegroom to the gay, sympathetic, and affectionate young Pearl—a fifteen-year-old who found ways to demonstrate her love of Kuang Hsu that his icy first consort could never have achieved. Since etiquette demanded that the young empress accompany the dowager on her frequent sojourns at the new Summer Palace, then being built, the carefree young lovers amused themselves happily in the Forbidden City and at the Sea Palaces, attended special theatrical performances, held picnics on the lakes, and shared frequent private suppers. This closeness was not overlooked by Tz'u Hsi, who received practically hourly reports of the lovers' activities. Concubines *could* be a threat—Tz'u Hsi had been one herself. On top of that, her own niece, Yung Lu, while not caring a whit for Kuang Hsu, nonetheless did not enjoy the emperor's flagrant preference for another. There was nothing that could be done about it, except keep a watchful eye on the Pearl—especially if she gave birth to a son. But the years slipped by, and though the Pearl bore no child, she held her place in the heart of the emperor.

Feeling sure of her position, the Pearl finally grew bolder, enlarging her activities by entering the political sphere through her brother's liberal young friend K'ang Yu-wei. When the Hundred Days of much needed reform came to a tragic end, and the emperor was banished to the Sea Palaces, the Pearl was forced to remain in the Forbidden City as an unworthy, outcast female. Not long after, she created an unpardonable scene by begging the aging dowager to spare Kuang Hsu from any further indignities. And not content with making the actual appeal, she had the temerity to point out that Kuang Hsu *was* the lawful sovereign —a reproach that stung the arrogant Tz'u Hsi to unforgiving anger and made her scream out in a burst of recrimination.

The Pearl was banished at once to a section of the palace-city where communication of any kind with the imprisoned emperor would be impossible. For the next two years she remained in disgrace and loneliness. Nevertheless, her eunuchs kept her informed of the Boxer movement, the siege of the legations, and the antiforeign policy of the throne. Gradually she concluded that the collision course against the Western powers would not only defeat the narrow objectives of the hard-headed Tz'u Hsi, but eventually the victorious Allied armies would lay the entire responsibility for the debacle on the shoulders of the old lady. On the evening of August 14, 1900, the Pearl learned that the foreign troops had entered Peking and that the empress dowager was in a grim conference with the only three members of the Grand Council who had not fled the capital. As she waited for more news, she was startled to hear the sound of weeping rising over the pavilions of the concubines. Then wild reports began to seep into the palace enclosure: many Chinese and Manchu ladies had thrown themselves into wells, terrified lest they be ravished by the barbarians.

About midnight the Pearl was summoned to Tz'u Hsi's apartments. For the first time in many months she saw her beloved emperor, pale from prison life, sullen, and powerless as ever in the hands of his enemies, the eunuchs. While the young empress busied herself, helping to hide her aunt's treasures in the secret grottoes, Tz'u Hsi was occupied with frantic last-minute instructions and preparations for departure. Then, while both the dowager and the empress were garbing themselves in the dress of peasants, the Pearl decided to make a last desperate appeal for the emperor. Throwing herself on her knees before the old dowager, she begged: "I dare suggest that His Majesty remain here. He has nothing to fear from the foreigners."

The dowager stopped short and glowered angrily at her. Possession of the emperor's person was her one hope: to bargain with the Allies to save her own life, to retain freedom and the power to which she had been long accustomed. If the Pearl were left behind and fell into the hands of the "Foreign devils," she could be dangerous, and doubly dangerous if permitted to accompany the imperial party into exile. She would be constantly with Kuang Hsu; she had courage where he did not; and anything might come of such a cabal.

Exactly how the Pearl met her fate was never officially disclosed by the few present at the time. The last act of the tragedy took place in a small courtyard leading to the Household Gate, by which the Dowager left the Forbidden City at dawn. Later the body of the unfortunate Pearl was found in a small, stone-curbed well. Of necessity, the decision as to her death was a hasty one. And since the grand eunuch Li Lien-ying was present, he and his assistants would have executed his mistress' command without the slightest compunction.

As time passed, several accounts of the Pearl's death emerged. One claimed that after the unhappy concubine had begged the dowager to leave the emperor behind, the old lady was so outraged she had ordered her thrown down the well at once. This was done while the young emperor, with a wretched, stricken face, stood helplessly watching. A eunuch who claimed to have been present told a slightly different story. The murder took place, he later stated, immediately after the last audience of the Grand Council. Having sent for the Pearl, Tz'u Hsi told her she was to be left behind, but that she could save her honor if she committed suicide by jumping down the well. As the kneeling girl rose to her feet, protesting she had committed no crime, her cries were smothered by shouts of: "Obey Her Majesty's command!" Then, at a sign from Tz'u Hsi, a eunuch seized the struggling victim, carried her screaming to the well, and stuffed her headfirst down its shaft—as the old lady grimly watched her death struggles.

Though an air of romantic mystery has shrouded the last moments of the Pearl Concubine, to anyone familiar with the characters of the Empress Dowager Tz'u Hsi and her chief eunuch, the only obvious conclusion was that the young woman was brutally murdered. She stood in the way of other plans and had to be eliminated. Since the Pearl had grown quite plump during the two lonely years of her exile, and since the well was too small even to permit the easy passage of a ten- or twelve-year-old child, Li Lien-ying and his eunuchs had had to use considerable brute force to carry out Tz'u Hsi's orders. After the occupation of the Forbidden City by foreign troops, the battered remains of the concubine were found and removed. Though there were few sources of water in the Great Within, the "Well of the Pearl"—being haunted by the Pearl's spirit—was never used after her death.

She was buried in the Western Tomb Enclosure in an unobtrusive grave, beside one that later held the remains of her imperial consort. With the passage of time a solitary cypress pushed the grave's crumbling bricks askew, as if to emphasize the pathos of her life and death. Years after her death, her sister, the Lustrous Concubine, in order to appease the Pearl's weeping ghost, erected a tiny shrine at the site of the murder.

Embarrassing stories of the Pearl's unfortunate end continued long after the return of the court from exile in the provinces. A troublesome aspect of the affair that the superstitious old dowager actually feared was that the angry spirits of the dead could be extremely vengeful—and this preyed on her mind. After many days of agitated consideration, an imperial edict awarded the Pearl a posthumous title and a promotion of one rank in recognition of her "virtuous conduct in committing suicide when she found herself unable to catch up with the court on its flight."

PART 7
The Western Section of the Palaces

THE APPROACHES

THE HALLS OF MARTIAL GRACE

THE IMPERIAL HOUSEHOLD DEPARTMENT

THE INNER COURTS OF THE WEST
The Palace of Peace and Compassion
The Garden of Dispossessed Favorites
The Great Buddha Hall
The Empress Dowager Tz'u An

THE TOWER OF RAINING FLOWERS

THE HALL OF THE NURTURE OF THE MIND

THE SMALLER PALACES OF THE WEST

THE APPROACHES

Identical in size to the eastern section of the Forbidden City, the western section was devoted to residential apartments, temples, the offices of the Household Department, numerous storehouses, and quarters for the many thousands of eunuchs, maidservants, gardeners and sweepers—in short, all those who looked after the needs of the emperor's family.

The West Flowery Gate, a double-towered counterpart of the East Flowery Gate and overlooking a wide road leading to the Sea Palaces, was reserved almost entirely for the comings and goings of the imperial family. Balancing the Halls of Literature and Learning in the eastern section, the Halls of Martial Grace faced an open, parklike expanse between the Meridian Gate and the southwest Corner Tower. Behind them were many small, unpretentious buildings that housed the palace workshops and the offices of the Household Department, and the south garden of the residential apartments. The garden was a charming, private retreat, with a gently flowing stream, gracefully arched bridges, pavilions, and tree-bowered shrines.

Separated by a "street" and protected by high walls with few gates, the great Western Palace consisted of many enclosures, small halls, towers, gardens, courts, and residential palaces. When the emperor's family was large, as during the reigns of K'ang Hsi and Ch'ien Lung, the entire area was crowded with consorts and imperial children. Later, sections were either closed off or buildings used as storehouses for the vast accumulated treasures.

Adjacent to the western and northern ramparts of the Forbidden City, and secluded from the residential apartments by high walls, were the food storehouses, the kitchens, a few stables, the Punishment and Mourning Palaces, and the West Flower Garden. Between them and the Imperial Rest Garden was a small two-storied theater, built in the early Manchu period and antedating the Great Theater by more than a century.

A nearby residential palace, called the Hall of the Nurture of the Mind, was used by the last three Manchu emperors during their minorities. The empress of P'u Yi, the boy-emperor, lived in the adjoining group of buildings to the north, and his secondary consort in a series of apartments to the west. As their complicated arrangement afforded great privacy to their inhabitants, these were the traditional living quarters for concubines of high rank.

The deep tunnels of the Gate of Spiritual Valor, with its flanking guardrooms, gave entrance to the palace-city for all supplies, servants, and eunuchs. The emperors used this busy portal only when they visited the enclosure of Coal Hill and the nearby pleasure palaces of the Northern Sea. A part of these great gardens were once Kublai Khan's—and of such beauty that they were immortalized by the pen of Marco Polo. However, the north gate was one of ill omen: it witnessed the ignominious flights of the last emperors of both the Ming and Manchu dynasties.

The original northern lake of the Sea Palaces had been created by Kublai Khan in the twelfth century, and the Ming Emperor Yung Lo expanded it to include two additional bodies of water. Fed by the clear springs of the Jade Fountain and called the Pools of Great Fertilizing Spume, their waters reputedly partook of the male and female principles, Yin and Yang. Pavilions, palaces, gardens, and terraces made the entire park a fairyland of rare beauty. There the emperors, their families, and guests relaxed in a walled sylvan setting, completely surrounded by the teeming city, yet shut away in privacy.

A fanciful, poetic quality characterized many of the landmarks. The Pavilion of Perpetual Southern Melodies was erected in memory of the legendary Emperor Shun (2317-2208 B.C.), who invented the five-stringed lute and composed many songs of the south.

In a grove of mulberry trees at the Altar of Silkworms, the empress and her ladies offered annual sacrifice to the goddess of sericulture—a function as important to women as the sacrifices at the Altar of Agriculture were to men. According to the *Book of Poetry*, the cultivation of the mulberry tree and the manufacture of silk were discovered in 2602 B.C. by Hsi Ling, the wife of the legendary Huang Ti. Whether or not this origin is correct—which is doubtful—records of 782 B.C. indicate that silk culture and the connected development of the mulberry tree were well established at the time.

THE HALLS OF MARTIAL GRACE

(THE IMPERIAL TREASURE STOREHOUSES)

Adjacent to a tree-shaded park, the Halls of Martial Grace reared their lacquered pillars and yellow roofs above an I-shaped, white marble connecting terrace. The twin halls escaped the conflagration that marked the defeat and flight of Li Tzu-ch'eng at the fall of the Ming Dynasty. It was in these beautiful old buildings that Li proclaimed himself emperor and founder of what he called the Ta Shun dynasty, which lasted for less than forty-eight hours. It was also there that the victorious Manchu regent, Prince Jui, gave his first audience to the remnants of the conquered Ming dynasty. But aside from these two episodes, the twin structures, despite their name, had few associations with the military aspects of the imperial court.

Martial displays and receptions traditionally took place in the quadrangle before the huge Meridian Gate, which was outside the "threshold" of the Great Within. Since military demonstrations were never stressed within the palace-city, the name of these two halls was probably inspired by the Chinese love of balance, for they were placed opposite the Halls of Literature and Learning in the eastern section. The military complemented the civil, and the name merely represented an acknowledgment of the fact that good government was based on their harmonious adjustment. Though the halls were not concerned with glorifying leaders in battle, they were definitely associated with the spoils of war and the fruits of empire, for it was beneath their intricately coffered ceilings that the emperors stored and inspected their treasures.

In theory, and in accordance with their own personal attitudes, the wealth of the dynastic rulers of China consisted of all the lands, all of the people, and all of the riches of both. Their personal resources were composed of the national treasury in its entirety; their income, the accumulation of all taxes and tribute paid either in kind or in bullion. In other words, the emperors simply owned *everything*. They possessed an incredible fortune in gold and silver ingots in the treasure houses and unused wells of their ancient palace at Mukden; in Peking, a fabulous store of jewels and precious stones, and an enormous collection of works of art. Some of the treasures had been inherited from former dynasties. Much came from annual tribute and gifts. And much was specially ordered from the imperial factories. In addition, because of the inherent risk involved in shipping supplies over long distances, the huge granaries of Peking, as well as those of the provincial capitals, were maintained and replenished with each harvest.

The Ming emperors were not only avid collectors of art, but frequently artists themselves, and they took an intense interest in adding to this hoard of wealth. In one year, for example, the Emperor Wan Li ordered 26,350 bowls, with saucers to match, 6,000 pitchers, 6,500 wine cups, and 680 fish bowls, all at a cost that today would run well over two million dollars.

Throughout the Forbidden City there were bulging storehouses. Some were specially constructed to withstand dampness and vermin. Others were mere side rooms in the larger courts and seldom-used palaces. In addition to the hundreds of tons of daily household supplies, so many articles of necessity or ornament were in constant use, and so many in storage, that no emperor—not even the watchful Ch'ien Lung —ever knew the extent of his valuables. Pictures, like clothes, were changed according to seasons; porcelains and bronzes were rotated to suit the ceremonies they enhanced.

The storehouses in the Halls of Martial Grace were formally opened on such special occasions as the raising of a consort to the rank of empress, the birth of a prince, the celebration of a birthday feast, or an imperial wedding. At the New Year, when presents from the emperor were given to everyone at court and to all high officials throughout the provinces and vassal states, the treasure rooms were raided.

Should His Majesty wish to make a gift of furs, hundreds of crosses (unmade fur robes) or separate skins would be brought from their special storehouse for his inspection—rich Manchurian and Siberian pelts of red, silver, black, and white fox, gray squirrel, dark and lustrous sable, priceless sea otter, the softest ermine, heavy bear, and splendid tiger skins. On other occasions he might choose to examine his pearls and jade, as did Emperor Kuang Hsu when he ordered a cape of pearls for the Pearl

Concubine. The sealed doors that guarded the brocades, silks, and satins from Soochow, Nanking, and Hangchow were the most frequently opened.

When the Son of Heaven visited his treasures, scarlet-robed eunuchs of the Presence spread the silks and satins, or displayed deep-glazed potteries and delicately designed porcelains, before a low throne for his inspection. When they unrolled the scroll paintings, they had to be careful not to scratch the silk or paper with their long fingernails. On occasion the emperor might be in search of something for his own wardrobe or to use at a great review—perhaps a new robe ornamented with a net of coral and ivory beads, or a new saddle cloth woven with gold thread, or a new set of embroidered cushions for a favorite throne chair. At times it was rare tea, and quite often special ink and paper for his verses and paintings.

In 1680 the Emperor K'ang Hsi established workshops within the Forbidden City for many of the crafts. He summoned skilled workers from all the provinces and set them to work on ceremonial scepters, glass in many forms, watches, clocks, cloisonné, enamels, lacquers, carved jades and ivories, gold and silver filigree, lanterns, and the countless trifles the court desired. These "factories" continued to operate for over a century, but were finally closed one by one, as the artistic ambitions of succeeding emperors waned. The last to remain open was a studio where a corps of artists was kept constantly at work until the last days of the Manchus. These artists produced portraits of the imperial family, which were hung in a special hall used in connection with the ancestral rites. They also decorated lanterns for the halls and festivals, fans for use in the palace, and gift scrolls for those whom the sovereign chose to honor. Tz'u Hsi employed eighteen court painters divided into three groups—each team of six on duty at the palace for ten days out of every month. In addition to their artistic tasks, they also acted as art instructors for the emperor's ladies and children.

At the elaborate inventories of palace treasures, the court officials in charge of the storehouses were held directly responsible for the contents —or for what they were *supposed* to contain. But many valuables existed only on paper, and their disappearance or theft could never be explained. During the last three reigns of the Manchu dynasty, the losses were staggering. Great was the consternation when the boy-emperor began to call for certain pieces chosen at random from the lists. Those in charge panicked. They not only feared that they would be held to account for their own peculations, but for those of their predecessors and their subordinates as well. Though they hedged and procrastinated, P'u Yi persisted, and cases that had been in storage for decades, containing tribute from long-forgotten vassal princes and gifts from long-deceased viceroys, were unearthed. The emperor soon found innumerable discrepancies between what was in the storehouses and what appeared on the inventories; and in anger and indignation he announced he would make a personal inspection of the treasure houses, the first to be the Palace of Established Happiness in the northwest quarter. In order to hide their wholesale thefts, the eunuch guardians set the halls of this palace afire a few days before the appointed time of the imperial inspection, and they were completely destroyed. The apartments of the empress would have suffered the same fate had not the fire brigade of the Italian legation arrived promptly at the scene.

According to the inventories, great quantities of irreplaceable works of art were lost or ruined in the fire: twenty-five hundred gold images of Buddha, more than a thousand paintings of Buddha, fifteen hundred gold altar vessels and ornaments, four hundred pieces of porcelain, bronze, and jade, many of which were from the Chou, T'ang, Sung, and Yuan dynasties, an uncounted number of books, boxes of sables, and ceremonial robes.

Shortly after P'u Yi's marriage in 1922, the treasures of the Forbidden City were rather casually estimated to be worth fifty million American dollars. Some seventy thousand items at the Jehol and Mukden palaces were at the same time valued at a mere one and a half million dollars—for their number and known quality, a ridiculously low figure. The great store of gold and silver ingots that had been laid aside by prudent emperors and empresses had completely vanished.

More serious attempts have been made to estimate the worth of the imperial treasure at the height of the Emperor Ch'ien Lung's reign—the mid-eighteenth century—prior to the rampant thefts of the eunuchs; but all such efforts have proven impossible. What figure can approximate the value of one of the greatest libraries in the world of the eighteenth century? Or the most fabulous collection of jade, jewels, gold, and silver that has ever been assembled? Of brocades, porcelains, paintings, and bronzes so perfect in quality they can never be duplicated? The imperial treasure of that opulent period really had no value, because—being beyond all value—it represented the synonym of the word "priceless."

After P'u Yi's abdication in 1912, the Three Great Throne Halls and the Halls of Martial Grace were nationalized and reserved as a museum by the Republic. The Halls of Literary Glory housed the Mukden and Jehol collections—"on loan" from the imperial family. Since the vast collection was too extensive to be displayed in its entirety, a Western-type brick structure was erected near the old Ming buildings. Finally, in 1924, when the emperor was driven from the Inner Courts by the "Christian" warlord Feng Yu-hsiang, many more priceless objects were lost.

Following the expulsion of P'u Yi and the last of his family, a carefully selected government commission spent several years working on an inventory and a many-volumed catalogue of the remaining treasures in the Forbidden City. In the collection at that time were over one hundred thousand pieces of carved jade, including the two great blocks representing the Mountain of Longevity and the Ocean of Happiness. Among the enormous accumulation of bronzes was one piece known as the Nation's Honor, which had been cast in the Chou dynasty. There were innumerable fine paintings from every dynastic period since A.D. 600, and some that were ascribed to the Han dynasty. The extent of the hoard of porcelains and potteries was incredible, dating from before 600: rare unique T'ang and Sung pieces, exquisite blue and white Ming vases and wine cups, and a great number of perfect monochromes and polychromes from the Manchu period. Added to the above were thousands of carved ivories, works in lacquer, literally mile after mile of tapestries and brocades, ancient weapons and musical instruments, jewel trees of semiprecious stones and jade, and countless historical items.

In 1933, a few years after the seizure of Manchuria by the Japanese army, the Chinese government decided to move the finest items of the imperial treasure to Nanking for safekeeping. The waggish gossips of the teahouses dubbed this operation the "loot of Peking"—and with considerable justification. Not only did priceless pieces unaccountably become the property of the wives of highly placed officials, but many works of art soon went up for sale in the protected markets of the foreign-controlled cities of Shanghai and Hong Kong. However, enough of the vast collection remained intact to provide the great London Exhibit of 1935 with the greatest display of Chinese treasures ever shown in the Western world.

Today, what little of the imperial collection may remain, the former palace-city of the emperors of China can serve only as an unappreciated background for official receptions of the present Communist government.

THE IMPERIAL HOUSEHOLD DEPARTMENT

Behind the Halls of Martial Grace are the long, narrow office buildings of the imperial Household Department; though roofed with yellow tiles, they are without architectural distinction of any kind.

During the Ming dynasty the entire palace staff consisted of eunuchs —from the controller of the imperial household and the captain of the imperial bodyguard down to the lowest menials in the kitchens and the stables.

When the Manchus seized the throne, they looked upon the eunuch corps with a distaste and distrust to be expected from any vigorous military people. Hence, the first regent appointed a prince of high rank and proved loyalty as controller general. He was assisted by six assessors, all either kinsmen or nobles, who directed the multiple activities of the Household Department.

Under the reorganization the head office was divided into seven principal departments. One supervised the privy purse; another the bullion and jewel storehouses; a third the collection and storage of tea, rice, spices, medicines, silks, furs, porcelains, and the buttery; a fourth, in charge of the Office of Worship and Ceremonials, made all arrangements for sacrifices and—rather curiously—operated the fruit office; a fifth, head of the Pasturage Department, supervised the flocks and herds for palace use and for sacrifices; the sixth managed the imperial stud; and the seventh was in charge of building, construction, and repairs. Among the many subdivisions were the office of the imperial bodyguard, which managed the properties of the Banner troops and collected their rents, a division that controlled the bondsmen (mostly gardeners, sweepers, and maidservants); and a special department that ran the operation of the eunuch corps and its many activities.

The senior heads of the Household Department accompanied the emperor whenever he left the palace; attended imperial ladies on excursions to the Sea Palaces or on rare visits to their families; directed the management of the living quarters; and supervised the education of His Majesty's younger children, and saw to it that designated officials—including themselves—were in attendance at all sacrifices. They also arranged for all banquets, festivals, and the daily supplies required by the vast household. At the height of Manchu power the palace population consisted of over ten thousand people: nearly a hundred in the imperial family itself, between two and three thousand guards, as many as six thousand eunuchs, and over two thousand maids, sweepers, and gardeners.

Every individual living in the palace was granted a food ration appropriate to his rank and dignity. Each day the emperor was entitled to thirty pounds of meat, one and one-third pounds of "hog's fat and butter each," two sheep, two fowls, two ducks, the milk of eighty cows, and seventy-five parcels of tea. The empress received twenty-one pounds of meat on platters and thirteen pounds boiled with vegetables, one fowl, one duck, twelve pitchers of water, the milk of twenty-five cows, and ten parcels of tea. Though the Emperor Ch'ien Lung complained that every egg he ate cost several ounces of silver, profiteering on food during his reign was slight compared to that in later reigns.

The Emperor Tao Kuang, annoyed by the huge expenses of the palace, once strenuously objected to the cost of his favorite noodle soup, which his eunuchs had persuaded him was obtainable only from one restaurant in Peking at forty coppers the bowl (several U.S. dollars). In fact, the soup was a common dish—available for a few coppers at any restaurant—and was, in any case, prepared for the emperor in the palace kitchens, most of the forty coppers being squeeze. Seeing an opportunity for graft on a truly royal scale, the eunuchs told His Majesty that in order to make the soup in the Forbidden City it would be necessary to build a special kitchen at a cost of six hundred thousand ounces of silver and that its upkeep would amount to fifteen thousand ounces a year.

"Order it from the restaurant at forty coppers!" the emperor directed.

Miffed at the loss of such potential graft and in order to spite their master, the eunuchs told the empeor that the "one restaurant" in Peking had closed and that its proprietor had gone out of business. The penurious Tao Kuang sighed in resignation and did without his soup, as did the eunuchs without their squeeze.

A tin of English biscuits, procured by the eunuchs at the only foreign store in Peking before 1900, cost Tz'u Hsi twenty ounces of silver; "Fruits of glory"—eggs poached in chicken broth—to which the dowager was very partial, cost twenty-four ounces of silver in Her Majesty's accounts. But she merely shrugged her shoulders, knowing only too well that to deprive herself of these delicacies would simply transfer the squeeze to other items. When outrageously cheated on the elaborate theatricals at the Pavilion of Pleasant Sounds, where the accounts for a single entertainment might be so flagrantly padded as to absorb the annual revenues from an entire province, she raised a cynical brow and shrugged again. The tax collectors would soon refill her coffers with the hoard of gold they constantly extracted from the people, so why bother?

The only foreign shop permitted to operate during the era of the aging Tz'u Hsi was the popular Kierwulf's Store on Legation Street, which carried a wide assortment of tinned delicacies, mechanical toys, clocks, and odds and ends of Western manufacture. It was always crowded with dignified, gorgeously robed Manchu and Mongol princes, accompanied by their shyly tittering concubines, eunuchs, and retainers. They wandered about the shop in naive fascination, delightedly purchasing every mechanical toy that struck their fancy.

Tz'u Hsi's attitude toward taxes was carried on by those who followed her in authority with the establishment of the Republic. In 1937 and 1938, in order to ensure that his treasury—and his own pockets—would never be empty, the warlord governor of Szechwan province had collected local taxes for thirty-five years in advance. Another of his ilk, the semi-independent Han Fu-ch'u of Shantung, who was spoken of as a "good governor," demonstrated his paternalism by only demanding taxes for a mere four years in advance.

During the Manchu dynasty it was the duty of high officials of the Household Department—and in their interest—to prevent all peculations from palace accounts. Being aliens, they would be certain to share in the emperor's collapse. But instead, the short-sighted Manchu officials helped themselves generously at all opportunities, and Chinese officials and eunuchs never had any scruples about robbing their foreign overlords. The thought of true service and high principles was usually subordinate—though not always so—to personal aggrandizement.

The Household Department supervised the palace eunuchs, who were divided into forty-eight grades and classes. The eunuchs of the Presence, who served the emperor, were the highest. Having achieved court rank, they had the greatest opportunities for squeeze. The attendants of the empress were next in rank, followed by those who served the secondary consorts and concubines. One of the principal duties of the senior eunuchs was to preserve order and discipline among their subordinates. Since infractions were punished by beatings, a yellow silk bag containing bamboo whipping rods always accompanied the court when it traveled. Legions of lamas, actors, tailors, gardeners, footmen, and chair bearers made up this semimilitary organization of emasculated men, each class of which was distinguished by its own uniform.

The eunuchs of the Manchu court received a bonus of five ounces of silver on entering palace service. Their usual starting wage was one ounce a month and was increased annually.

They could ask and be sure of receiving assistance in time of need. If a grandfather died, they were granted an allowance of at least ten ounces of silver to help defray funeral expenses; if a brother, only five ounces. When a eunuch died on duty, his funeral was paid for by the palace treasury.

Among the duties of the chief eunuch was that of supervising the maids, the pretty young girls who waited on the empress and her ladies. He paid their wages, and when they left the palace to marry, provided them with a proper dowry of clothes, ornaments, and a present of money.

Under the feminine regencies during the last fifty years of the dynasty, the eunuchs regained most of the power and consequence they lost with the fall of the Ming dynasty. Their rapacity got so completely out of hand toward the end of the boy-emperor's residence in the Forbidden City, that after the disastrous fire which destroyed the Palace of Established Happiness, he decided to dismiss the entire corps. At the time of his abdication in 1912, the number of eunuchs had been reduced to one thousand.

Since it was feared the eunuchs might avenge their dismissal by burning or looting the palaces, they were expelled from the precincts with no prior notice by a well-disciplined unit of Nationalist troops who accomplished the orderly dispersal of all but fifty. These were retainers of the three surviving concubines of the two preceding emperors—fat old ladies spoiled by lives of luxurious idleness who pleaded that they simply could not live without the servants who knew their ways so well. When one of these old has-beens died in October, 1924, her attendants took merciless advantage of the situation by stealing all her effects.

After the departure of the eunuchs, it was found that the deplorable state of the imperial treasury was not entirely their doing. The incompetence of Manchu officials in charge was an important contributory factor. For almost a century the Household Department, many of whose members could scarcely read, write, or add a column of figures, had muddled along in hopeless ignorance. Despising accounts of any kind, the Manchu princes were at the mercy of stewards even in their own homes. They seldom deigned to ask about the state of their personal affairs. As long as they could depend on cash grants from the imperial coffers and huge allowances of rice and grain from the granaries, they deceived themselves into believing that their lives would continue to run in the same well-worn channels as at the time of the conquest.

This same attitude of distaste and ignorance toward commerce pervaded the Household Department, as its fumbling Manchu administration went from bad to worse and as the reckless greed of lesser officials steadily increased.

THE INNER COURTS OF THE WEST

The Palace of Peace and Compassion

The Palace of Peace and Compassion was the private home of every Manchu emperor's family; it was, therefore, a place to be treated with dignity and respect. The domain of the emperor's mother, his wives, consorts, and younger children, the palace buildings were secluded behind high, rose-colored walls inset with yellow and green medallions. Having escaped the disastrous fires at the fall of the Ming Dynasty, the main structures retained a grace and lightness not characteristic of the heavy Manchu hand despite the fact that palace records indicate it was either rebuilt or completely renovated in 1653.

A pair of six-foot-high bronze mythical beasts—half lion, half dog, with winglike projections on head and back—stood guard on marble pedestals at the outer portals of the palace, alert and ready to spring to the defense of the women and children who dwelt within. "Only the pure in heart could pass their fiercely bulging eyes without faltering." Beyond the gate the main hall of the household courts loomed in pillared dignity above conventional, white marble terraces, and a "spirit staircase." Great bronze incense burners, sundials, a pair of handsome cranes, and huge vats for burning oil marked its exalted position among all the buildings of the Inner Courts of the West. Flanked by side structures and gates, the eaves of its yellow-tiled, double roofs supported processions of decorative animals and high finials. These proclaimed that the female world of the palace-city was no less important than the all-male Palace of Cloudless Heaven.

The interior was frescoed with a wide band of golden phoenixes encircling its rose-colored walls—the flying bird creatures of the empress replacing the dragon motif of the emperor's halls. When last redecorated by Ch'ien Lung for his mother, the massive beams and coffers of the painted ceiling were of multicolored patterns etched in gold, and the walls were hung with embroidered banners and long pendants.

On all formal occasions the empress dowager and the reigning empress presided over the prescribed rituals in this hall. When great ladies joined their ancestors, their earthly remains lay in state in the Palace of Peace and Compassion. There, imperial princes, amidst a throng of white-robed relatives and officials, offered wine and called upon the spirit of the departed one to absorb its essence.

During the Manchu period the formal decree announcing promotion to the rank of empress or empress dowager was presented in this hall, and for the first time, the wife or mother mounted the throne to receive the obeisance of her ladies. On the happy occasions of New Year receptions and imperial birthdays the great room was filled with the laughing chatter of little princes in tiger-face caps, tripping and stumbling about in the long, silken robes whose wide skirts entangled their pattering feet. When an empress-bride saluted her august mother-in-law for the first time, the walls seemed to echo her trembling fear. And when a princess of the blood departed the Forbidden City for a husband and a life outside its gates, the sadness of a permanent farewell filled the air. There were gayer moments, though. It was there that Father Ricci entertained the aging Wan Li, of porcelain fame, and his ladies with delicate melodies on his spinet. And there that the court eunuchs, confused and bewildered, were given lessons on how to finger the ivory keys so that they, too, could amuse their master with its strange foreign music.

During the Emperor K'ang Hsi's long reign, there were numerous palace ladies. Their virile master had a roving eye, a liking for variety, and passionate urges. In addition to his empress, there were as many as fifty ladies at any one time—consorts of the first order, and concubines of the second, third, fourth and fifth ranks. But despite the emperor's insatiable desire for nocturnal delights, some concubines did not succeed in attracting his attention and soon became little more than handmaidens to his mother or to the empress. The empress dowager, the most important person throughout the Inner Courts, was a stern matriarch who ruled his ladies and guided his daughters until they reached marriageable age. Even the little princes did not escape her grandmotherly attention until they were old enough for lessons in the imperial schoolroom.

The first wife—the empress—who had shared the sovereign's nuptial wine, was always a young lady of quality, carefully reared, and fully conversant with court etiquette—as were his other senior consorts. However, the empress dowager was not necessarily of noble birth; she could be a former concubine of secondary rank. This was a circumstance that did not always make life easy for some of the more aristocratic empresses. It was hard to look up to one's mother-in-law, who attained and held her exalted position as mother of the palace only because she had given birth to the reigning Son of Heaven.

Because filial piety gave the mother great influence over her son, the empress dowager wielded enormous power. In a position to take revenge for petty slights and spites, her whims often controlled the careers of all other palace ladies. If beauty, charm, intelligence, and worldly wisdom were helpful to newly arrived concubines, a timely bribe to a powerful eunuch close to the old dowager could be a much quicker path to success.

Filial piety prescribed that the young empress serve her haughty mother-in-law like a loving daughter. That meant, among other things, that she accompany her on all excursions outside the Forbidden City. It was a tense and restricted life for many unless they were the dowager's favorites. Because the Dowager could award promotions and order punishments, two Manchu empresses were demoted by their mothers-in-law to the rank of concubine. Until death relieved her of subjugation, Ch'ien Lung's first empress was at the mercy of his spoiled mother's whims for thirteen years. His second wife was degraded because the old lady indulged herself in selfish annoyance and took it out on the helpless young empress. After his abdication, the first wife of his successor Chia Ch'ing was luckily without the iron demands of a dowager. A year later she died and was succeeded by the daughter of a Manchu noble of the first class, who became a dowager herself and lived to a great age.

On one occasion, the young Emperor Kuang Hsu violated the sacrosanct privileges of the Dowager Tz'u Hsi by attempting to defy her selection of his secondary consorts. This event occurred in the throne hall of the Palace of Peace and Compassion, already festive with decorations for his approaching wedding. Surrounded by all the senior ladies of the court and the eunuchs of the Presence, Tz'u Hsi, with young Kuang Hsu on a stool at her side, accepted the obeisances of the young girls as each was presented in accordance with her previously determined rank. On a table before the dowager's throne lay a gold filigree scepter inlaid with jade, which would honor the maiden chosen as the first consort. There were also two brocaded red purses in the shape of lotus leaves for the next two in rank. Turning to the Emperor Kuang Hsu, Tz'u Hsi handed him the scepter and said: "Present this to your first choice."

With the proper degree of self-deprecating formality, he replied in the prescribed manner: "I would not dare! This is a very delicate matter. I beg my august mother to decide for me."

In accordance with court etiquette, she then insisted he make his own choice—since this public exchange of exaggerated but hollow courtesy was expected.

Knowing that the ladies had already been placed in line as befitted their birth and new rank at court, Kuang Hsu deliberately offered the scepter to the second girl. Shocked at her nephew's utter disregard of proper convention, and smarting under the deliberate rudeness, Tz'u Hsi called out sharply, "Your Majesty!"

As the emperor hesitated, she indicated the first lady with a peremptory gesture. Then, fearing he might repeat a similar violation and complicate the future with his preferences, she brusquely ordered him to hand the lotus purses to the third and fourth girls, completely passing up his choice of the second, who was later relegated to a low rank of concubine. Thus the sisters—the Pearl and the Lustrous concubines—received unexpected promotions.

On this occasion the dowager was within her rights. While the em-

peror saw his ladies only when he wished, they were in constant attendance on the mother of the palace. It was considered proper that she
should say whom she would or would not have about her. Therefore, his
personal preference was not only rude but ill-advised. The matter of love
or affection on his part was inconsequential and actually beneath the
dignity of a true Son of Heaven. His only duty to his consorts was to sire
sons; theirs, to respond, regardless of their feelings.

The long, low buildings extending northward to join the Great Buddha Hall were the "warm rooms," heated by a system of flues under a
raised platform. On the bitter winter days, when the northwest wind
swept through the courts, these rooms were colorful and teeming with
court ladies and their eunuchs. As a lonely old man, the Emperor K'ang
Hsi frequently lingered there to warm his chilled bones. But there was
no real peace for him anywhere in the palace. His sons and their various
ambitious mothers were involved in such deep intrigues for the succession that he feared for his life and seldom slept two nights in the same
apartment.

A separate enclosure of this palace group contained three south-facing
pavilions, each with its small, private court. These and the quarters in the
adjacent Palace of Vigorous Old Age were the main residential apartments of the Palace of Peace and Compassion. Space was allotted with
great care and in accordance with the rank and age of the occupants.
Senior ladies were given preference, and newcomers often shared apartments with as many as four or five others. However, mothers of young
children—even of low rank—received adequate quarters for their needs.
It was rare, indeed, when a few princely moppets did not rule these
household courts in their own arrogant fashion. Like most Chinese fathers, the emperor was usually an affectionate parent who delighted in
playing with his children and took a keen interest in the education of his
sons.

The petted and pampered little princesses learned to read and write,
to paint and embroider. When they grew older, they were given the
choice of marrying a Manchu nobleman or a Mongol prince. If they
chose a Manchu, they lost their imperial rank; if a Mongol, they retained
it, but were exiled for life to a crude and harsh land. Both the Ming and
Manchu emperors gave the husbands of their daughters and nieces special titles. The man who married the emperor's daughter by his empress

could wear two four-clawed dragons in profile embroidered on his court robes; if he married a daughter by a concubine, he was entitled to wear one four-clawed dragon, the insignia showing kinship to the imperial house.

The Garden of Dispossessed Favorites

To childless, middle-aged ladies, life in the Inner Court was a dreary succession of days, weeks, months—even years. The emperors never rid themselves of senior women by bestowing them on high officials, as was done at other Oriental courts. In China the fact that she had shared the bed of the Son of Heaven and, therefore, a measure of his godhead, set her apart as one whose body could never be sullied by another man. Though childless concubines of the lowest rank were sometimes returned to their families after the age of twenty-five, the the higher ranking ladies were never allowed this happy release from boredom. They were doomed to a lingering, monotonous life of virtue and piety, listening to the meaningless chants of interminable masses and spending endless hours in meditation before shrines.

Day after day they wandered listlessly in the spacious South Garden, better and more aptly known as the Garden of Dispossessed Favorites. No doubt they had seen its exquisite loveliness so many times that they became blind to its appealing beauty. The altars of the largest shrine were elaborate, canopied with intricately carved and gilded lotus petals; the frescoed walls were brilliant with color. The walls were permeated with the scent of burning incense that was destined to last for centuries, and the bronze wind bells gently tolled with each fitful breeze. Once in a while an unhappy woman might set her gaze on the stately white pines standing proudly near the gateway, thrusting their dark foliage high above the other trees. Native only to China, the bark of these trees, like the hair of the aged, turns a pale, silvery gray after fifty years of growth. But at best that was a prophetic and depressing sight, as were the fragrant, pink blossoms of the catalpa tree, from whose wood the palace coffins ("longevity boards") were made. The great magnolias, with their glossy leaves and early blossoming flowers, provided some pleasure and distraction: in the autumn, when their flailed branches became mere sticks, the bored women set themselves busily to work making silken replicas of the real blossoms, which they fastened to the naked limbs to create the illusion of a second spring. There was little else for the "discarded ladies" to do but stroll about, staring unseeing at the garden with its many shrines.

Until after the fall of the Manchu dynasty, the halls of the main building in the garden and its twin, two-storied temples contained a complete pantheon of eight hundred bronze images, each standing solemnly in its own framed niche. A great rarity outside Tibet, the images were cast in the eighteenth century by order of the Emperor Ch'ien Lung. Hooded lamas of gold smiled faintly from behind tables that held gilt incense burners, candlesticks, and vases adorned with stylized lotus petals and flowers. The shrines of the upper stories were surrounded with frescoes of Tibetan deities so menacing in design that all transgressors were frightened back to the paths of righteousness. Thin curtains, aglitter with semiprecious stones, jade, coral, lapis lazuli, and ivory beads, hung before their threatening figures. Filling the recessed cupboards in all this grisly elegance were rich, priestly vestments of red, mulberry, and orange brocade, scepters shaped like thunderbolts, drums, and votive cups made of human skulls.

In the Tower of Auspicious Clouds the tiny faces of ten thousand images of Buddha, made with a special claylike dirt from Tibet, gazed down without expression on the bowed heads of the dispossessed favorites. A nearby garden shrine contained an image surrounded with the eight treasured symbols of those who followed Buddhist laws. In another, spanning a marble pool facing a terrace of peonies, a gentle Buddha seemed to listen for the ripple of water in an unseen stream beneath. This was a favorite device of Chinese landscape gardeners who wished to surprise unsuspecting visitors with the murmuring sound of a hidden brook.

These forgotten ladies had daydreams, of course, wandering around, half listening to chants, praying before shrines; the present was dead, but the past—which was all they had to sustain them—often must have come alive in their minds. Long ago scenes of happier times surely passed like bright, silken streamers though their thoughts: childhood joys, fond parents, family celebrations, laughter, girlhood chatter, and that radiant moment when they stood trembling before the empress dowager, waiting for the emperor to drop the blue silk handkerchief at their feet—a signal that they had been chosen to live, however briefly, in the sunshine of his presence. And what sunshine that had been! Those glorious weeks at the great Summer Palace of Jehol! Fluttering about the emperor as he gaily walked here and there in the hillside gardens! Boating on the lakes! Informal picnics in the pine-shaded parks! And with the autumn hunting season about to begin, prostrating themselves before the shrines of the Potala, praying they might accompany His Majesty and his thirty thousand troops as they pushed far out on the Mongolian plains in search of game of all kinds. Some had been chosen—his favorites, of course—but for those left behind there was always another season ahead and another chance. But somehow they had missed the great chance. And here they were, ending their lives amidst the gloomy trees and shrines—once lovely girls grown sallow and drawn, frustrated by idleness and hopeless boredom, grown fat from overeating.

How had it all come about? Once every three years the eligible daughters of all Manchu Bannermen were commanded to present themselves at the office of the Imperial Household Department. Those whose qualifications and personalities proved satisfactory were then introduced to the empress dowager. Only she could admit a young girl to the palace family. Selection brought honor to maiden and her parents. If the girl later bore a son, she might wield great power and attain high rank. At the palace, as the young maidens waited with downcast eyes before the empress dowager, the first act in what was often a long, drawn-out tragedy began. From that day on, it was by special imperial decree only that a chosen girl could revisit her home. However, on one occasion her mother could enter the Inner Court, for the dynastic house law provided that if a daughter was about to bear a child, her maternal parent could be with her at the time of the birth. But even this concession was far from satisfactory. Mother and daughter could never be alone: a eunuch had to be in constant attendance, as eunuchs were responsible for the welfare of all imperial consorts.

After the child was born, the emperor was notified by the registry office and asked to choose a name for the infant. This he did, but only after consulting with the court astrologers. The name had to be appropriate, auspicious, and preceded by the distinguishing character of the child's generation. The latter requirement was in accordance with a dynastic law promulgated by the Emperor K'ang Hsi. It was he who had chosen the designation by which each of the succeeding generations of his family should be named. Therefore, his sons were all given the generation name Hsuen. His grandsons and their cousins were given the generation name Yun. And the following generations were respectively, Hung, Yung, Mien, Yi, Ts'ai, Feng, and P'u. These arbitrary prefixes served the purpose of keeping an orderly record of sons of the same generation, who often overlapped in age. When the boy-emperor was born in 1906, his selected name was preceded by P'u, as were all imperial children of the same generation. He became known as P'u Yi, though his official reign title was Hsuan T'ung. K'ang Hsi prescribed prefix-designations only as far as the ninth generation, and one can speculate as to his vision, because the ninth generation was the last of his dynasty.

It was the duty of the Household Department to formally announce the birth of a child. The emperor then acknowledged his parenthood by commanding that its name be inscribed on a jade tablet. This was known as the jade spirit, and bore a record of the hour, day, month, and year of the birth, as well as the name of the mother, to whom the tablet was given for safekeeping.

The names of all the sovereign's ladies—first wife, secondary consorts, and concubines—were engraved on jade tablets and kept on a table near the entrance to his private apartment. Each day he chose his partner for the evening by turning face down the tablet on which was inscribed the name of the girl he desired. This was an unspoken order to the eunuch in attendance, who then hastened off to the chosen one, notifying her of the honor about to be bestowed upon her. At the proper time the girl—stripped naked—wrapped herself in a large yellow brocade quilt or cloth and was lifted onto the back of a eunuch, who trotted off with her to the emperor's apartment. She was then deposited at the foot of the emperor's couch. After the eunuch had left, she tossed the quilt aside and, now stark naked, crawled up beside the emperor, where she usually spent the entire night. Since "a nude woman carries no weapon save one," the safety of the Son of Heaven and his pleasure were assured. The visit was duly entered in the connubial record. The day and hour were noted, as was the exact time of the young consort's departure. A look at these records confirmed the legitimacy of any child she might bear.

Though the less important consorts were but twelve to fifteen years old when they entered the palace, the imperial bride was usually older than the emperor. Since few of the young girls had had much schooling, they were given lessons in painting, calligraphy, and the classics. Their tutors were required to sit behind a screen of black gauze, which hid the pupils from sight, but the young ladies could plainly see the written characters pressed against the thin curtain. A knowledge of court etiquette and of the seven forms of salutation was required of the girls, and the empress dowager kept a stern eye on their progress and behavior. Tz'u Hsi's senior lady in charge of instruction was given authority to raise or lower the status of the girls, and to degrade, humiliate, or even have them whipped by eunuchs.

Once a year the emperor visited a special hall in the grounds of Coal Hill to examine samples of needlework accomplished by the women of his household. The younger concubines awaited this day with excited eyes, flushed cheeks, and fluttering hearts. The pretty ones who had so far escaped the sovereign's attention hoped now to catch his eye, and the plain ones feverishly prayed that the delicacy of the flowery designs their soft little hands had achieved would make him see deeper than their homeliness. They did not always pray in vain. In a court that ordered the erection of splendid marble arches in memory of virtuous widows, goodness, intelligence, and talent were encouraged, and many noble hearts, though plain of face, found their way into the emperor's bed.

THE GREAT BUDDHA HALL

The interior of the Great Buddha Hall was a place of rich carvings, handsome brocades, satin hangings, and gold-lacquered images—a glorification in sumptuous beauty that exacted yet belied the simplicity of the life and philosophy of the god. The calm face of a great golden image of Buddha smiled from the center altar, its benign expression a contrast to the clutter of elegant cloisonné vessels, candlesticks, gorgeous brocade curtains, and six-foot-high, nine-storied pagodas of polished bronze. Against the walls, glowing with a thousand images of the teacher, stood life-sized statues of the eighteen lohans—the disciples of Buddha—each face reflecting the deep serenity of those who had found light and wisdom under the law.

For years the Emperor Ch'ien Lung had lavished fortunes in taxes on the ritual objects, which made this the most opulent of all the shrines of the Great Within. The eight treasures of the Laws of Buddha were carved in wood and heavily gilded to enhance the altars—the umbrella, the twin fish, the vase, the lotus, the conch shell, the mystic diagram, the banner and wheel, and the silver-toned bells and lacquered fish-head drums. High stemmed plates that held pagodas of cakes, fruit, and painted bread crowded the altar tables. Red candles of mutton fat flickered on images and walls, flaring high or casting their dim gleam on gold and bronze, on the multicolored satins of embroidered hangings and the thick kneeling cushions.

Buddhism had long been accepted as a spiritual refuge by the residents of the palace-city. Its philosophy of gentle tolerance infused a warmth into the chilly formality of court life, and its spiritual grace cheered many a lonely heart. The most humble of servants was as welcome as his imperial master to burn a stick of incense, tell his beads, and recite a chapter of the scriptures. The noblest of Buddhist gospels, with their abstract ideas and involved dialectic, were far beyond the understanding of many who knelt in quiet prayer before the altars. But "even the sound of good words is good," according to Buddha, and so the making of copies of the holy books was a work of great merit.

Centuries before the Forbidden City was built, the rational Chinese had rearranged Buddhist learning to suit their own needs and clothed its symbolic ideals with familiar human characteristics. In the villages, the dwellings of the gods, like those of the country folk, were humble; in the palaces, deities lived in halls as spacious as the emperor's. Eventually, the Buddhist gods came to resemble those that were indigenous to China, and they all reigned together in happy confusion. To place a pair of shoes beside a barefoot, sleeping Buddha for his use when he awakened was as natural as any Taoist ritual. Waves of religious fanaticism seldom embarrassed the relations between the gods. At times Confucians banded together to keep the Buddhist priesthood in its place or to curb the extravagant hocus-pocus into which Taoist doctrines so easily degenerated, and responsibility for the ancestral cult always rested in the hands of the rather sedate Confucian priests.

The Mongol dynasty had sponsored the young and vigorous cult of Tibet in preference to the purer and longer-established form of Chinese Buddhism. The red and henna robes of the lamas added a strident note to the already crude clash of colors at their barbarous court. Being Chinese, the Ming emperors favored their own, more gentle sects. But the Tibetan hierarchy could not be ignored. Hung Wu, the first Ming ruler, had been a priest under Mongol rule. For several generations the various forms and sects of Buddhism prospered in peace. Then, a fanatic, a rare phenomenon in Chinese history, sprang into action. He was a Taoist who threw the golden Buddhas out of the shrines and had them melted down to provide the means to build a palace for his mother. After his death, he was quickly forgotten; but from that time on Taoism had little direct influence on the court, though its deities—the god of the heavenly ladies and the kitchen god—continued to receive official homage.

The Manchus had adopted Tibetan Buddhism before they conquered China. Henceforth both sects were patronized: the ancient, aggressive red-gowned one and the reformed, peaceful yellow-capped school. As the Manchus were not a peaceful people by nature, the grimly gorgeous rituals of Tibet, which blended admirably with their own savage Shaman rites, strongly attracted them. Its great potentates exercised temporal as well as spiritual power, and were represented by a score or more of their own eunuch-lamas in the Forbidden City.

In the Great Buddha Hall of the Palace of Peace and Compassion, masses were sung with unfailing regularity whenever senior ladies were in residence. Prominent among the participants was Tz'u An who, by her own standards was deeply religious. One of her greatest pleasures was to visit the temple and meditate alone before its elaborate altar, or bowing her head in piety, to listen to the lama choruses chanting the sutras in a turgid drone.

When the Empress Dowager Niuhulu, the mother of Ch'ien Lung, set up her Court in the Palace of Peace and Compassion, the Great Buddha Hall glowed with fresh tones of gold and rich bronzes. Though her doting son accepted her authority with indulgent affection, the blood ran hot and full through his virile veins, and his burning desire caused him to transgress the dynastic laws during one period of his reign. He deliberately offended the basic principles of filial piety and introduced a strange woman into the imperial household.

Curiosity began it all. After a successful campaign in Sungaria, word of the famous Fragrant Beauty reached the emperor. She was the widow of the great khan who, rather than surrender with his defeated army to the Chinese and Manchu forces, had committed suicide. Supposedly as lovely as she was loyal, the widow was known among all the wind-tanned tribes of the frontier lands for her great beauty, the delicate perfection of her complexion, and for the faint odor of a rare perfume that emanated from her person. Ch'ien Lung thought but briefly on these reports and then commanded that she be brought to the capital in slow, comfortable stages, "lest the hardships of the journey impair her beauty."

On arrival, the great khan's widow was installed in a pavilion by the Southern Lake, and the emperor hurried off to see her. Though she stood aloof and resentful, and eyed him with icy disapproval, within seconds he had fallen in love! Like all enamored men, he busied himself to make her as happy and comfortable as possible. Since she was a Moslem, he had a mosque built close to her two-storied apartments so that she could hear the five daily calls to prayer. Luxuries were piled upon her: silks, the most delicate of foods, jewels. She was the widow of a khan, a lady of high rank, and nothing was too good for her. Despite the glowering disapproval of the empress dowager, Ch'ien Lung had the great beauty moved into the Forbidden City and he promptly ordered a bathing pavilion to be constructed in the Turkish style—the Hamman Bathhouse —in the southwest part of the palace.

Maintaining the transparent fiction that she was a royal guest rating every honor and courtesy, Ch'ien Lung began an ardent, though gentlemanly courtship, pressing his suit through discreet messengers. Then he had Castiglione paint a portrait of her and bring it to him the instant it was finished. This the Jesuit priest did, depicting the famous beauty as a warrior garbed in European armor, helmet, and plumes. Though this alien costume may have jarred the emperor a bit, he nonetheless sat staring at it with the moonstruck concentration of an adolescent. None of this performance escaped his mother, the empress dowager; and her annoyance grew. Not only was this behavior unseemly and undignified for a Son of Heaven, but the Fragrant Beauty's answers to his pleas were alarming.

"Inform His Majesty," she had told his emissaries, "that I will never yield to him. If he does not cease troubling me, I shall kill myself. But I will not enter the Gate of True Freedom like any meek peasant girl perishing by the roadside. When I go, His Majesty goes with me!"

Undaunted, Ch'ien Lung continued—more boldly now—to seek her favor. He sent a court artist to paint another portrait of her, this time in Chinese dress leaning against the lattice of a palace window and gazing longingly over a lotus-filled lake toward her distant home. He had it framed as a table screen and, always kept it close beside him. Even when he reached a very old age, it stood on the writing table in his private apartment.

As the months passed and the short days of the winter solstice approached, the old dowager grew so agitated that she decided to end the whole affair. There was no question but that her son was deeply in love, and love was a serious affliction! It could do nothing but warp his judgment, as it had many a man's in a responsible position.

On the day before the great sacrifice at the Temple of Heaven, while the emperor was occupied with the prescribed ceremonial purifications in the Hall of Abstinence, the dowager sent for the beautiful stranger.

"I am told that you have dared to refuse the emperor's favor!" the dowager reproached her. "And that you say you would rather die than yield to him."

"I dare reply that this is the truth," the Fragrant Beauty answered.

"Then," said the dowager, "an end must be made to this trouble! You are granted the privilege of committing suicide!"

The unhappy woman fell on her knees before the throne and with brimming eyes, said: "Your Majesty shows me great understanding and compassion. I would have traveled the road of no return before now, but to avenge my Lord's memory, I had hoped to take the emperor with me. This was a vain hope. What use is there for me to linger on alone! It is far better to join my Lord in the Other World. There I shall not forget Your Majesty's benevolence."

Unmoved by the woman's dignity and virtue, the dowager summoned a eunuch and commanded him to conduct the unfortunate beauty to an inner room where a silken cord lay waiting.

Meanwhile, notified by a faithful eunuch that his mother had sent for the Fragrant Beauty, Ch'ien Lung was instantly alarmed. Dispensing with tradition, he hurried out of the Hall of Abstinence long before he had finished with the purification rites and reached the dowager's throne hall wild of eye. Grimly she sat waiting for him, her eyes as hard as his were frightened. When he tried to speak, she rose with rigid dignity and without a word motioned him to follow her. He did—to the room where the Fragrant Beauty's body was hanging from a rafter. The great emperor looked up, paled, and turned away in silence. As he staggered from the throne hall, his weeping echoed in his mother's ears—but her expression did not change.

Later, when his first harsh grief had softened, he sent the Fragrant Beauty's remains back to her distant homeland—a last tribute to her serene loveliness and unswerving fidelity—where her body was interred near that of her lord, the khan. And the Son of Heaven knelt for long hours before the golden altar of the Great Buddha Hall seeking in prayer and tears a solace he never found.

The Empress Dowager Tz'u An

In the days of the empire posthumous portraits of all the emperors and empresses were preserved in a special gallery of the Great Within. No shadows touched the full-face portrayals, for shadings should never mar the serene countenance of the Son of Heaven and his consort. Shown wearing the dynasty's official robes of state and seated stiffly on throne chairs, the character and likeness of each subject, in spite of the rigid rules under which the artist worked, was often caught with surprising realism. The procedure used in painting a posthumous likeness was both unique and a trial to any artist. (The painter who had had an opportunity to observe his subject during life was indeed fortunate, since it was considered unseemly and disrespectful for a mere craftsman, no matter how capable, to stare at the face of a departed ancestor.)

For example, after a grandfather had been placed in his gigantic, satin-lined coffin, the sons, grandsons, and their wives gathered for a consultation on his portrait. For the occasion the artist brought along a large book containing every conceivable type of carefully drawn eye, ear, nose, mouth, chin, forehead, and facial contour. Starting with the drawings of the right eye, perhaps, the entire family would pore over the book. Arguments followed about this or that eye, and when in tentative agreement, the eldest son was despatched to compare the selected drawing with the eye of the deceased. If satisfied, he instructed the artist to note down the one chosen. The same course of action—with the usual verbal uproar that accompanies any difference of opinion among the Chinese —marked the selection of each facial feature. Finally, after hours of patient helplessness, the painter had a sort of jigsaw assortment of features from which he was expected to assemble a reasonable likeness. The pose, hat, robes, and insignia of rank presented no problems. Tradition prescribed them down to the most minute detail.

All the noble and wealthy families followed this same practice—which explains the large number of ancestor portraits sold to foreigners by impoverished descendants.

In the mid-1930's, when a few foreigners for amusement commissioned their own "ancestor portraits"—to be done in the old style—they found the results startling. Never having painted a blond subject, the Chinese artists produced faces with glaring, electric-blue eyes, over-sized noses, straw-colored or bright henna hair, grim, slitlike mouths, and overly pink skins. The heads were set on shoulders as formal as those of any imperial prince. But being craftsmen rather than true artists, they did not object to altering the portraits in any manner to please the buyer.

The posthumous portrait of the pious dowager Tz'u An was an excellent likeness. It showed her delicately high-bred face and sensitive features, the thin nose, small lips, and rather weak, pointed chin. Her magnificent costume and hat—the latter surmounted by an intricate spike and two phoenixes of pearls—seemed to weigh down the slight figure, and the rich colors contrasted with the pale weakness of the wearer.

Tz'u An and Tz'u Hsi, though wives of the same husband, were completely dissimilar in character and appearance. Tz'u Hsi was healthy, vigorous, charming when she wanted to be, and gifted with executive ability. Her neat little figure radiated strength and energy. In contrast, Tz'u An was always ailing, a slim, willowy girl grown thinner and more austere as an older woman. By nature she was passive, almost to the point of indolence. Had it not been for the prestige of high birth and the fact that her sister Sakota had shared the nuptial wine with the emperor Tz'u An would never have achieved her position. When Sakota died a month before Hsien Feng's accession to the throne, Tz'u An (then called Niuhulu) was not promoted to empress until after the death of her mother-in-law, the old dowager. Tz'u Hsi, called the Yi Concubine, was expecting a child—but her rank and origin were far too humble to qualify her for the great position merely on the chance that the unborn baby might be a male and thus heir to the Dragon Throne.

At Tz'u An's promotion to empress, a ceremony was conducted for the ladies of the court, with no men present. The princesses of the blood, imperial princesses, and wives of high officials were led by a mistress of ceremonies to the throne hall of the new empress' apartments in the Palace of Peace and Compassion. There they were received by her chief eunuch and assembled according to rank. Then the mistress of ceremonies intoned: "I humbly beseech the empress on behalf of this assembly to appear and place herself on the throne." Dressed in magnificent robes of state, Tz'u An, the new first lady of the palace, then seated herself on the chair of state to receive the imperial decree confirming her appointment. The ladies were formally presented, each bowing twice, then dropping to both knees touched their heads to the floor—after which they repeated the bow and returned to their places. When all the silent obeisances had been completed, Her Majesty descended from the throne and withdrew.

When Tz'u Hsi's son—the heir—was born a few months later, the motherly instincts of Tz'u An were roused to ecstasy and delight. She adored the baby. While his mother played at power politics, Tz'u An constantly had the little prince T'ung Chih in her apartments, hugged him to her loving heart, spoiled, pampered, and petted him. Tz'u An knew well that Tz'u Hsi had more or less forgotten the child, turning his care, rearing and education over to the eunuchs. She reveled in Tz'u Hsi's neglect and basked in the knowledge that her own appropriated role of "mother" was completely escaping the other woman's attention. But once Tz'u Hsi saw what was going on, she was furious. It was not that she cared for the child—she had made little effort to see him—but he was *hers*, and Tz'u An's proprietary activities annoyed her. Thus the first seed of discord was sown between the two women.

In 1860, when the court fled the Old Summer Palace at the approach of an Allied Expeditionary Forces—made up principally of British and French troops and bent on avenging mistreatment of their diplomats as well as imposing a more advantageous treaty on China—Tz'u An took charge of the five-year-old child, his own mother having forgotten him in the wild confusion of escape. Though the emperor was quite ill, the flight was undertaken anyway—and without any real preparations. The departing imperial cortege was simply a panic-stricken mob, with everyone clinging to his own bundles of treasures and motivated by the single thought of getting as far away from Peking as possible. As the imperial family fled through a side gate, the foreign troops approached the main entrance, demanding vengeance on those who had killed or badly treated their truce bearers. When the first European troops broke into the parklike palace, the emperor's opium pipe was barely cold. His fan lay where he had left it; his papers and possessions were spread about in disorder.

At some time during the hasty flight to Jehol, Tz'u Hsi craftily obtained possession of the Great Seal of Lawfully Transmitted Authority. Having accomplished that, she remembered her son, the heir, and set out to track him down. To her annoyance she found him happily asleep in Tz'u An's arms. There was almost nothing about Tz'u An that didn't exasperate Tz'u Hsi, including this touching scene. Tz'u Hsi regarded the empress as a fool—a narrow, pious creature who had no interest in politics and was as lazy physically as she was mentally.

Tz'u An, for all Tz'u Hsi's bad opinion of her, was a fine classical scholar and took great pride in examining the essays of candidates for literary honors. By her supervision of the emperor's early education and her joy in watching his young mind develop, the bond and love between them was strengthened more and more. But her self-appointed task afforded her little satisfaction and much anguish.

In the first place, the boy had been born stubborn, and selfish. On top of that he had been spoiled, even corrupted, by the eunuchs; nor had her own pampering and petting helped. It had weakened what basic character he might have had. Decorum and propriety were the breath of life to Tz'u An, and she was horrified at the growing lad's lack of morals and his irresponsible attitude toward life. As he grew to young manhood, his idleness and dissipation increased. While she did all she could to counteract the evil influence of the eunuchs, his own mother seemed to applaud his wild escapades and aberrations. Knowing Tz'u Hsi so well, Tz'u An could not help but feel that there was a selfish motive behind her encouragement of conduct that could lead her son to but one end— the grave. What Tz'u Hsi's scheme was, she did not know; Tz'u An could only tremble in fear and wait and see.

As senior empress dowager, Tz'u An presided over all activities in the Palace of Peace and Compassion. While fingering the beads of her rosaries, burning incense at the altars of the Great Buddha Hall, and conducting her life with the dullness and dignity befitting her high birth, she not only looked on Tz'u Hsi's zest for pleasure and power as vulgar but found her manners and taste offensive. As her dislike for her co-regent grew, she missed no opportunity to subject Tz'u Hsi to sly mockeries and sarcasm, and on occasion, delivered stinging and well-deserved sermons on behavior.

Tz'u Hsi was impervious to all slights and corrections. She continued her own reactionary political ambitions and, having no scruples about violating any proprieties that might interfere, insisted upon complete freedom in her private life. Tz'u An's decree that caused the execution of An Teh-hai, Tz'u Hsi's chief eunuch, was the last straw. Tz'u Hsi's hatred of Tz'u An erupted. The Inner Courts of the Great Within then abruptly and sharply divided into two camps.

After the death of the dissolute young Emperor T'ung Chih, Tz'u Hsi thrust her nephew, the four-year-old Kuang Hsu, on the throne, with the tacit agreement of Tz'u An. The latter quickly won this child's affection, just as she had gained that of T'ung Chih. Tz'u Hsi was again too busy with politics and pleasures to be personally bothered with the boy, but the bond between him and Tz'u An lit another spark of hatred.

At the annual visit to the Western Tombs in 1880, during which the two ladies took part in the memorial services for their deceased lord, Hsien Feng, the six years of constant bickering came to a climax and broke out before the whole court. This open quarrel, in the presence of the imperial dead, occurred when Tz'u An tried to force Tz'u Hsi to take third place at the sacrifices—the first being reserved for the spirit of the senior empress, her departed sister Sakota. Tz'u An cuttingly reminded her junior co-regent that since she had acquired her rank after the death of Hsien Feng, she was entitled only to what she had enjoyed during his lifetime. The emperor had been dead for eighteen years, and Tz'u Hsi angrily refused to submit to such an indignity. She insisted on taking her place beside Tz'u An, which she did; but in doing so, she lost face before the entire entourage of officials, princes, and nobles.

Soon afterward Tz'u An successfully encouraged an intrigue between Duke Jung Lu and one of the palace ladies. She reasoned in her vengeful mind that such a scandalous indiscretion on the part of Tz'u Hsi's cousin and lover would deal her enemy a mighty blow. Not only would it deprive Tz'u Hsi of a staunch and able partisan, but would injure her vanity and personal feelings in the bargain.

The imperial tutor Weng T'ung ho, who detested Duke Jung Lu, hastened to inform the Dowager Tz'u Hsi of her favorite's philandering. In a blind and screaming rage, she banished Jung Lu from the court for seven years. And as time dragged on, the loss of her friend and lover became almost unendurable, and her hatred of the woman who had deprived her of his company grew beyond all bonds.

In the following year Tz'u An stooped to quarrel with Tz'u Hsi's new chief eunuch, Li Lien-ying, openly accusing him of usurping imperial prerogatives. But even an empress dowager could not always abuse a grand eunuch with impunity. A shaky peace was finally restored, and the two women were seemingly on friendly terms again. But it was clear to the palace family there was no longer room enough in the Forbidden City for both dowagers.

Sometime later Tz'u An visited her colleague in her apartments. The two women chatted as pleasantly as if they did not despise each other, reminiscing about the Tsai Yuan conspiracy, which had so nearly cost them their lives, but which had made their fortunes. They spoke of their girlhood and excursions to the Old Summer Palace; of Pewter Lane and the great compound of Muyanga; of jaunts to temple fairs and family feasts. As the afternoon grew late, Tz'u An said she felt hungry. Tz'u Hsi instantly called for a tray of sweet cakes, which had been made for her by her sister, Duchess Chao. Tz'u An ate a few of the dainty, flat discs and remarked they were far better than any served in her own apartments.

"If you like them, I will tell my sister to send you some," Tz'u Hsi said, politely brushing aside the usual protestations expected on such occasions. "My family is as your family. How then should you deem this an imposition on my sister?"

Within a few days several boxes of the same kind of cakes were sent to Tz'u An by the duchess. But after eating four or five cakes, she complained that they had a strangely bitter taste. On that morning, April 2, 1891, she had risen in perfect health and held audience alone, as Tz'u Hsi had felt indisposed. Before sundown Tz'u An was dead. Her physician, who had seen her only the day before, was shocked into a thoughtless exclamation: "I cannot believe such a sudden death to be a natural one!" Then, realizing what he had said, he rushed headlong from the palace and left Peking within a few hours—never to return.

As it was well known that the collection of poisons in the palace dispensary was an extraordinary one, many agreed with the doctor's opinion. Some of the palace poisons were legacies from the Ming times; others were reputed to have been brought from Europe by the early Jesuits. A number were so potent they produced instantaneous unconsciousness or death if only touched to the lips.

General suspicion pointed an accusing finger directly at the Empress Dowager Tz'u Hsi and her grand eunuch; but her part in this obvious case of poisoning has never been proved. Nonetheless, it was a strange coincidence that at exactly the right time all those who stood in Tz'u Hsi's path had a convenient habit of "mounting the dragon" to join their ancestors.

Tz'u An's desire for a simple funeral as a fitting conclusion to a modest life was not heeded. She was buried with all the imperial splendor suited to her high rank. Tz'u Hsi officially mourned the untimely death of her colleague with every outward show of grief. If fears of the tales that ancestors might hear in the shadowy realms of the Nine Springs troubled her pragmatic heart, she never showed it. At last, Tz'u Hsi was free from all authority—the sole regent and ruler of China.

THE TOWER OF RAINING FLOWERS

During the early years of the Ming dynasty a saintly Buddhist priest of Nanking became renowned throughout the empire for his ceaseless, day-and-night chanting of the sacred sutras of Buddha. Falling like a constant rain of flowers upon the altar of his little shrine, the fragrance of the priest's holy words was accepted by the truly pious as the inner, glowing light of many blossoms. Filling the people's hearts with a happy warmth, the "miracle of the flowers" soon caught the court's attention. Eager to share in the spiritual grace of the priest, the Emperor Hung Wu built a shrine to him: a three-storied pagoda—the Tower of Raining Flowers—in the midst of the great palaces by the Yangtze River. Later, the Emperor Yung Lo, to show his devotion to the Buddhist faith, set aside an enclosure in the Forbidden City for the construction of a three-storied tower to honor "the benevolence of the Lord Buddha that drops from Heaven as gently as the falling petals of a flower."

The first Tower of Raining Flowers in Peking disappeared into the silent shadows of history as quietly as did the venerated priest, whose holy spirit had inspired its erection. During the latter period of the Ming dynasty it was replaced by one more suited to the altars before which the Tibetan-Mongol lamas could perform their barbaric rites. The highest building in the Inner Courts, its peaked, square roof of yellow tiles was surmounted by a gilded shrine to Buddha under a miniature golden umbrella with a high, decorative spike. Four elegantly designed dragons of gilded bronze stood upright on each of the curving eaves, their twice-arched tails creating a touch of feline grace. More of these fantastic creatures from the watery world thrust their necks through the outer pillars to raise fierce bewhiskered heads under the projecting roofs. Repeated on all three levels, the writhing dragons stood poised to defend the graceful tower with angry, threatening jaws.

Last repaired at great expense by the Emperor Ch'ien Lung, the upper balcony offered the confined palace family its only unbroken view of the world beyond the walls and courts of the Great Within. From this balcony unhappy women gazed sadly over the undulating sea of yellow roofs toward the homes of their parents in the city; or, secretly restless ladies, straining their eyes toward the high horizons of the Western Hills, dreamed of carefree, sunny days at the Old Summer Palace.

As early morning light pushed through the hovering gray of dawn, the city and the wide plain beyond were clothed in a shimmering, glistening mist; and the radiance of the setting sun turned yellows to gold, rose-colored walls to deep wine-red, and hazy shadows to inky black. The varied light rested gently on the shrines of all faiths that the emperors, with the characteristic tolerance of the Chinese, endowed and supported throughout a long history. The universal attitude toward rival religions and sects is exemplified in a simple story of the sixth-century scholar Fu Hsi. A happy, carefree soul, he wandered about the empire wearing a Taoist cap, a Buddhist robe, and the large, upturned shoes of a Confucian. When summoned to the court, the sovereign asked if he was a Buddhist.

Pointing to his Taoist cap, Fu Hsi said nothing.

"You are a Taoist, then," said His Majesty.

Pointing to his shoes, Fu Hsi again remained silent.

"Then you are grounded in the rites and wisdom of the Great Sage," the Emperor said.

But for answer, Fu Hsi merely pointed to his Buddhist robe.

Had the old scholar lived during later centuries, he might have carried a lama drum of human bone in one hand and a Christian cross in the other. Such emblems of various creeds never disturbed the tolerant K'ang Hsi. He accepted them all with an understanding smile. Like the great Mogul Emperor Akbar in India, he selected the best from each religion or sect in the hope of uniting them to form a national faith. If Buddha, Lao Tzu (the founder of Taoism), and Confucius were able to sit peacefully together in wayside shrines, he saw no reason why Christ and assorted Tibetan incarnations should not join them with equal affability. Until the Japanese invasion and the subsequent Communist wars between 1937 and 1949 disrupted the entire land, it was not uncommon to find a statuette of the Christian Virgin Mary beside one of Kuan Yin, the goddess of mercy. If asked to explain this association, the usual answer was: "They are both good; both kind; both merciful and understanding. Why should they not be together?" Such an ecumenical attitude, however, did not exist during the brief period of the Boxer movement in 1900.

Such Jesuit priests as Ferdinand Verbiest, Louis Buglio, and Gabriel de Magalhaens, following the tradition set by Ricci, had led K'ang Hsi by skillful rationalizations to believe the principles of all faiths might be united in Christianity. Pointing out that the exalted Oneness of Heaven and its sovereign representatives on earth could be likened to the relationship between God and the Roman Catholic pope, the priests reasoned that the popular worship of many gods could be combined in the veneration of one—their One—as a Supreme Deity. They were willing to tolerate the ancestral cult as being social rather than religious, its rites being reverence rather than worship—a concept to which His Majesty fully subscribed. But when the rivals of the Jesuits—Dominicans, Franciscans, and Lazarists—arrived in China, they did not agree with the interpretations of the Jesuit pioneers and angrily reported the matter to the pope in Rome.

The ensuing discussions, known as the Controversy of the Rites, were strongly influenced by internal politics at the Vatican and extended over a period of many years. Papal legates came and went. Papal bulls first supported one faction and then the other. But eventually, when the discussions became acrimonious, the emperor was completely disillusioned. The picture of semieducated, hair-shirted, priestly bigots in bare feet, relentlessly pressing for their own political ends and authority against the intelligent Jesuit effort to spread the words of Christianity among countless millions of Chinese, was beyond K'ang Hsi's understanding. Broad-minded though he may have been, he was emperor because his subjects acquiesced to his Mandate from Heaven. This could not and must not be threatened by the autocratic and uncomprehending nature of a distant conflicting authority. If Rome condemned the ancestral cult, the power of the Catholic Church could penetrate Chinese society and endanger the rule of the sovereign himself—and K'ang Hsi recognized this at once.

It was Pope Clement XI who decided against the Jesuit rationalizations and K'ang Hsi's own interpretations of the ancestral rites. In a papal bull he ordered all Chinese Christians to conform rigidly to the existing laws of the Church. At this point the emperor had no choice but to order the expulsion of all missionaries from his empire. He would accept no interference with internal politics or with the customs of his people, on which the very foundations of his government rested. However, he exempted the court Jesuits from the edict, with the condition they were to make no further attempts to win converts. Sadly, K'ang Hsi told them to "be happy with what is given, and lament not over what is denied." The hopes of both Jesuits and emperor for an idyllic, all-embracing faith ended in a deliberately nurtured political squabble.

The priests remained in the palace as teachers, interpreters, and authorities on technical and scientific matters; but the old amity and trust were destroyed. The Jesuits found their duties both tedious and trying —and their every move jealously watched by Rome for signs of participation in "heathen practices."

Today, in a harsher repetition of history, Mao Tse-tung has ordered the expulsion or imprisonment of all Catholic priests and missionaries from Communist China. Thus the efforts of the first heroic Jesuits who reached Peking over three hundred years ago have come full circle to nothing, because of fear of the power and hold over its communicants by the same Roman authority.

At the death of K'ang Hsi, when Father Ripa went to console the new Emperor Yung Cheng and to mourn for his deceased friend, he was assured that there would be "no improper or idolatrous sacrifices, no papers burned, and no libations of wine performed." As the deceased monarch lay in state in the great hall of the Palace of Peace and Compassion, Father Ripa followed a host of officials through the west gate of the Court of Cloudless Heaven and joined them outside the throne room which contained the coffin. Later, he wrote:

> We found a vast number of mandarins upon their knees. They were all habited in mourning, and weeping; and from time to time, upon a signal from the master of ceremonies, they all at once raised a howl of lamentation as filled the sky, after which they performed their prostrations.

In the most sincere Christian spirit, Father Ripa was able to add his own genuine grief to theirs but, to his horror, he learned that a libation of wine had been made and poured upon the ground while his own head was lowered in a deep obeisance.

On hearing that we had, even unconsciously, taken part in this work of superstition, I was grieved and alarmed to a degree which it would be impossible for me to express. In order to preclude the re-occurrence of such a misfortune, I resolved to quit that Babylon at any risk and as soon as possible.

Fortunately, Father Ripa never set foot inside the Tower of Raining Flowers. Had he done so, he would have been convinced he had stumbled into Satan's holy of holies. The lowest of the three floors was the most ornate lama chapel in the palaces. Like the ball of an ivory puzzle, it contained shrines within shrines. It was a dim, mysterious place illuminated by lamps made from human skulls. There were handsome carvings on the inner colonnade, and numerous paintings of ferocious Tibetan deities crowded the main hall and its two chapels. These exotic shrines, one circular and the other square, were the settings for the most darkly exotic rites of the higher orders of the lama hierarchy. An elaborate altar was cluttered with incense burners, vases, candlesticks, urns for holy water, cups of human bones and skulls, drums covered with human skin, symbols of bone and bronze, and thunderbolt scepters, all for ceremonies that were said to invoke magic in the worship of the devils of the Eighteen Hells.

During the reigns of K'ang Hsi and his son, Yung Cheng, the lamas were much in evidence in the Forbidden City. At one of the feasts before the New Year, when the people indulged themselves with the traditional pottage made from eight different grains, five hundred monks from the lama temples of Peking entered the palace grounds through the Gate of Spiritual Valor in grand procession—members of the old sect wearing crimson and henna robes; those of the reformed sect in yellow and orange. The senior lamas wore high hats with stiff crests like those of the ancient Greek and Roman officers. Their procession was a noisy one. The echoes of their sonorous chants broke in waves against the halls and courts, and their shuffling feet sounded like doleful sighs. Along the route were huge braziers with burning incense, which rose in clouds of smoky veils over the walls.

The alliance of the Manchu court with the Tibetan and Mongolian lamas dated back to the earliest years of the first emperor's reign when the fifth Dalai Lama visited Peking. At the time the young sovereign built a special temple for him in the capital. Years later the seventh Dalai Lama was presented with a golden tablet and seal to confirm his honors and sovereignty, and K'ang Hsi set aside a special suite of rooms in the Garden of Earthly Repose for his reception and provided an additional building near the Tower of Raining Flowers for his vestments.

All this imperial interest in the great lamas and their sects was not entirely pious; nor was it sentimental. The Tibetan and Mongolian priests had great influence and power in the restless border lands of the west and northwest, and the emperors knew it only too well. In later years, these religious leaders and their followers acted as buffers against the growing pressure of the Russians, and this was a great deal less costly to the Chinese than sending out large expeditions to maintain order and authority in those distant spheres of trouble.

The Dalai Lama was supreme in spiritual matters, the Panchen Lama in temporal affairs. The death of either made the question of their successors a matter of tremendous concern to the emperors in their frequently troubled relations with Tibet and Mongolia. Because of his unique spiritual character, the Dalai Lama was usually venerated as the more important of the two.

When a Dalai Lama died, emissaries scoured all central Asia in a search for the predestined boy-child into whose newborn body the priest's soul had entered. This "heir" had to have been born at exactly the right astrological hour and of exactly the right parents. He had to have been able to speak and walk at an extremely early age—preferably immediately after birth. Though several likely candidates might be found, all portents in the heavens and on earth had to favor and point to one only. With the countless required tests, it sometimes took years to find the true reincarnated child.

When a boy exactly fitted all the requisites of this heavenly jigsaw puzzle, he was proclaimed the new Dalai Lama, taken to Lhasa at once, and educated by specially trained priests. Though only a minority of the Chinese subscribed to Lamaism, the Buddhist background of that faith created a deep respect and a measure of fear throughout China for both the Dalai and Panchen lamas.

At his accession, the Emperor Yung Cheng gave his enormous princely palace in the northeast quarter of Peking to the Yellow Sect. Known afterward as the Lama Temple, it was an extraordinary collection of magnificent buildings, both in architecture and content. Its most treasured and unusual symbolic figure was a seventy-five-foot-high statue of Maitreya, the manifestation of Buddha that is destined to return to the world—a rather startling link with the Christian prophecy of the second coming of Christ.

After his father's death, believing that the questionable loyalty of a growing number of Chinese and Manchu Christian converts menaced the strength of the throne, Yung Cheng did not revoke the decrees restricting the activities of the Jesuit priests. In the first place, one of his troublesome brothers was reported to be a Christian—a prince who had been the ringleader in a serious disturbance during his father's last years. The loyalty of several other imperial kinsmen had also been found wanting, and the emperor attributed their defection to the influence of the missionaries. He became convinced that no matter how good Christianity might be for some, it was not necessarily beneficial for all. Two years after his accession to the throne, he confirmed the edict forbidding Catholic priests to make converts. Those Jesuits still attached to the court became alarmed for their future.

To allay any fears for their personal safety, Yung Cheng granted them an audience and, in a speech that lasted for fifteen minutes, as reported by Father Ripa, made his attitude very clear:

> What would you say if I were to send a troop of *bonzes* and lamas into your country in order to preach their doctrines? How would you receive them? The converts you have made recognize no one but you, and in time of trouble they would listen to no other voice than yours. My father suffered much in reputation among the literati by the condescension with which he allowed you to establish yourselves. He could not make any changes in the laws of our sages, and I will not suffer that even in the least degree there be any cause to reproach my reign on this score. When my sons and grandsons are on the throne, they may do as shall seem best to them. . . . You are aware how I used to act on your behalf when I was only a prince. What I do now, I do in my role as Emperor. When the time of mourning for my father is over, perhaps I shall be able to see you more often.

The succeeding emperor, Ch'ien Lung, adhered to the same policy. Unlike his father and grandfather, he was probably more Confucian than

Buddhist at heart; but not being basically religious at all, he paid tribute to all faiths with an impartial and tolerant condescension.

In June, 1779, the sixth Panchen Lama set out with a gorgeous retinue and fifteen hundred escort troops to honor Ch'ien Lung on his seventieth birthday. Traveling slowly and accepting the homage of the border tribes, he was finally greeted by a splendid advance guard of honor as he approached the great Summer Palace at Jehol. The emperor, then in residence, received him regally and ensconced the holy man in an enormous monastery that had been patterned after the vast temple-palace of Lhasa. Being both a saintly reincarnation and an astute diplomat, the Panchen Lama had many matters to discuss with his imperial host and sovereign lord. In order to talk freely—and as a compliment to his guest —Ch'ien Lung had studied the Tangut dialect for several months before his guest's arrival. Among other items, His Holiness, having connections with the powerful East India Company, wished to arrange for the reception of a trade mission from their nearest headquarters. But the emperor, determined to continue relations with his distant lieges on an exclusive basis, refused the request.

At the end of the summer the sovereign and the pontiff journeyed in state to Peking. There His Holiness was shown the wonders of the capital and some of the marvels of the Forbidden City. The unsophisticated honored guest took a childlike pleasure in the fireworks displays at the New Year solemnities. At one of the lakes of the Old Summer Palace, he witnessed a naval demonstration, with a specially built warcraft discharging its guns in imitation of an actual sea engagement. In return, the Panchen Lama consented to receive the imperial ladies from behind a screen of yellow gauze to give them his blessing. Then quite suddenly, in 1781, in the midst of all this pomp and ceremony, His Distinguished Holiness fell ill with smallpox and died within a few days.

Horrified over the possible reaction in Tibet and Mongolia to this unfortunate event, Ch'ien Lung took great pains to show his grief. He personally offered incense before the corpse, provided a lavish coffin, and attended the magnificent memorial masses at the Yellow Temple, just north of the city walls, and the Tower of Raining Flowers. To preserve forever a relic of the saintly man, he ordered that a sumptuously carved, white marble stupa be built at the Yellow Temple to contain the garments of his lamented guest. And with a final gesture of unprecedented generosity, His Majesty commanded that all gifts to the deceased pontiff

—from the princes and khans of Mongolia, from the great nobles of the empire's eighteen provinces, and from himself (to the value of about a million ounces of silver)—be sent back with the coffin to Tibet. Thus he forestalled any inference that the Panchen Lama's death might have been too timely to be natural.

A strange superstititon clung like moss to the visits of the Dalai and Panchen lamas, known as the living Buddhas. In his own palace, the emperor was frequently referred to as the Old Buddha. According to an ancient and ominous prediction, two Buddhas could not live in the same place at the same time—meaning that one had to give way to the other. In the case of Ch'ien Lung's visitor, this handy explanation of his hasty departure to the world of shadows was generally accepted—much to the relief of the emperor. In 1908, during the visit of the Dalai Lama to Peking, when the deaths of both the Empress Dowager Tz'u Hsi and the Emperor Kuang Hsu occurred, the sovereign, rather than the pontiff, "gave way." Considering this old superstition, it is curious that the Manchu dynasty collapsed two years later, and Tibet regained its independence. On the former occasion, the death of the Panchen Lama in Peking presaged the complete Manchu domination of his mountain country!

No longer do petal-like prayers fall from the Tower of Raining Flowers; nor is its silence broken by the chanting of henna-robed lamas. One by one the fiercely protective dragons have wasted away into broken shards of tarnished gold, to lie amidst the ruined colonnades and cracked tiles.

THE HALL OF THE NURTURE OF THE MIND

The Hall of the Nurture of the Mind, a small, compact palace of Manchu architecture, was an informal apartment for the emperors. Selected with great care, the name was derived from an admonition of the philosopher Mencius (372–289 B.C.): "In the nurture of the mind, it is of first importance to refrain from self indulgence." The present building was constructed in 1802 during the reign of the Emperor Chia Ch'ing as an unpretentious residence for the sovereign, and usually was so used throughout the remainder of the dynasty.

The throne room of this dark and ill-omened palace was associated with some strange and unprecedented events during the last thirty-five years of the Manchu regime. The nomination of Kuang Hsu in 1876 to the Dragon Throne was the most notable. On a bleak and freezing January night, a few hours after the death of T'ung Chih, his mother Tz'u Hsi summoned the Grand Council to this hall to name a successor to her son.

From the black, ragged clouds of a threatening sky, Heaven and the spirits of the ancestors frowned down in wrath on the imperial family that night. Howling winds shook the windows, and blinding waves of gritty dust swept in from the Gobi desert. The hanging lanterns outside the hall swayed noisily with each angry gust. Their chains creaked in violent protest, and guttering candles splattered hot wax, which burned the painted panels. The torches of the guardsmen, leading the imperial princes and high dignitaries through the darkened courts, flared and streamed cometlike trails of sparks under each fresh blast of the bitter gale.

Once inside the throne room, the great officials of the empire shivered in the chill of the tightly closed hall. All were short of breath in the burnt-out air of the glowing charcoal braziers and struggled not to gasp aloud as they knelt on the cold stone slabs of the floor. The Dowager Tz'u Hsi had commanded Duke Jung Lu to double the guard at all the entrances to the Forbidden City, and word had been spread that her loyal and powerful friend, Li Hung-chang, had seized control of the city gates with his hardy troops from Anhui province. The assembled officials were aware of these measures, and their hearts were heavy with fear that this ambitious woman was about to circumvent the guiding spirits of the past.

When all were gathered together at last—the Grand Council, imperial princes, heads of the boards, three viceroys from the south—the two empress dowagers took their places on the thrones behind curtains of gauzy yellow silk, just as they had sat together when taking over the government after the death of their imperial consort Hsien Feng.

Tz'u Hsi opened the audience. Her first words left no doubt she meant to dominate the session. In a cutting manner, her phrases as sharp as knives, she announced that an emperor must be named without delay.

It would be foolish to leave the throne vacant on the chance that the young Empress Aleute's expected child might be a son. Since a son was so greatly desired, doubts could be raised as to his legitimacy. The Grand Council meekly agreed, even though her statements cast an unwarranted slur on the first consort of the deceased emperor. Urgency was vital, she continued; recent rebellions in the south required the establishment of a valid central authority at once.

The Dowager Tz'u An then proposed as emperor the son of Prince Kung and grandson of the Emperor Tao Kuang. He was seventeen years old and therefore could almost immediately assume the reins of government. Furthermore, Prince Kung, his father, had helped the two imperial ladies thwart the Tsai Yuan conspiracy in 1860. On the other hand, Prince Kung had lost Tz'u Hsi's favor for his part in the death of her grand eunuch An Teh-hai some years before, and his son was of the same generation as the late Emperor T'ung Chih and thus not qualified to fulfill the ancestral obligations.

Convention, of course, required Prince Kung to deprecate the worthiness of his own son. With becoming modesty he protested the boy was unfit for the Great Bequest, and proposed, instead, the infant Prince P'u Lun. Tz'u Hsi quickly took advantage of Kung's meaningless courtesy, agreeing with him about his son but raising objections to the baby P'u Lun. Even though this child was of the proper generation to succeed the late emperor, he was the offspring of an adopted heir of the eldest son of the Emperor Tao Kuang, and therefore not of direct blood descent.

"What precedent can any of you show for placing on the throne the son of an adopted heir?" she asked.

Undaunted, Prince Kung quoted the case of Cheng Te from the Ming dynasty.

"That is a bad precedent. His reign was an era of disaster," she said abruptly.

It was now the turn of the infant's father, Prince Tsai Chih, to apologize for the shortcomings of *his* child.

With growing impatience, Tz'u Hsi turned to her co-regent, Tz'u An, and fastened her with a piercing black gaze. "As for me," she stated firmly, "I propose as heir, Tsai Tien, the son of Prince Ch'un, and advise that we waste no more time."

Tsai Tien was Tz'u Hsi's own four-year-old nephew, the son of her sister and Prince Ch'un, the seventh male offspring of the Emperor Tao

Kuang. Being a first cousin of the recently deceased emperor, he bore the character "Tsai" in his name; but it was the character "P'u" that designated the generation that was eligible to conduct the ancestral rites.

Tz'u Hsi's proposal brought forth an immediate protest from Prince Kung.

"Is the privilege of seniority to be completely overlooked?" he asked in an astonished voice. By age his son was obviously better qualified to ascend the throne, even though he was not qualified to fulfill the filial rites due the departed T'ung Chih. The difference in their ages, of course, explained Tz'u Hsi's preference for the younger prince. The four-year-old would require a regent for many years.

None of those present supported Prince Kung's objections. Tz'u Hsi had made her wishes known. She was ready to ask for what amounted to a vote. Since the grand councilors, the Duke Jung Lu, and the viceroys from the south owed their offices, rank and wealth to her, she knew she could rely on them. Seven of the princes, led by Prince Ch'un, pronounced for the baby P'u Lun; three supported the son of Prince Kung; but the remainder agreed with the dowager's choice of Tsai Tien.

Her choice confirmed, Tz'u Hsi immediately commanded Duke Jung Lu to take a strong detachment of household troops and, carrying the imperial yellow chair with them, bring the child from his father's palace to the Forbidden City. Then turning to Prince Kung, she ordered him to take charge of the late emperor's funeral. Occupied with the same ceremonies that had handicapped the Tsai Yuan conspirators, Kung would be unable to circumvent her plans.

The child's first official act as emperor was to bow before the coffin of T'ung Chih. Then he expressed "dutiful thanks" to the two dowager empresses for consenting to "resume" the regency. To indicate her "reluctance" to assume this responsibility, Tz'u Hsi ordered work on the new Summer Palace stopped at once. State affairs, not pleasure, would thenceforth absorb all the united energies of the two ladies. The last act in the farce was to bestow an honorific title on the widowed Empress Aleute.

Two months later, on March 27, 1876, Aleute died from unknown causes. Vague stories of her suffering and indignities at the hands of Tz'u Hsi began to be whispered about. The sympathy that had been denied her in life suddenly swelled to a storm of outrage. Her death brought forth memorials by the score, protesting the eligibility of the new emperor. In order to quiet the Board of Censors, Tz'u Hsi was obliged to promise that as soon as an heir was born to the new sovereign the infant would be decreed a son of T'ung Chih by posthumous adoption—thus creating the unusual biological phenomenon of two men (one long dead by the time this could happen) as cofathers of one offspring. The strongest protest came four years later with the suicide of Wu K'o-tu, a scholar and a member of the Board of Censors. Since this event aroused public opinion more strongly than had all the previous written memorials, Tz'u Hsi was forced to make a solemn promise that the spirit of T'ung Chih would not be neglected forever. (This unusual accommodation—utterly absurd as it sounds to Western ears—was accepted, if somewhat unwillingly, as a political adjustment to public opinion in the completely make-believe atmosphere of the court.)

The young Emperor Kuang Hsu spent most of his boyhood and youth in the Hall of the Nurture of the Mind. The rooms opening off the throne hall were small but comfortable. His bedroom was draped with yellow silk and dragon-embroidered brocades, and the playroom—later used as an informal study and lounge—was full of books and toys. The buildings about the courtyard housed his personal attendants and provided additional space for the large foreign mechanical playthings in which he delighted.

After the establishment of the Republic in 1912, this hall became the state apartment of the boy-emperor. It was partially modernized and furnished in semi-Western style. Its tables and stands, as well as the floor, were covered with blue and white linoleum. When P'u Yi was forced to flee from the palace-city in 1924, he abandoned some pathetic objects: a bright pink, celluloid kewpie doll; a long-dried out Christmas tree still draped with tinsel; lesson books in English and Chinese; and numerous small reminders of his childhood. The last pretense of majesty was destroyed. The spirits of the ancestors were doomed to neglect for all time.

THE SMALLER PALACES OF THE WEST

A group of smaller palaces, charming with painted lotus blossoms, phoenix birds and delicately carved screens of scented sandalwood, was normally reserved for the less important ladies of the emperor. Decorated with silk-paneled lanterns, trees of jewels in enamel bowls, blue silk hangings, large round mirrors to symbolize well-rounded conjugal bliss, and finely carved lattices at the windows, the Palace of Eternal Longevity was one of the oldest in the Inner Courts. After the death of her son, Tz'u Hsi lived there for a time. But she left only a handful of personal mementos to mark her stay: a few elaborate carvings, finely embroidered cushions, and a beautifully paneled throne screen flanked by peacock-feather fans.

Another palace, the Hall of Sympathetic Harmony, was used as a study by the boy-emperor's young consort. A third, the Palace of Treasured Beauty, contained her bedroom and bath. A fourth, known as the Porch of the Beautiful View, had two principal apartments: a Western-style dining room for P'u Yi, the boy-emperor, and a private room, which was dwarfed by an enormous bronze bed with a mosquito net of woven gold threads.

In 1487 the Ming dynasty Emperor Hung Chih was born in the nearby Hall of the Most Exalted. Its last occupant was Yu T'ai, one of the widowed concubines of T'ung Chih who had made her home in this unusually large palace until she was evicted by the uncouth General Feng Yu-hsiang on November 5, 1924.

During the early period of her life in the Forbidden City as the Yi Concubine, Tz'u Hsi lived in an adjacent small palace. Many years later the same apartments were assigned to E-erh-te-te, the untouched secondary concubine of the myopic and reputedly misogynist P'u Yi. She had been brought into the palace as a companion for the young empress on the insistence of four old concubines of former sovereigns. Once there, she settled down to utter loneliness and misery. A few years after the last members of the imperial family were expelled from the Great Within, the unhappy friendless girl retired to a Buddhist monastery.

For centuries many junior ladies took pleasure in studying the intricately painted scenes, from the well-known *Dream of the Red Chamber*, that decorated the balconies of this palace. Among such ladies of the court was Li Fei, the favorite concubine of the Carpenter Emperor of the Ming period. In those opulent times the large palace family had filled all the buildings and courts with gay and active life. But at the end of the Manchu dynasty only seven members of the imperial clan lived in the vast complex of halls and palaces that made up the Forbidden City. Four of these were spoiled old dowager consorts who ate, slept, and dreamed of the past—and two of them died before they could be evicted. One of the survivors was the Lustrous Concubine, the sister of the Pearl; the other an aged widow. Though the two women stormed, wept, and threatened suicide, they were given three-hour's notice to get out. Most of their possessions were abandoned when they were forced to take refuge in the city palace of a kindly prince. Some years prior to her abrupt expulsion, one had appropriated apartments in the Studio of Pure Fragrance, directly opposite the old open-air theater with its gaily painted stage and delicately carved friezes. As a boy, the Emperor Ch'ien Lung had lived in the adjoining Hall of Mighty Glory, where later he feasted his adored mother on her birthdays and arranged for special theatrical performances in her honor.

West of these halls stood the blue-roofed Mourning Palace, to which members of the imperial family retired at times of grief. Nearby was the Punishment Palace, whose façade and gate faced the ill-omened north. The second empress of Ch'ien Lung—a dutiful daughter-in-law and consort for fifteen years—was imprisoned there for inexcusable behavior. During a state progress to the south, in 1765, she had created a number of violent scenes, all culminating in such unbearable conduct at Hangchow that she was dismissed, demoted to the rank of concubine, and returned to Peking under guard. A year after her incarceration, she died —disgraced and unforgiven.

The site of the Palace of Established Happiness, destroyed when the palace eunuchs burned the treasure storehouses to cover their thefts of imperial possessions, was converted into a tennis court for the boy-emperor, his tutor, and princely relatives. The old concubines were horrified at such undignified activity. The sight of even a much reduced Son of Heaven sweating and mopping at his face like a peasant and hurtling himself about the court was almost beyond their endurance.

PART 8
Last of the Emperors

THE GATE OF SPIRITUAL VALOR

The great two-storied tower of the gate of Spiritual Valor has risen proudly above its triple-tunneled portals and the crenelated outer walls of the Forbidden City for five and a half centuries. Before the death of the Emperor Ch'ien Lung in 1799, this northern entrance to the palace was called the Gate of the Dark Warrior—an allusion to its astrological association with the Warden of the North, which the Buddhists called the Heavenly King or the Far Gazer and which the Western World calls the North Star. Since a character in the old name of the gate was the same as one in Ch'ien Lung's personal name, Chia Ch'ing, his son and heir, decreed that it be changed. But the soothsayers strongly disapproved. Later they attributed the waning luck of the gate, the Forbidden City, and the Manchu dynasty to this change in names—and for once, perhaps, they were right.

For centuries the busiest of all four entrances to the Great Within, it guarded the informal comings and going of the court. It stared down at the heralds and banners, the yellow-curtained sedan chairs, and the sleek, handsomely appointed horses from the palace stables. It had even witnessed the departure of the last Ming emperor.

As the "kitchen," or household, entrance of the palace-city, the Gate of Spiritual Valor's western tunnel gave daily entrance and exit to countless small officials, eunuchs, and servants. Great ladies, accompanied by their wide-eyed children and occasionally escorted by noble lords, used the more dignified eastern portal. The central, arched sallyport was reserved solely for the emperor.

Everyday activity around the Gate of Spiritual Valor was always full of color and movement, but the arrival of delegations from the northwest frontiers created an air of splendid pageantry beneath its high, gray walls. Then, turbaned khans and henna-robed lamas brushed against camel caravans from Kashgar, Khotan, and Outer Mongolia, carts loaded with supplies for daily use in the palace or tribute from the south, and camel trains carrying coal from nearby Mentoukou. Quarrelsome voices of carters and cameleers vied with priestly chants, deep-toned Tibetan horns, and the clank of heavy brass bells. Under the sharp eyes of Manchu guards, grimy men went swiftly about their tasks of unloading their carts and beasts, for all feared the lash of whips across the backs of the slack and unruly. But the milling crowds always fell silent and stepped back to clear a path—"to give light"—at the appearance of even the most humble funeral, since all who died within the Forbidden City were carried through the portals of the Gate of Spiritual Valor to a final peace many had never attained in life.

At dawn on August 15, 1900, the old gate witnessed the strangest procession of its long history. The courtyard between the inner and outer entrances was jam-packed with dozens of blue-hooded Peking carts, each with a sturdy mule between its stout shafts. Hardened drivers, their headbands dirty and sweat-soaked, waited at each cart, ready to flick their long whips to set the shaggy-haired beasts in motion. As the sun had not yet risen, a pearly dimness shadowed the scene of scuffling and confusion. The drivers in their ragged garments were little more than silhouettes as they waited patiently for the order to move. There were muffled, harsh noises, too; anxious, rasping cries; subdued weeping. But finally, screeching wheels rumbled out of the courtyard toward the stone causeway that led to the outer gate—the Empress Dowager Tz'u Hsi, and the Emperor Kuang Hsu, disguised as lowly peasants, were fleeing before the victorious troops of the Allied Expeditionary Force.

The last act of the drama in the palace, and the collapse of the Boxer movement, had started at midnight on August 14 at a hastily summoned audience in the Hall of Imperial Supremacy. And now, a few hours later, the imperial party passed through the outer porch of the Gate of Spiritual Valor huddled behind the closed hoods of a long line of mule-drawn carts. Tz'u Hsi had disguised herself in the typical short cotton jacket of a peasant woman, trousers bound neatly around her ankles. Her long hair was rearranged into the conventional knot at the back of her head and secured by a plain band of black satin that fitted low over her brow. Regretfully she had clipped her long, elegant fingernails so that their jeweled sheaths could not attract attention. Except for the fact her hands were soft and delicate, few could have suspected that this squat, little old woman was the empress dowager.

The emperor hid inside one of the carts, peering out now and then through the forward opening, which was covered with a loosely woven screen. The surly heir apparent, looking mean and ill-tempered, dangled his legs over the shafts of the dowager's vehicle. As Tz'u Hsi took her place under the hood, she told her grand eunuch Li Lien-ying to take care of himself. Then turning to the carters, she said: "Drive your hardest. If the foreign devils try to stop you, say nothing. I will tell them that we are only poor country folk fleeing to our homes. First, go to the Summer Palace."

Within a short time the carts were lost in the general exodus of refugees escaping from the city. Jolting over the massive blocks of stone that paved the old road to the Summer Palace, Tz'u Hsi sat in seething rage, her heart black with hate. As in 1860, she again had been defeated by her own bigoted policy toward foreigners. And again, she had been forced to leave the comforts of a luxurious palace. Long days lay ahead—miserable ones under the drenching downpours of much-delayed summer rains —before she could reach a safe haven.

It was not until January 7, 1902, that Tz'u Hsi felt safe in returning to the Forbidden City from her wanderings. Meanwhile, the reactionary old dowager, making a virtue out of necessity with astonishing aplomb, decided to constitute herself the leader of the reform movement.

Refusing to blame herself for the debacle, she was convinced the entire fault lay with the "disloyal" imperial princes who had given her bad advice. Perhaps some slight doubts crept into her stubborn mind—a few brief fears that the predictions of the astrologers should have been heeded, for they had foretold that the year 1900, because of ill-omened combination of signs in its intercalary month (which occurred in August that year), would be an unlucky one. Despite these portents, Tz'u Hsi had refused to fall back on the safe Taoist doctrine of nonaction. Instead, she had foolishly encouraged the Boxers, the secret society of fanatics whose avowed intention was to drive all foreigners ("old hairy ones") and all Chinese Christians ("secondary hairy ones") into the sea. And that was exactly what Tz'u Hsi wanted! The Boxers were first organized as trained bands of village militia in north China after the disastrous Sino-Japanese War of 1894-95. Then, united into a blustering, swashbuckling mob, they affiliated themselves with the White Lotus, Triad, and other secret societies having semireligious connotations in their rituals.

The majority of the Chinese people, seldom having anything to make them feel personally important, were strongly driven to secret organizations, which held a special appeal for the illiterate and superstitious. These organizations seemed to fill the comparable need for regalia, secret signs, passwords, benevolent deeds, and ringing titles that lodges and orders do for millions of men in the Western world. Some of the Chinese societies offered complicated initiations and other hocus-pocus to cloak and excuse robbery and gangsterism. But a few, like the Kuan Yin Society, with its millions of members, exercised a genuine and powerful influence for good throughout China.

The Boxers, or Society of Righteous Harmonious Fists, practiced a debased form of Taoism. They welcomed any bully or malefactor into their brotherhood and, working themselves up into an hysterical pitch of excitement, grew determined to pit their protective magic against foreign bullets. These were the allies of the Dowager Tz'u Hsi when she resumed the regency, imprisoned the Emperor Kuang Hsu, and revoked the reforms of the Hundred Days. The constant pressures brought by the foreigners were an unbearable strain, and hearing of the reputed magic powers of the Boxers, she saw a way to counteract those pressures. At the drop of a handkerchief, she had been told, the Boxers could set fire to buildings, or, for that matter, rise to Heaven on a cloud—achievements that fully justified her blessing and encouragement.

After many sporadic assaults on missionaries in the provinces, the Boxer movement reached its climax in June, 1900, with the assassination of the German minister. The ensuing bloody massacre of foreigners and Christian Chinese in the north, the siege of the legations in Peking, and the repeated attacks on the Tientsin concessions at long last aroused the angry indignation of the Western world. A hastily organized expeditionary force, made up of troops from six great powers (the United States, Britain, France, Germany, Russia, and Japan), assembled at Tientsin. After some sharp fighting in that area, and a slow, inept march, this relief army eventually reached Peking and assaulted its ancient walls. Typical of the blind, unreasoning hatred for Europeans and their Christian converts was the attitude of the Bannerman Hsu T'ung, a grand secretary and tutor of a former emperor. He loudly proclaimed his desire to cover a sedan chair with the skins of "foreign devils" and refused to set foot on a newly macadamized street leading to the main gate of his residence. Instead, he used an old back alley of "honest Chinese dust and mud" that led to the servants' and tradesmen's side entrance. On the day the Allied armies entered the city, he and his entire family committed suicide.

Another leading spirit of the movement, Prince Chuang, delighted in supervising drumhead courts for the "trial" of Christian converts outside the gates of his palace. On one afternoon alone, over nine hundred men, women, and children were "convicted," sentenced, and executed as Chuang gleefully watched the carnage. After the collapse of the Boxers, he fled to the interior. But he was tracked down, brought back to Peking under arrest, and given an imperial decree to commit suicide.

In the meantime old Tz'u Hsi, convinced at last that she had been badly advised in choosing the losing side—even though she stubbornly refused to admit its purposes were wrong—was having trouble with her rough, undisciplined allies of the Righteous and Harmonious Fists. She continued to wear their secret talisman, and each time she muttered one of their incantations, her eunuchs exclaimed: "That's for another dead foreign devil!" Though she used all of her persuasive powers over Duke Jung Lu, they failed for the first time. He had always disapproved of the Boxers and, despite her pleas, flatly refused to use his artillery against the Catholic cathedral—a sanctuary for fifty French and Italian marines, a hundred seminarists, thirteen missionary priests, and about three thousand Chinese converts. Somehow they held out for seventy-two days against the constant assaults of many thousands of Boxers and the fire from fourteen artillery pieces. The only respites in their heroic defense were when screaming attackers began to fight wildly among themselves or when Tz'u Hsi twice ordered a cessation of the bombardment because the noise of the guns gave her a headache during her boating picnics on the lakes of the nearby Sea Palaces.

The siege of the Legation Quarter lasted fifty-five days, from June 20 to August 14, 1900. About 900 Europeans and Americans, and some 3,000 Chinese Christians, were defended by 525 Legation Guards and volunteers against over 6,000 badly organized and poorly directed Boxer attackers. The Chinese spent much of their time in a general looting of the city, hunting down converts, or quarreling among themselves.

The crude manners of the Boxer leaders were soon adopted by many of the court eunuchs, who openly flaunted the Society's insignia of red headbands, waist bands, and military-type coats, and became insufferably arrogant. Tz'u Hsi bore up under this, but men like Duke Jung Lu began to sympathize with the reform plans of Kuang Hsu, which formerly they had bitterly opposed. During that hot, dry summer, when tempers and nerves were frequently on edge, honest advisers tried desperately to dissuade Tz'u Hsi from her stubborn course of supporting the Boxers. The situation in the Forbidden City had become almost as dangerous as that in the Legation Quarter. On one occasion a group of palace guards with Boxer leanings tried to seize the emperor himself! But the old dowager stood like a stone wall between them and the sovereign, her basilisk-like eyes forcing the guards to withdraw in shame.

THE DOUBLE DEATH

The last act in the two-hundred-and-fifty-year-old history of the Man-chu dynasty unfolded itself, not in the Forbidden City, but in the adja-cent Sea Palaces, whose lakes and parks extended far into the northern section of the city. The double death of the Emperor Kuang Hsu and the Empress Dowager Tz'u Hsi occurred within a few hours of each other. Those two events marked the end of all real power for the once-great imperial family and the deterioration of all strength in the clan organiza-tions that had sustained the regime. For a few years longer, a shadow of formalities lingered on, but the gleam of gold had become the tarnished glitter of tinsel, ready to be swept away before the harsh winds of revolu-tionary change.

During the entire summer of 1908, the teashops and inns of Peking buzzed with rumors and gossip: Tz'u Hsi was failing; the emperor was seriously ill. As tongues wagged endlessly, the hopes of one party rose as those of the other withered. If Kuang Hsu outlived Tz'u Hsi, he would be able to revenge himself on all those who had mistreated him. Small officials of the court and hangers-on were besieged for news. Carters and chair bearers at the village of Hai Tien, near the Summer Palace where the sovereigns were in residence, were anxiously questioned. Since the emperor was childless and the heir apparent had been dismissed after the Boxer trouble, the whole question of the succession would again be raised.

Outwardly, affairs were conducted as usual. At the end of the summer the foreign ministers were granted an audience. On October 20, the court returned to the capital, but Tz'u Hsi left the country reluctantly. As her barge moved slowly along the canal, she glanced time and again over her shoulder toward the magnificent palaces, lakes and parks of her own designing.

Though she tried to ease the strain of life in the capital by taking up residence in the Sea Palaces, she became heavily involved in preparations for the celebration of her seventy-third birthday. The city was to be decorated in her honor. Elaborate plans for long plays in the Great Theater involved many hours of supervision. And on top of that, the Dalai Lama had just arrived from Tibet.

On the day of the Dalai Lama's reception the emperor was too ill to see him and was represented by one of the princes. The disappointed pontiff, who had journeyed to Peking heavily laden with gifts to win personal favors, had hoped to be excused from making the *k'o-t'ou* and to be received as a sovereign on equal terms with the emperor. But he was given no choice and had to make an unwilling obeisance to an empty throne.

His gift to the empress dowager was an image of Buddha that was reputed to possess miraculous powers. It was a timely offering. She had caught a chill while picnicking on the lakes, and its ill effects were aggravated by a too hearty intake of clotted cream and crab apples. The Dalai Lama advised her to place the golden Buddha on the altar of her tomb, assuring her its influences would overcome the unlucky conjugation of the stars that menaced her longevity. Superstitious as always, she ordered Prince Ching to carry out the Dalai Lama's advice. But the prince, who later earned a reputation for rapacious greed, was reluctant to leave the capital while both the dowager and the emperor were indisposed, in case they died and he should miss a plush appointment bestowed by the new emperor.

Tz'u Hsi was enraged. "I am not likely to die within the next few days. I am feeling better already. In any case, you will do as you're told!" When he bowed and departed, the old dowager smiled grimly. This was not the first time she had taken satisfaction by reminding an imperial prince that "his tail was too heavy to wag."

But Ching's misgivings were justified. On November 13 the Grand Council summoned him. The emperor had had a relapse. His condition was very serious. The dowager was again indisposed, though cheerful.

The vein of iron in her body had not yet rusted with age. On the prince's arrival, she called a special meeting of the Grand Council to nominate a successor to the ailing sovereign.

Five days later an edict in the name of the dying Kuang Hsu announced the selection of his heir—the two-year-old P'u Yi, the son of Prince Ch'un by a daughter of Duke Jung Lu. By this choice not only did the elder branch of the imperial family suffer again at the expense of Tz'u Hsi's loyalty to her own clan, but she also fulfilled a deathbed promise to her friend and lover that his loyalty would be nobly rewarded. P'u Yi's mother could have been Tz'u Hsi's own daughter—the secret issue of her long-ago trysts with Jung Lu. She could, indeed, have been that girl baby born in secrecy in the dowager's apartments and reared by Duke Jung Lu in his own palace. Though open to question, the probability is strong that the newly selected boy-emperor was actually the grandson of Tz'u Hsi.

Three more edicts followed in quick succession.

The first of these, issued by Tz'u Hsi, conferred the regency on the boy-emperor's father, Prince Ch'un, and raised the status of the widowed Yung Lu to that of empress dowager.

The second, also in her name, announced the approach of her death. It began: "I, a person of small importance, received the favor of Hsien Feng and was placed in an exalted position in the palace as his second consort." It then recapitulated her past successes and told of the coming change in the government. "Reflecting on the past fifty years on how I have striven for the good of my country without taking any ease, I notice how small a result I have achieved." Regarding the youth of the new emperor: "Now is the time for him to study; not one to be wasted in sorrow and mourning. Let him proceed with his studies so that in the future he may add to the glory of his country." Mourning for her death, she ended, should be for twenty-seven days only.

The third edict was issued in the name of P'u Yi, whose reign title was to be Hsuan T'ung. Dated November 15, 1908, it announced the death of Kuang Hsu, at six o'clock on November 14 and prescribed that mourning for his departure should be "in accordance with ancient custom, the three year period . . . which shall be kept in memory of him."

Still another edict of the same date set forth the mourning regulations in detail and stated that despite his hope the Empress Dowager Tz'u Hsi would enjoy good health forever, she had taken medicine to no avail. "Unfortunately, owing to her sorrow at the death of the Emperor Kuang Hsu, her sickness increased and her spirit was handed to Heaven on the twenty-third day [November 15] at two P.M."

On November 18, the four imperial doctors who had been attending the dowager were degraded by two ranks for permitting her to die, but were allowed to retain their posts.

Though these edicts represented the official version of the unusual events in the Sea Palaces on November 14 and 15, much strange information later came to life. The only definite evidence as to the true sequence of the imperial deaths was the assertion by court officials that His Majesty's "kitchen fire" was the first to be extinguished.

At the time palace gossip indicated that the physicians of the emperor, fearful of their responsibility when they found "His Majesty's nose twitching and his stomach rising," had urgently pleaded for outside help. Though it was obvious his end was approaching, Kuang Hsu refused to don the Dragon Robes, as tradition demanded of a dying sovereign. Could this have been a last futile protest against all the indignities and injustices he had suffered? Or could it suggest that the emperor was not actually dying at all—that he was murdered by the powerful clique that would have suffered his wrath had he survived the dowager?

On the morning after the emperor's official death Tz'u Hsi rose sufficiently refreshed to grant an audience to the Grand Council. She condoled with her widowed niece, chatted with the regent and his wife, and issued the first edict in the name of the boy-emperor. In it she was named empress grand dowager. She had apparently suffered a slight stroke during the preceding summer—word of which had increased the rumors of her failing health. Now, after her early rice, she suffered a second attack. But she rallied sufficiently to dictate a valedictory decree giving her niece, the new empress dowager, the right to overrule the regent in important decisions. Finally, she was prepared to admit that her days, perhaps even her hours, were numbered. However, her mind fastened on the future and remained active and alert. She was going to die and knew it, but she still schemed for the power and glory of her own family.

As her kin and attendance crowded into the apartment, she was dressed in her "longevity finery": a long, gold-embroidered gown and short waistcoat of the same material. In accordance with age-old custom, her family begged her to pronounce her last words of advice—a sacred utterance to be obeyed and cherished, since the speaker, on the threshold of the world of spirits, supposedly no longer had any personal interest in the riches of the earth. They waited patiently, as her lips began to move with slow agony and a terrific effort of will: "Never again allow any woman to hold supreme power in the state. Never again permit eunuchs to meddle in government affairs."

Then, still mindful of her dignity, Tz'u Hsi straightened her limbs and turned her face to the south in the proper attitude for a sovereign about to greet the finality of death. As she gasped for breath, still loath to depart the life she had always loved, the innumerable clocks in her apartment ticked off the passing of her last moments. When at last she ceased to breathe, her mouth remained open, a sure sign to those around her bedside that her strong spirit had left this life with great reluctance.

Tz'u Hsi had entered the Great Within an unknown girl who had been living on charity on Pewter Lane and left it a dowager empress in a massive coffin. As outward symbols of a life of intrigue, of deceit and of cruelty, the pontifical sonority of the titles that accompanied her empty soul to the abode of more visionary spirits of the past, rang with a hollow tone: Motherly; Auspicious Orthodox; Heaven Blessed; Prosperous; All Nourishing; Brightly Manifest; Calm; Sedately Perfect; Long Lived; Respected and Revered; Worshipful; Illustriously Exalted.

When the Empress Dowager Tz'u Hsi died, the first news made the Western world give a sigh of disbelief. She had held China together so long that she seemed indestructible. She had had a wicked, ruthless reputation; she could be bent only a little, she did not break. The people of her own city of Peking, however, loved her, because they understood her. They sensed that the imperial court had been no more than a magnificently dramatic transformation from her childhood home and this, somehow, made her seem close and one of them.

The instinct for theatrics had been strong in her, and, in spite of her position, she relished taking part in the stage productions of the Great Theater. As a child she had been so convincing at simulating emotion she had often been invited to weep and keen at the funerals of friends and relatives.

Tz'u Hsi's own death and funeral was the epitome of theatrics. If, as was believed in China, departed spirits were never very far away, then Tz'u Hsi must have looked down and reveled in the panoply of the court.

The great Hall of Imperial Supremacy was draped in white, and its floor spread with heavy cocoanut matting. Her enormous coffin was placed under a huge catafalque whose white curtains could be separated when mourners came to make their last obeisances. Emperor Kuang Hsu, who had died the day before Tz'u Hsi, lay in state in the Palace of Cloudless Heaven. As the Forbidden City devoted itself to long months of mourning ceremonies, the entire empire observed the regulations issued in the following edict published in the *Peking Gazette*:

> The ceremonial for the funerals of the late Emperor and the late Empress Grand Dowager shall be arranged by the Board of Rites.
>
> Members of the Imperial Household shall wear mourning dress.
>
> The Emperor [aged two] shall wear mourning dress with his hair unplaited.
>
> Females dwelling within the Gate of Cloudless Heaven and females of the families of imperial blood shall wear mourning dress, with their hair unplaited.
>
> The whole State Affair of the funerals shall be prepared.
>
> A red flag is to hang in the Imperial Household and a tent of yellow cloth with dragon embroidery shall be set up, the same having white edges.
>
> All officials shall remove the red threads from their official hats. Within the next twenty-seven months no marriage shall take place among members of the Imperial Clan; and among officials during the next twelve months. No feasts shall be given, nor music played; nor shall members of their families wear ornaments.
>
> All officials, scholars, monks and Taoist priest shall assemble at the Shun Tien Fu [a large temple in the city] for three days, and shall there mourn.
>
> All the common people in the Capital shall obey the following: Males shall remove all red buttons and the like; females shall not wear ornaments for a period of twenty-seven days.
>
> For one hundred days no marriage shall take place, no feast be given or music played; nor shall shaving of the head be permitted. During twenty-seven days no worship of ancestors in the temples will be allowed, and every temple bell shall be tolled with twenty thousand strokes.

Each day, for almost a year, four imperial princes performed the *k'o-t'ou*, wept loudly, and made the prescribed offerings before the empress dowager's sealed coffin. One took the morning watch, the second relieved him at noon, a third came on duty in the evening, and the fourth was available as a substitute in case of illness. Lesser nobles were assigned to assist the princes. Twenty maidservants and thirty minor palace officials were designated for duty in the throne hall. All wore coarse white robes, white belts, white felt boots or shoes, white sheepskin coats in winter, and no insignia of rank or office.

The duty of the maidservants was to arrange on various tables placed before the funeral bier the food offerings of Mongolian and Chinese dishes, wine, tea, and Tz'u Hsi's favorite fruits. They also opened and closed the white curtains for each of the thrice daily rites.

This done, the women moved to the west side of the open doors of the Hall of Imperial Supremacy and the men to the east. The prince on duty raised a small glass cup of wine, then poured it into a larger basin, and dropped to his knees to perform the nine-fold *k'o-t'ou*. At the same time his ten noble assistants and all those on the terrace prostrated themselves in obeisance. But officials from the provinces remained upright on their knees and removed their hats to indicate shame for their absence from the capital when the great spirit departed.

The officiating prince then poured the basin of wine onto the steps of the terrace. This was called "feeding the earth," from which the sovereign and the offerings had sprung and to which they now returned.

Aside from the prescribed weeping, the rites inside the hall and on the terrace were conducted in complete silence. But the outer courtyards reverberated with funeral dirges and chanting prayers.

For each ceremony three Buddhist abbots and 108 priests alternated with three Taoist chief lamas and 108 lamas. They stood silently at the Gate of Peaceful Old Age and its outer court. Having already "left the world," they wore their customary robes of red and purple, gold brocade, brilliant yellow and, if chief lamas, imposing felt headdresses. Outside the Nine Dragon Screen numerous musicians from the great temples in the city set up a constant din with percussion instruments and nine-foot-long Tibetan horns.

Once every twenty-seven days—at each moon period—robes of silk and brocade as well as gold and jewelry were placed before the coffin for

Tz'u Hsi's use in the spirit world. These articles were then carried by the eunuchs to a brazier in the courtyard, where they were consigned to the fire. And as the eunuchs raised their arms, they slipped most of the gold and jewelry up their long, loose sleeves.

Since the presence of all nobles was required at least once while the coffin lay in state, the terrace was thronged with mourners at every ceremony during the first few weeks of the long deathwatch. But as the months slipped away, fewer and fewer grieving subjects participated. Under the early emperors only those of certain ranks had been admitted, but toward the end of the dynasty, etiquette was gradually relaxed and a motley element of the city, disguised in hempen robes, surged into the palace grounds to enjoy the spectacle. As long as the essential rites were duly performed each day, the deceased dowager was thought to be content. Typically Chinese, the appearance, the form, and the illusion were all that really mattered.

THE FUNERAL OF AN EMPRESS

For many years, a handsome three-hundred-pound coffin of catalpa wood had awaited the death of Tz'u Hsi. Comfortably lined with a thick mattress embroidered with pearls, it was covered with an embroidered silk quilt also sewn with pearls and a lace sheet on which a figure of Buddha had been worked in still more pearls. When the body of the Dowager Empress was laid in the coffin, a jade lotus flower was placed at her head, at her feet a jade lotus leaf, in her arms eighteen tiny Buddha images of pearls, about her brow an elaborate chaplet of pearls, and encircling her body nine times a long rope of large pearls. To show their devotion, her family and followers offered a vast amount of treasure to be buried with her. The old grand eunuch Li Lien-ying made a faithful record of these gifts before they were put into the coffin so that each would occupy a suitable place in relation to what it symbolized. One hundred and eight gold and jade carved jewel-Buddhas were placed at her side; a water melon, fruit and two sweet melons of jade at her feet;

two hundred peaches, pears, apricots, and dates of semiprecious stones, a jade cup from which sprang leaves and flowers of jewels, and a jewel tree with coral blossoms at each side; and dozens of precious stones and pieces of jewelry in the remaining spaces. The last gift was made by an imperial princess: eighteen jade carvings of Buddha and the fabulous "eight horses" so frequently depicted by Chinese artists.

After the coffin was closed, it was borne from the Sea Palaces through the Gate of Spiritual Valor to the Hall of Imperial Supremacy in the Palace of Peaceful Old Age, where it lay in state for almost a year.

In simpler style, the body of the Emperor Kuang Hsu was laid in state in the Palace of Cloudless Heaven. On a sunny day in May, 1909, which had been selected by the court astrologers, his funeral cortege filed through the Gate of Spiritual Valor toward his last resting place in the Western Tombs. Unlike the Ming emperors, who were all buried in a single, beautiful valley, the Manchus had two sites for their tombs, the eastern site and the western. Successive sovereigns were usually alternated at the locations, the father in one, the son in the other.

According to legend, the imperial tombs were modeled on that of the Emperor Ch'in Shih the builder of the Great Wall, for whom in 207 B.C. an entire mountain was hollowed out so that he could take with him as much of his wealth as possible. At the Emperor Ch'in Shih's tomb, cities of jewels and rivers of quicksilver were laid out on the polished bronze floor. Before his sarcophagus, lamps, filled with enough dolphin oil to burn for two hundred years, raised their flames toward a high vaulted ceiling into which were set the stars and planets in gleaming gold and silver. Following an ancient custom, his consorts and servants were buried with him—crucified against the walls, lest in death their corpses assume unseemly attitudes. A great stone slab closed the entrance, earth was heaped over it and the whole slope planted with grass and trees. All those who had had any part in creating this magnificently barbarous tomb were killed. No living man was allowed to know in what mountain fastness it lay—and, though it has been sought for over twenty-one centuries, no man has ever found it. But the legend of its beauty and riches inspired each successive dynasty when their last resting places were being planned.

Later dynasties made no effort to hide their tombs. They placed them in great parklike enclosures shaded by evergreen trees and cared for by special detachments of troops. In front of each "jeweled city," as the earth mound over the coffin was called, a miniature palace with a tiny throne hall, yellow chairs of state, waiting rooms, and storehouses were constructed. A highly esteemed official was appointed to take charge of the Manchu tombs, and beyond the outer walls of the huge park were built special villages to house the guards and their families. Thus the imperial dead were assured of an undisturbed rest.

The building of an imperial tomb was an elaborate and expensive operation—not only because vast numbers of skilled workmen and fine materials were employed, but also because the ancient geomantic studies, known as the "wind and water" influences, had to be consulted. Occasionally, because of new interpretations of these signs, a chosen site had to be discarded, the partly finished mausoleum dismantled, and the whole project begun over again at a new location. Tombs were usually built during the lifetime and under the supervision of their future occupants. Tz'u Hsi fussed over the details of her last dwelling place for years; and to ensure that her departed spirit would always be comforted by the style and grandeur of the appointments, she spent fabulous sums on its construction and embellishment.

The barbarous practice of burying consorts and attendants with deceased royalty had long been abandoned. From the beginning of the Han dynasty to the end of the Sung dynasty—a period of nearly 1500 years—numerous symbolic figures of clay and tile filled the tomb chambers—guards, horses, priests, officials, ladies, and attendants of every kind to serve or entertain the spirit of the master. It was said that the first Manchu emperor was followed into the spirit world by many of his ladies, servants, and eunuchs. But some years later, when several ladies signified their wish to accompany one of his deceased dowager consorts to the Nine Springs, the horrified Emperor K'ang Hsi indignantly forbade any such action. Instead, spirit attendants, and treasures made of paper were burned at the graves and symbolically joined their masters and mistresses.

On Buddhist All Souls' Day, 1909, while Tz'u Hsi's huge coffin still rested in the Hall of Imperial Supremacy, many such paper effigies—a barge carrying officials, ladies in robes of state, furniture and a throne chair—were burned with great ceremony and chanting of prayers. Early in November, before the funeral cortege left the Great Within, more paper servants, guards, horses, camels, and all the trappings of imperial life, including an enormous supply of "spirit money," were sent to join her soul through great clouds of smoke and incense. Thus, well attended with fabulous treasures, she would not be ashamed to appear in the company of the Illustrious Shades.

At seven o'clock on the morning of November 9, Tz'u Hsi's funeral processesion started through the Gate of Spiritual Valor on its slow march to her tomb some eighty miles away, and the valiant old dowager passed through the gate's portals for the last time. The cold, gray day matched the spirit and grief of countless mourners in the almost endless column. Stricken dumb with sorrow—and perhaps fear—her grand eunuch walked before her bier like a broken figure for whom life no longer held the prospect of either joy or sorrow.

The gorgeous array—hundreds of chanting Buddhist, Lamaist, and Taoist priests, embroidered state umbrellas, banners, and the yellow brocade draperies of the mighty catafalque, which was borne by eighty-four bearers—were far more magnificent than had been those of her nephew, the emperor, a few months before. For four days the regent, great officials, and members of the imperial family led the long, winding procession over a specially constructed road that crossed the fields and farms of the countryside, the entire length of which was strewn with yellow sand.

When the cortege finally reached the tomb, the coffin was placed on its jeweled bed and surrounded with treasures of bronze and porcelain, sacrificial vessels, and embroidered saffron-colored hangings. The new empress dowager—Kuang Hsu's widow—and the imperial ladies performed the last rites within the tomb chamber as the male members of the family and high officials made their solemn obeisances outside. A massive wedge of stone was dropped into place in the masonry and sealed. Tz'u Hsi was alone forever.

After the court returned to the Forbidden City, Tz'u Hsi's spirit tablet was installed with due ceremony in the Ancestral Hall. With four hundred prostrations, the entire court informed the ancestors that the Empress Grand Dowager Tz'u Hsi had reverently joined their company. The new dowager and the imperial family were content. They had performed all the prescribed rites with the greatest filial piety. The Great Ancestress lay in her magnificent, well-guarded tomb, surrounded by all her heart could desire of mortal pomp. Little did the court dream that before twenty years had passed, her shriveled body would lie stripped and naked in a looted, broken tomb, mocked by rude soldiery who cared nothing for the ways and precepts of their ancestors. And little did these poorly clad scoffers of their own great past foresee that in another twenty years their shoddy moment in history would have passed; their rapacious leaders would lie dead and dishonored; and their children would serve new masters far more exacting and far more ruthless than those who had ruled from the Dragon Throne of the Great Within.

IMPERIAL YELLOW TO COMMUNIST RED

After the funeral cortege of the Empress Dowager Tz'u Hsi passed through the Gate of Spiritual Valor, all that happened within the Forbidden City degenerated into a shadowy and synthetic imitation of the past. The gate itself became a symbol of the rapidly changing times, for it was thereafter used as the official entrance of the palace-city, regardless of its unlucky north direction. The great court between the inner tower and the outer porch was usually silent and deserted. The tribute caravans bearing riches from all quarters of the empire came no more. But when the boy-emperor held formal court on feast days, despite his abdication, the ancient portals regained a few signs of former prestige. Again the carts and sedan chairs of imperial relatives filled the wide space below the tower, and for the first time in its long history, it was honored when the phoenix chair of an imperial bride was borne through its tunneled sally-ports for his marriage in 1922.

The two years that followed the marriage passed quietly. Though the court was pinched for revenue and reduced to a mere skeleton of its former greatness, P'u Yi acquired an education of sorts and grew up to become a thoughtful, if rather spineless, young man. After his expulsion from the palace and flight to the Japanese legation in Tientsin, he became the creature of his ambitious hosts. Weak and seemingly content—at least apathetic—in his later role as the Japanese-installed puppet emperor of Manchukuo he docilely went through a second marriage to a Korean "princess" of his masters' choice and ended his life a hapless victim of the Chinese Communists. On his death in 1966, this last descendant of the Manchus departed humbly and with shame to join his ancestors. And the mighty warrior race that conquered all of China has either disappeared or been so absorbed in the limitless human quicksands of Asia that today almost no Manchus remain on earth. In the long span of history their brilliant star flared briefly—and then was gone.

In time the illiterate warlord troops in the palace were replaced by shabby, black-uniformed police of the city government. Before the capital of the Republic was officially moved to the south, its leader, Sun Yat-sen, announced to the spirit of the founder of the Ming dynasty that the Manchu aliens had ceased to rule the land.

The Great Within became a tourist attraction, a place of desolation and mockery of the spirits of the past. The curious and the uncouth entered through any gate near which a ticket booth might be located. Crowds streamed through the portals of the massive Meridian Gate, snapping photographs of this and that as they trudged across deserted courts and terraces. On many occasions, when the guards were not alert, leather-clad feet climbed the "spirit stairways" that not even the foot of a priest-emperor had ever dared to touch. And once, in thoughtless disrespect for the exalted faith that had surrounded the emperor, a group of Westerners staged an evening picnic and danced to the music of a portable phonograph on the sacred terrace of the Altar of Heaven. For centuries only the Son of Heaven and the one God of the Universe had communed in reverent silence on its open marble platform.

Today the courts and palaces of the Forbidden City stand mute and forlorn, their walls and towers ablaze with slogans of a new order and a new regime whose masters regard the once-hallowed buildings as no more than a theatrical backdrop for their own domination. To the present rulers the lacquered pillars and yellow tiles represent an era of history for which they have neither sympathy nor understanding—over five centuries of waste and frivolity that ignored an oppressed and down-trodden people. The elegant dignity and formalized ceremony of imperial yellow has been replaced by the loud clamor of shouting parades and red flags. But with the stoic patience of its years, the high rose-colored walls still stand nurturing the secrets of time; as if awaiting a future that may bring forth new occupants and a new greatness in a new world whose change they can accept.

BIBLIOGRAPHY

Arlington, L.C. and Lewisohn, William. *In Search of Old Peking.* Peking: Henri Vetch, 1935.

Bell, Sir Charles. *Tibet Past and Present.* London: Oxford University Press, 1927.

———. *The People of Tibet.* London: Oxford University Press, 1928.

Bitchurin, Iakinth. *Description of Peking.* London: 1829.

E.L. Bland and O.P. Backhouse, *China Under the Empress Dowager.* Philadelphia: J.B. Lippincott Co., 1910

———. *Annals and Memoirs of the Court of Peking.* Boston and New York: Houghton Mifflin Company, 1914.

Bouillard, G. *Le Temple de Ciel.* Paris: 1930.

Bredon, Juliet. *Peking.* Shanghai and Hong Kong: Kelly and Walsh, 1931.

Carl, Katherine A. *With the Empress Dowager of China.* New York: The Century Company, 1905.

Cordier, Henri. *Letters from Peking.* Paris: 1874.

Crow, Carl. *Handbook for China.* Shanghai and Hong Kong: Kelly and Walsh, 1933.

Der Ling, Princess. *Two Years in the Forbidden City.* New York: Moffat, Yard and Company, 1911.

Du Halde, Jean Baptiste. *History of China.* London: J. Watts, 1736.

Hayes, L. Newton. *The Great Wall of China.* Shanghai and Hong Kong: Kelly and Walsh, 1929.

Hubbard, Gilbert Ernest. *The Temples of the Western Hills.* Peking and Tientsin: La Librairie Française, 1923.

Johnston, Sir Reginald. *Twilight in the Forbidden City.* London: Victor Gollancz Ltd., 1934.

Kingdon-Ward, F. *The Mystery Rivers of Tibet.* London: Seeley, Service and Company, 1923.

Lamb, Gene. *Tabloid History of China.* Tientsin: Peiyang Press, 1936.

Loti, Pierre. *The Last Days of Peking.* Boston: Little, Brown and Company, 1902.

Malone, Carroll B. *History of the Peking Summer Palaces under the Ch'ing Dynasty.* Urbana: University of Illinois Press, 1934.

Matignon, Doctor Jean Jacques. *Superstition, Crime and Misery in China.* Lyon: A. Storck and Company, 1900.

Porte-Petit, C. *La Femme qui commande 500 millions d'hommes.* Paris.

Rennie, D.F. *Peking and the Pekingese.* London: John Murray Ltd., 1865.

Ripa, Father Matteo. *Memoirs of Father Ripa.* New York: Wiley and Putnam, 1846.

Scidmore, E.R. *China the Long-Lived Empire.* London: Macmillan & Co., Ltd., 1900.

Simpson, Bertram Lenos (Weale). *Indiscreet Letters from Peking.* New York: Dodd, Mead and Company, 1907.

Sirén, Osvald. *The Walls and Gates of Peking.* New York: Orientalia, 1924.

————. *The Imperial Palaces of Peking.* 3 Volumes. London: John Lane, The Bodley Head Ltd., 1926.

Smith, Reverend Arthur. *Chinese Characteristics.* New York and London: F. Revell Company, 1894.

————. *China in Convulsion.* 2 Volumes. New York and London: F. Revell Company, 1901.

Varé, Daniele. *The Last of the Empresses.* New York: Doubleday, Doran and Company, 1936.

INDEX